Youth Marketing to Digital Natives

NEW HORIZONS IN MARKETING SERIES

Books in the New Horizons in Marketing series make a significant contribution to the study of marketing and contexts in which it operates. As this field has expanded dramatically in recent years, the series will provide an invaluable forum for the publication of high-quality works of scholarship and show the diversity of research on marketing.

Global and pluralistic in its approach, this series includes some of the best theoretical and analytical work with contributions to fundamental principles, rigorous evaluations of existing concepts and competing theories, stimulating debate and future visions.

Titles in the series include:

Social Marketing and Advertising in the Age of Social Media
Edited by Lukas Parker and Linda Brennan

Youth Marketing to Digital Natives
Wided Batat

Youth Marketing to Digital Natives

Wided Batat

Professor of Marketing, Entrepreneur and Keynote Speaker

NEW HORIZONS IN MARKETING SERIES

Edward Elgar
PUBLISHING

Cheltenham, UK • Northampton, MA, USA

Published by
Edward Elgar Publishing Limited
The Lypiatts
15 Lansdown Road
Cheltenham
Glos GL50 2JA
UK

Edward Elgar Publishing, Inc.
William Pratt House
9 Dewey Court
Northampton
Massachusetts 01060
USA

Paperback edition 2022

A catalogue record for this book
is available from the British Library

Library of Congress Control Number: 2021944950

This book is available electronically in the **Elgar**online
Business subject collection
http://dx.doi.org/10.4337/9781839109300

ISBN 978 1 83910 929 4 (cased)
ISBN 978 1 83910 930 0 (eBook)
ISBN 978 1 0353 0816 3 (paperback)
Printed and bound by CPI Group (UK) Ltd, Croydon, CR0 4YY

Contents

Figures

Tables

Boxes

About the author

Dr Wided Batat is a professor and doctor of experiential marketing and the ultimate leading expert in youth marketing, customer experience, and digital transformation. Wided is one of the best marketing experts in the world: as a university researcher, she carries out important work all over the world. As entrepreneur and international keynote speaker, Wided directs and carries out significant research in experiential marketing in France, Europe, the United States, Asia, and the Middle East. With over 15 years of experience in the field, and combining scientific research and field experience, Dr Batat transforms organizations by providing innovative market research and consumer insights. Her expertise can help businesses to have an eternal perspective of innovation, profitability, progress, and performance. She has also published many books in the field, and her 2019 best-selling book *Experiential Marketing* is invaluable for consumer behavior, marketing experts, and executive teams.

Introduction to *Youth Marketing to Digital Natives*

In this book, I offer new lenses to decode the youth market from the perspective of digital natives and their youth consumption cultures. Whether you are a researcher, a student, a business professional, or a brand manager, you will find in this book novel tools and a new segmentation method that can help you deal effectively with this paradoxical, digital, emotional, ethical, and collaborative youth group.

In line with studies in the marketing field that have examined digital natives, this book aims to deepen the reflection on the world of consumption and the behaviors of different groups of young consumers, whether they are children, tweens, pre-adolescents, adolescents, post-adolescents, or young adults. This approach, which centers on the different stages of the lifecycle from childhood to post-adolescence, is essential as it allows the reader to understand the evolution of these young consumers across different youth cultures in which their purchasing and consumption behaviors are shaped and rooted. The main contribution of this work consists in establishing an in-depth analytical review of existing studies on digital natives' behaviors in the consumption field and how they learn to become full and legitimate consumers and brands' partners. Whether they are French, American, Italian, or Danish, young consumers who belong to the same Western culture constitute a generation of digital natives for whom new technologies and social media platforms represent an integral part of their socialization and consumption activities. The purpose of their consumption is above all symbolic, emotional, and relational, and not purely utilitarian. For digital natives, the consumption of brands is a means that facilitates the integration and conformity of the young person to a particular youth consumption culture. It is through their shared consumption practices and brands that a digital native youth identity is created.

This digital native identity is then constructed and shaped by the codes and norms shared by the members in each youth consumption culture and breaks with previous generations' practices. Beyond a definition delimiting the age group of digital natives, in this book I introduce the idea of consumption practices anchored in a youth culture, which seems, at first glance, to homogenize all digital natives by contrasting them with older generations, such as their parents and the Baby Boomers. Thus, digital natives share an identical attraction for the consumption practices and brands adopted by their group. As a result, they participate in the creation of common generational references. Although digital natives are currently a hot topic and the subject of several forums and columns in various magazines for marketing managers, human resources managers, institutions, and educators, to our knowledge no professional and scientific reference has examined digital natives' consumption practices from the perspective of youth cultures. Therefore, to fill this gap in both business and academia and thus enhance our understanding of digital natives, I examine in this book the concept of digital natives by considering a youth-centric approach where consumption practices, as well as the adoption and/or the rejection of brands, are strongly embedded in several interdependent youth cultures that should be decoded to capture the meanings these young consumers assign to brands and their paradoxical behaviors.

Youth Marketing to Digital Natives, therefore, provides the reader with new horizons when it comes to marketing strategies and segmenting the youth market. The book does so by considering a unique and innovative field guide to decode youth norms and codes that businesses can use to promote their brands, implement engaging communication campaigns both online and offline, and create new products and services that are meaningful for digital natives – ones that fit with the different youth consumption cultures they belong to. In this book, I offer an overview of youth consumption cultures and new tools to segment the youth market. I introduce a new segmentation method, called "segmenculture", based on the characteristics of youth cultures, which marketing and brand managers can implement to better target the youth market. Segmenculture is a holistic technique that allows companies to segment the youth market into four major interconnected youth consumption cultures, namely childescence, adonascence, adolescence, and adulescence.

Numerous cases, figures, and tables illustrate each chapter.

This book focuses on a new way of thinking about youth marketing that could be a strategic framework and a tool to help businesses targeting the youth market design and implement successful products, services, and experiences aimed at digital natives. By offering a critical analysis of existing works that examine young consumers' behaviors, the book provides answers through the development of the following themes: who are digital natives, and how should the youth market be segmented? How do these young people become consumers? Why should brands learn more about young consumer socialization and the learning process in youth cultures? How can companies shift from offering products to designing suitable experiences and co-creating with digital natives to create a strong competitive advantage?

In this book, I have combined my professional expertise and my prior work on digital natives and youth consumption cultures in different fields. This book provides an extensive review of the existing knowledge in this field and examples. I hope the book will help readers gain an in-depth understanding of the paradoxical behaviors of digital natives shaped by the norms and the codes in different youth consumption cultures.

1. Why youth culture beats age segmentation when it comes to marketing to young consumers

CHAPTER OVERVIEW

In this chapter, I present the limits of the traditional segmentation by age of the youth market and discuss a new, effective segmentation approach that integrates youth culture instead of age. I also introduce the various definitions of the concept of youth culture to overcome the weaknesses by identifying the typologies of youth cultures that marketing and brand managers can take into account in the segmentation of young people and thus prevent a "myopic segmentation." Examples from different cultural settings and theory boxes are also provided to illustrate and explain why it is important for companies to rethink their segmentation strategies and tools when targeting young consumers.

1. WHY SHOULD MARKETERS CHALLENGE AGE SEGMENTATION?

The first questions that come to mind when it comes to youth segmentation are related to the profile of young consumers and the characteristics of their behaviors, the age groups to which they belong, and the way brands are targeting and implementing marketing strategies to attract this youth segment: what do we mean by segmenting young consumers? Are we talking about the kid, the pre-adolescent, the tweens, the adolescent, or the post-adolescent segment? And what about high-school and college students as well as young adults; do they still belong to the youth segment? Should marketers target them as a homogeneous generation such as Generation Y (millennials), Generation Z (post-millennials), or Generation Alpha? These questions highlight the ambiguous and fluctuating nature of the definition of the "young consumer" segment and youth consumption patterns and behaviors that marketers and brands need to consider in the implementation of their segmentation and marketing strategies.

The definition of youth differs according to different disciplines. Sociology, psychology, cultural anthropology, and marketing scholars use different terms and define the youth group in various ways. The definition of youth can even vary from one study to another published by the same author. It is, therefore, crucial to question the definition of youth and the established segmentation by age range to help marketers in defining effective marketing and segmentation strategies that capture both explicit and implicit features of these young consumers – and in turn provide them with suitable products and services with both tangible (e.g., quality, design, functionality) and intangible (e.g., socialization, symbolism, self-esteem) characteristics, valuable to today's youth cohorts.

Marketers and businesses targeting young consumers should then challenge the well-established "age segmentation" approach by considering a holistic youth marketing approach, which goes beyond the idea that young consumers as individuals belong to a set of segments with homogeneous expectations that can be defined by socioeconomic status (SES) or by physiological criteria such as gender and age.

The limitation related to age segmentation has been highlighted by Batat (2017a), who identified in her research focusing on young consumers the need to distinguish a person's "real age" from the person's "perceived age." What Batat refers to as "biological age" is defined by the chronological age of the individual (real age). However, this is often out of step with an individual's subjective age (perceived age). This is especially true when it comes to the youth group because young people can, at some points and in certain situations, feel older than their real ages and vice versa.

Therefore, the next section explores three main issues, specifically youth conceptualization, cultural impact, and the disciplinary discrepancy underling the limitations related to age segmentation, that marketers and brands targeting young consumers should take into account when rethinking their traditional segmentation approaches.

2.   CONCEPTUALIZING YOUTH: INVESTIGATION OF DEFINITIONAL ISSUES

This section attempts to question the universal and well-established character of the "youth" figure, which has certainly not been examined in marketing and consumer behavior studies. In doing so, I first take a sociohistorical perspective on the rise of the concept of "youth" to highlight its erraticism, complexity, and the difficulties it raises. Then, I introduce the cultural approach to examine the impact of culture on the construction of youth identity. Finally, the concept of the "digital native" generation will be explored from a marketing and consumer behavior perspective to examine how scholars study young people as consumers within today's high-tech consumer society so as to define the main features of youth consumption and attitudes towards brands.

2.1   The Rise of Youth: A Sociohistorical Perspective

Adopting several angles by analyzing the multidisciplinary literature rooted in history and psychosociology allows us to clarify the concept of youth: what it is, and what it is not. Although questioning the essence of the way that youth is defined may seem fundamental, the answer is not obvious given the ambiguous nature of this notion, whose definition may change from one discipline to another, from one author to another in the same discipline, or even from one study to another by the same author. The rise and evolution of the concept of "youth" have been affected by various cultural, social, historical, and political factors that have shaped its definition throughout history (Batat, 2010). Although the reality of youth is nowadays widely accepted in our modern societies, when examined more closely, every aspect related to it contributes to giving the concept of youth the appearance of artifice that requires scholars to develop an in-depth comprehension of its historical and social foundations to explain its emergence and evolution across cultures and time.

Thus, age ranges, which classify youth stages into homogeneous segments (e.g., kids, pre-adolescents, adolescents, post-adolescents), distinguish the stages of life and set the boundaries between youth and adult generations, vary over time. Even in terms of physical characteristics, youth is influenced by history. For example, the age when a person matures (puberty) and the norms of child empowerment and emancipation vary from one century to another. As a result, the line between youthhood and adulthood has changed over the course of history, according to eras, social contexts, and cultural settings. To be convinced of this observation, it is only necessary to evoke, even briefly, the evolution of the meaning of "youth" and its representation across history and cultures.

From a *historical perspective*, authors who have studied youthhood (e.g., Feldman-Barrett, 2018, 2019; Heilbronner, 2008) have found that it appears in literature, explicitly or implicitly, from antiquity. Since then, the concept of youthhood has continued to evolve over time. If the original word "adulescence," already existed in ancient Rome, the analogy ends there. Etymologically, "adulescent" refers to an individual who is in the process of growing and does not include any particular age group.

• In Rome, only young men between the ages of 17 and 30 years were so named, and by no means were they pre-adults or post-adolescents. Thus, these young men acquired citizenship at the age of 17 years old and the right to marry from puberty. A woman, on the other hand, became directly "*uxor*" – that is, a wife – without having to pass through youthhood or the adolescence stage. The use of the term youth then disappears;

- Later, throughout the Middle Ages, the population was divided into children and adults around the natural age of puberty. The terms used to designate young people are, therefore, more frequently linked to belonging to a group or a social class than to an age group (Batat, 2010, 2017a). This evolution clearly shows that youthhood is an indefinite concept, multifaceted, and tough to define from a physiological (age and gender) perspective. If the physical transformations that accompany puberty still mark the onset of transitioning from childhood to adolescence, the same is not true for its upper limit, signaling the transition from youthhood to adulthood, which shows complete ambiguity;

- On the other hand, whereas puberty is universal, and is found in all times, youthhood is a recent phenomenon, specific to Western societies, and appeared in the middle of the nineteenth century. Throughout this period of history, puberty marks the transition from childhood to adulthood. Through learning, a young person is introduced to adult know-how. In fact, the word "youth" itself occurs only occasionally in Latin writings of the Middle Ages to describe very imprecise age groups of people between 15 and 60 years old;

- It was not until the mid-nineteenth century that the word youth appeared in the vocabulary of Western societies to designate young college students who were financially dependent and continuing their education. It was at this time that industrialization boomed and life expectancies increased. Simultaneously, a particular type of attire at this age could distinguish young people from children and adults. However, youthhood was far from being a phenomenon of generation but rather a marker of social class because it still only defined a very small number of individuals belonging to the bourgeoisie. The nobles and the poor, on the other hand, continued to benefit from training acquired through contact with adults through preceptors and supervisors.

- The term "youth" to designate an entire age group of both boys and girls only came into use later in the twentieth century with the generalization of schooling. Indeed, youthhood and schooling are strongly related and evolved together;

Progressively, the structuring of the educational system and the training of an increasing number of young people over longer periods has led to their physical and psychological isolation, facilitating the development of a particular youth culture for each age which, in turn, has reinforced the idea of the particularity of each group. The development of a young and supportive age group reached its peak during the 1960s. Thus, as it is understood today, youthhood is a phenomenon that is relatively recent and, in some respects, still evolving: young people in the 1950s did not live in the same way as young people in the 1970s or 1990s and 2000s. However, it is in terms of the psychosocial nature of youthhood that the historical changes are the most marked.

Over the last 200 years, people often started working at young ages and did not have access to education and school that continued until they were 16 years old. Therefore, it is the recent movement of mass schooling of young people, both males and females, that has had major effects on the rise of youth as a unique group of individuals and as a subdivision of Western societies.

From a *sociological perspective*, the contribution of sociologists such as Philipe Ariès (1973), who is known for his masterpiece *Centuries of Childhood*, has been important. In his works, Ariès contributed to the definition of youthhood by distinguishing it from childhood and adulthood. Thus, the major contribution of sociology is the shift of the focus on youthhood from a concept linked to a "class effect" to the emergence of a "generational effect." For sociologists, the cultural, historical, and chronological characteristics are considered as main factors in differentiating and defining different stages of life between childhood and adulthood, according to the following logic:

- The childhood stage is characterized by the child who belongs to the mother's world, from birth to adulthood. This stage includes people 7–8 years old. The stage is situated before entering adulthood and before going through the phase of adolescence;
- During the nineteenth century, the figures of the *school student* and the *conscript* (a person who is required to join the armed forces of a country) appear;
- Then, adolescence arose from the extension of both schooling and military service, which characterized the nineteenth century. The adolescence stage was still associated with childhood and considered to be the second phase of childhood;
- At the beginning of the twentieth century, youthhood was distinguished from childhood and adolescence and referred to a specific age group and a recognizable population. It is during this era that youthhood became a subject of research in sociology.

In the 1970s, sociologists defined the concept of "youth" and its distinction from adolescence was noticeably emphasized by authors in their studies (e.g., Nielsen and Thing, 2019; Debesse, 1972). Batat (2017a) argues that whereas adolescence is more psychological and physiological, youthhood is considered to be a social construction. As Figure 1.1 shows, in the sociology of youth studies, Roudet (2009) identified five major stages linked to the emergence and evolution of sociological studies that examined young people.

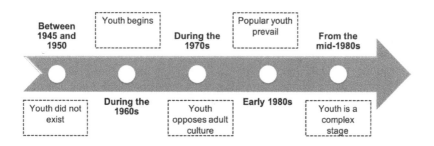

Figure 1.1   *The five stages of the rise of youth*

Since the 1980s, several studies on youth have been published by scholars in various disciplines, such as anthropology (e.g., Mead, 1935/1963; Rohrer, 2014), educational sciences (e.g., Wortham, 2011), cultural studies (e.g., Buckingham et al., 2015), and marketing (e.g., Batat and Tanner, 2021; Batat, 2008; Roedder-John, 1999). By examining these studies, we can define youth-hood as a period of transition into adulthood. This period relates to a process of socialization whereby young people learn to become adults in a society defined by social and cultural rules and norms specific to each society. This definition highlights the crucial role of the cultural facets of age and of youth identity, which go beyond the chronological and physiological notion of one's age range.

Following this definition, it is clear that each age refers to a different identity built around common values and anchored in a specific sociocultural setting (Batat, 2010, 2017a). Thus, youthhood is a social construction defining a social role and a social identity. As a result, youthhood does not refer to individuals with homogeneous behaviors and consumption patterns; rather, it is made up of several heterogeneous youth social realities: pre-adolescence, adolescence, post-adolescence, adulescence, studenthood, active youth, young parents, etc.

Also, in addition to the use of obsolete aspect of age to define youthhood, the American sociologist Parsons (1942) highlighted another difficulty linked to the expansion of the average duration of studies in American society, which has made it harder to define the status of youth. This observation is also accurate in the European context where the age criterion, which deter-mines the youth phase up to the age of 24 years, is no longer acknowledged. Indeed, entering adulthood by getting hired for your first job is no longer the sole criterion of this transition. Several criteria have been identified in demo-graphic studies (Tamesberger and Bacher, 2014) to precisely define the border between the youth phase and the entry into adulthood. Among the elements defining the entry into adulthood, four main criteria have been highlighted by demographers:

- Age. This refers to the chronological age at which a young person produces his or her first child. For instance, according to statistics from the National Institute of Demographic Studies (INED, https://www.ined.fr/en/), in 1970, a French woman, on average, bore her first child at the age of 24 versus at the age of 30.3 years today. In the United States, the average age of first-time parenthood increased from 22.7 years in 1980 to 30 or 40 years nowadays, according to the Centers for Disease Control and Prevention (CDC, 2015);
- Couple. This aspect is related to the age at which two individuals start living together and thus form a couple by getting married or cohabiting. Recent statistics reveal that the average age of marriage in Europe increased from 23 years in the 1990s to 28.5 years in the 2010s, and 38 years in 2018. In the United States, the median average increased from 25 years in 1998 to 30 years in 2019 (Statista, 2020);
- The departure from the parents' home and first permanent job. The age of departure has increased and is becoming later and later because of the economic situation and the difficulty newly graduated students are experiencing obtaining their first permanent jobs. This stage has been delayed due to the decrease in steady employment and fixed-term contracts. The average age of a person entering his or her first stable job fell from 26.5 years in the 1990s to an average of 28 years in the 2010s;
- The end of the course of education lengthened from 18.3 years in the 1990s to 23 years on average in the 2010s.

Youth is, therefore, a socially constructed concept and cannot be defined in absolute terms by applying an age principle, or even the aforementioned criteria. Indeed, these four criteria, including age, vary according to the structure and the organization of societies as well as the representations different societies have of youth. For instance, the stage of youthhood may exist in some cultures but not in others for the following reasons:

- The regulation of areas that affect young people's lives, such as schooling, education, or access to employment and housing, can vary considerably from country to another;
- The economic situation is also an additional differentiating factor;
- Historical and cultural factors are also indicators of the multiplicity of youth (e.g., the notion of youth in Northern Europe is different from that in Southern or Eastern Europe).

Consequently, marketing and communication managers must take into account the "youth experience" of young people according to the context in which they live, instead of using the age criterion to segment the youth population. Recent studies on youth show the existence of instability in youth, which can be progressive depending on two factors: time and space. Sociologist Van de Velde (2008), who analyzed four European countries, identified four forms of "youth experiences" that mark the transition to adulthood:

- The experience of *finding oneself* refers to the way of living one's youth-hood as a long period of exploration and experimentation of one's self and identity. The main objective of this experience is preparing young people's personal development and the definition of their identity on both an indi-vidual and social level. This type of youth experience has been identified in Nordic and Scandinavian countries such as Denmark;
- The experience of *asserting oneself* reflects how young people access individual emancipation and the different paths they take to achieve it. These trajectories are short and mainly centered on the employment search, thus guaranteeing autonomy, independence through self-financing, and the development of individual capacities and skills to navigate within society. This experience of youth has been identified in Anglo-Saxon cultures such as Great Britain and the United States;
- The experience of *placing oneself* refers to the race for a diploma, which gives access to meaningful work and high social status. Investing in extended schooling and advanced credentials pressures young people to find jobs as quickly as possible and thus exit their youth, which remains rather caricatural (e.g., irresponsible and inexperienced youth). This type of youth experience has been identified in French culture;
- The experience of *settling down* is very characteristic of Southern European countries, such as Spain or Italy, where young people are looking for a family affiliation, which slows down the departure from their parents' household. The departure is, therefore, conditioned by three main factors: marriage, buying a house, and achieving stable employment.

BACKGROUND BOX 1.1 HOW IS THE YOUTH POPULATION DEFINED IN EUROPE?

In Europe, the definition of the boundaries of the youth population varies not only according to cultures but also the institutions and the laws that govern each country. Sociologist Van de Velde (2008) examined the process of becoming an adult in the European context by comparing the period of entry into adulthood in different cultures to identify the key features that mark this shift. These are as follows:

- In countries such as France, Belgium, Ireland, the UK, and a few Eastern countries, an individual is considered to be part of a youth population until that person gets his or her first full-time job;
- In Scandinavian countries, individuals are considered youth until the day they decide to leave the households of their families;
- In Portugal, Poland, and Bulgaria, young people move into adulthood when they become parents responsible for their own family households.

From a business perspective, defining young people according to "youth experiences" rooted in different cultural settings provides an in-depth understanding of young people's consumption patterns and purchase behaviors and thus is much more relevant than a conventional definition based on the age criterion. The identification of different types of "youth experiences" calls into question the concept of youthhood as a phase or an earlier transitory state inscribed in a logic of "ages of life," in which age ranges are separated from each other by fixed boundaries and disconnected from future behaviors developed and adopted afterwards in adulthood.

Consequently, businesses aiming at young people should approach the youth segment as a cultural fabrication (e.g., Batat, 2017a, 2020; Batat and Tanner, 2021), which is understood from a perspective centered on individuals, their perceptions, expectations, behaviors, and meanings related to the consumption culture to which they belong. This consumption culture is shaped and rooted in a distinct sociocultural, economic, political, environmental, ideological, and technological context.

As a result, the criteria to be used to define youth groups and to segment young people are complex and cannot be limited to biological criteria such as age or the criteria defined by polling institutes (e.g., the age when giving birth to one's first child or obtaining one's first job). If we consider only these criteria related to transitional stages, how can we define and distinguish a young person who has never had children? Or, can we consider in the same way a young 20-year-old student unemployed and living with his or her parents, and a 20-year-old worker who is married and a parent? Are their consumption behaviors, patterns, and practices similar? Do they have the same consumption needs? Do they like the same brands? Do they constitute a homogeneous youth segment with similar expectations? How can brands adopt an appropriate offering and communication approach targeting such individuals?

These questions highlight the limits of the conventional segmentation applied by professionals who target young people by relying on a segmentation of the young population based on age groups with more or less variable limits:

15–29 years old for some and 11–25 or 10–18 years old for others. To overcome the gaps and ambiguities related to segmenting by age group, marketing and brand managers must rethink their segmentation approaches by adopting holistic thinking, which takes into account cultural and subcultural factors that shape the behaviors and attitudes of young consumers.

2.2   The Impact of Culture on the Construction of Youth

Culture is a polysemic notion that encompasses common behaviors and values, acquired and transmitted within a group for multiple purposes, such as cohesion, coordinated action, communication, and adaptation to the environment. Cultures are infinitely complex, with subsystems, such as social organization, language, or family, serving as focal points for observation (Schwartz, 1978; Hall and Jefferson, 1976).

According to Solomon et al. (2010), culture can also be defined as the accumulation of meanings, rituals, norms, and traditions shared among members of a society or organization. Culture includes abstract ideas, such as values and ethics, but also services and material objects, such as cars, clothes, foods, and sports valued by members of the culture. To Hofstede (2001), an iconic figure in intercultural research, culture refers to the collective programming of the mind, which distinguishes the members of one group or category from others.

BACKGROUND BOX 1.2 HOFSTEDE'S FIVE CULTURAL DIMENSIONS

To define his model, Hofstede relied mainly on an international survey, conducted in 1968 and 1972. The survey examined the attitudes of IBM employees in 72 countries (n = 116,000) and identified five major cultural dimensions:

- Uncertainty avoidance refers to the extent to which a society feels threatened by uncertain and ambiguous situations and tries to avoid them by providing greater career stability or establishing more formal rules. Nevertheless, societies in which avoidance of uncertainty is strong are also characterized by a high level of anxiety and aggressiveness, which creates, among other things, a strong internalized need to work a lot;
- Hierarchical distance indicates the extent to which a society tolerates an unequal distribution of power in organizations and institutions. It is also reflected in the values of the less powerful as well in those of the most powerful;

- Collectivism versus individualism captures a distinction between a tight social fabric, where people clearly distinguish those who are members of the group and those who are outside, and wait for their group (e.g., tribes, organizations) to take care of them in return for their loyalty (collectivism), and a social fabric where people are supposed to take care only of themselves and their immediate families (individualism);
- Masculinity versus femininity corresponds to the dominant values in a society. For example, masculine traits include the go-getting temperament and the taste for money and material goods, in contrast to a preoccupation with others or quality of life (the so-called "feminine" values);
- Long-term orientation measures the orientation towards the future, the present, or the past of a society (Hofstede, 2001, p. 354).

The advantages of the Hofstede model are widely recognized, such as its wide geographic coverage, its robustness, its rigor in research design, and its simple application in studies. Nevertheless, several researchers express reservations criticizing the method of the survey and the outdated aspects of the data. The scientific debate remains open on this subject, but the defenders of the model are more numerous, and many elements converge towards its validity.

Drawing on the conclusions of prior studies, we can distinguish cultures with a rich or poor context and examine them according to their temporal system, and distinguish between monochronic and polychronic cultures (Hall, 1956, 1976). While monochronic cultures tend to assign sanctity to organization, in a polychronic culture everything seems to constantly fluctuate, especially plans for the future. For example, whereas scheduling dominates the professional, social, and even the private lives of individuals in monochronic cultures, establishing precise schedules remains challenging in polychronic cultures. The same is also true in terms of individuals' social and professional interactions.

On the other hand, the GLOBE (Global Leadership and Organizational Behavior Effectiveness) Research Project led by House et al. (2004), which is the largest research project investigating the impact of culture on organizations and society, has conceptualized culture according to cultural dimensions, namely; power distance, uncertainty avoidance, human orientation, institutional collectivism, in-group collectivism, assertiveness, gender egalitarianism, future orientation, and performance orientation. Consequently, one of the major results of the GLOBE project was the identification of ten clusters of countries based on these areas: Eastern Europe, Middle East, Confucian Asia,

Southern Asia, Latin America, Nordic Europe, Anglo, Germanic Europe, Latin Europe, and Sub-Saharan Africa (for more details see House et al., 2004).

Acquired through a learning process, culture consists of a system of shared values that are invisible and stable over time, and a set of externally visible and evolving practices, such as symbols, heroes, and rituals. Based on these definitions, we can state that values are fundamental elements of cultures, especially when it comes to youth cultures. They are defined as a set of principles guiding young individuals in daily life (Batat, 2014; Roedder-John, 1999) and are related to enduring beliefs acquired and constructed by individuals through exchanges within their socialization processes (Batat, 2008, 2014). Transmitted mainly in childhood by family, but also by the school and the whole society, values are deeply rooted in cultures and change little over time (Hofstede, 2001).

Besides, the domain of the influence of culture can extend over several countries or regions or, on the contrary, be restricted to one country. Likewise, a culture can be divided into ethnic subcultures, such as the Hispanic and Asian subcultures in the United States, or by geography (e.g., southern and northern cultures) or lifestyle (e.g., urban and rural cultures). Following this logic and depending on the cultural setting, individuals' behaviors and practices, especially among the youth segment, are strongly influenced by various cultural factors that can be more or less important according to the significance of their effects on young people's purchasing behaviors, consumption patterns, and attitudes towards brands (Batat, 2014).

Thus, because markets are constituted by people and not products, culture affects consumer behaviors. However, it has been reported that consumers, especially young people, can develop similar behaviors and tastes (Elliott and Cova, 2008) because of their exposure to global ideas and images, as well as their consumption of media culture and social media content. For instance, studies show that in European consumption culture, there is undeniably the emergence of increasingly convergent consumption models for so-called *culture-free* products (e.g., high-tech and digital products), which are not affected by the local context. The same is true for luxury item consumption, although consumers' motivations can differ depending on whether they belong to an individualist or collectivist culture (Wiedmann et al., 2009).

Analyzing the impact of culture on youth behaviors, studies show that cultural values can be seen as a source of motivation for young consumers within the collectivistic Chinese consumption culture. Indeed, with the economy of the market and social developments in Chinese consumer society, it can be expected that individuals born into this society will acquire consumer values and behaviors that differ from previous generations but are identical to those of young people in individualistic Western societies. Using the work of Hofstede (2001), which highlights cultural values and the typology of cultures (distance from power, individual versus collective, male versus female, high versus low uncertainty), Elliott and Cova (2008) show that, unlike Western culture, the fourth dimension of Hofstede's typology (high versus low uncertainty) is difficult to justify in the Chinese context.

Therefore, the results of studies conducted on young consumers in the Western context do not reflect the behaviors of Chinese young people. The cultural values of young Chinese consumers are identical to those of previous generations. Unlike young Westerners, young Chinese consumers strongly embrace collectivistic values because these consumers need security and value compliance and goodwill. Thus, assumptions that the underlying values of young Chinese consumers have altered due to economic changes, the rise of new social trends, and their growing interest in Western products and culture are, therefore, contested. Indeed, Chinese cultural values remain extremely anchored and rooted in the national culture and are, therefore, transmitted from one generation to another, and to today's youth growing up in digital and contemporary societies while resisting changes and globalization.

BACKGROUND BOX 1.3 YOUTH ATTITUDES TOWARDS LUXURY BRANDS IN FRANCE VERSUS CHINA

Although youth are perceived as a homogeneous group with similar expectations, recent studies emphasize the differences among youth based on cultural and geographical disparities. The comparison of young consumers' attitudes towards luxury brands in two distinct cultural settings, namely France and China, reveals differences between French and Chinese youth in terms of their motivations for consuming luxury products due to their cultural perceptions and definitions of luxury.

In China, luxury goods are considered to be symbols of youth; in France, young people tend to perceive luxury goods both in terms of their symbolic and social values (e.g., the image and social status they project) and their functional aspects (e.g., quality, price, and promotion). At first glance, young Chinese consumers have, on average, less money to spend compared to French youth, although this is also due to the overall level of poverty, which is higher in China. However, among the Chinese living in big cities, many of them are financially comfortable. Due to the one-child policy, the children of wealthy Chinese people benefit greatly from their parents' income. These young people have the opportunity to study abroad and spend money on products they love. They purchase luxury goods to express their identities and styles and share them on social media. Luxury items are symbols of Western culture that allow young people who can afford them to demonstrate a higher social status and show their wealth and power in society.

In the French context, the youth population grew up in an economic context characterized by the recession caused by the 2008 financial crisis. They are, therefore, more careful about their spending and do pay attention to the price of products, unlike Chinese youth who grew up in a country that experienced, during the same period, economic growth and increased prosperity. The anxiety about the future, in terms of purchase power, differs in France and China among the youth population. It has been shown that French young people do not believe their incomes will increase in the short term. In contrast, Chinese youth are mostly optimistic about their incomes. This explains why young people in the French context are interested in good deals and promotions. For these people, the price remains a significant factor when it comes to purchasing luxury goods. In addition, French youth are less easily influenced by brands or role models. Thus, the main differences between French and Chinese youth when it comes to luxury consumption and purchases can be summarized as follows:

- Luxury purchasing behaviors. Whereas the purchasing process of French young people is more analytical and rational, young Chinese buyers exhibit impulsive buying behaviors in the purchase of luxury goods;
- Influence of role models (e.g., Instagrammers, ambassadors). Whereas Chinese youth are strongly influenced by the role models and online influencers they follow on their social media, French youth, who also follow influencers, are more analytical and do not necessarily purchase products due to influencers;
- Relationship with luxury. For French young people, purchasing luxuries is considered a dream that might come true or not, depending on their budgets. In the Chinese context, luxury is an obsession, and most youth end up purchasing the items that provide them with social status, and a powerful and attractive image.

Therefore, it remains important for luxury brands to deepen their understanding of the differences among youth populations within different countries, especially because the symbolic aspects of a brand, as a key determinant in the decision to purchase luxury goods is a powerful factor. This is the case among younger Chinese consumers. The Western image, social media influencers, and celebrities have a significant impact on the decision-making process of these buyers.

2.3   The Myth behind the Rise of the Digital Native Generation

Generational segmentation is not new. It is often at the heart of debates involving researchers from different disciplines, governments, and professionals in different sectors, such as tourism, luxury, food, distribution, textiles, leisure, culture, and so forth. For brands and marketers, each new generation raises new questions about transmission, continuity, and disruption in terms of people's social behaviors (e.g., their work habits and management, consumption practices, and daily lives). Since the late 1980s, we have witnessed a behavioral paradigm shift within consumer society accompanied by the emergence of a new youth generation, namely Generation Z (Gen Z), which is characterized by its values and beliefs acquired during its first years of socialization. Additionally, the simultaneous alignment of Gen Z and today's digital era has had a powerful impact that has created a large divide in terms of the values and traits of young consumers who belong to Gen Z and their predecessors, such as Generation Y, or millennials, and Generation X.

Several researchers who have studied the characteristics of Gen Z have given this age cohort different names, including the Net or Web generation, post-millennials, Nexters, Generation Next, the Digital Generation, and "digital natives" – a term retained in this section to examine the behaviors and consumption patterns of these young consumers. In some countries, such as Australia, the United States, and the United Kingdom, media and journalists have mainly contributed to the dissemination of the idea of generational differences by highlighting certain behaviors that are specific to digital natives, demonstrating a break from the codes of previous generations.

Although there is a claim of a specificity linked to each term used in the different studies, the authors agree on the common principle that individuals belonging to this generation were born after 2003 (Batat, 2017b). Furthermore, the emergence of this generation is a consequence of the democratization of digital technologies and their integration into the daily lives of a Web 2.0 generation whose members share a common digital culture. Therefore, digital natives belong to a youth generation that is creating a new consumption culture with codes and norms that differ from those of previous generations. Table 1.1 summarizes the birth years and the age groups of different existing generations.

This generational phenomenon highlights the distinctions between generations and creates new opportunities for marketing professionals to develop an in-depth understanding of the consumption characteristics of digital natives, their values, their attitudes, and especially the meanings they assign to their consumption practices and experiences, as well as their perceptions and attitudes towards brands. Indeed, the distinctive and specific characteristics of digital natives could have implications in terms of how this youth generation reacts and creates changes in consumer society. This, in turn, could result in a source of innovation for brands that succeed in capturing and sharing the core values of this generation.

Table 1.1   *Summary of the birth years and the age groups of the different generations*

Generation name	The age group of the generation in 2020
Silent generation	78–95 years old
Baby Boomers	60–77 years old
Generation X	39–59 years old
Generation Y	18–38 years old
Generation Z	17 years old and younger

Yet the idea of a homogeneous youth generation gathered under unique features and a common characteristic, namely familiarity with digital technology, has some limitations related to the generational theory used by scholars to define this age cohort. Although focusing on Gen Z, or the digital native generation, is a relevant approach for youth marketing, the concept is fuzzy, and its definition remains superficial and varies from one study to another. Indeed, the concept itself lacks sociohistorical and methodological depth, leading to disparate interpretations, conclusions, and recommendations.

To provide a better definition of the concept, it is essential to retrace the history of the concept via a multidisciplinary approach in order to introduce its implications for the marketing and brand managers targeting today's digital natives, who belong to Gen Z. Let us explore the foundations of the generational theory and examine its limitations.

2.3.1   Generational theory: a founding principle of digital natives

The generational theory introduced by Mannheim in 1952 allows both researchers and practitioners to understand and determine cohorts of people according to their belonging to a generation defined objectively by the criterion of the year of birth (Pendergast, 2009). It is a dynamic and sociocultural theoretical framework using a global approach that makes it possible to cover an entire generation, beyond individual characteristics.

This approach defines the generational models that are representative of the characteristics and trends across different generational groups. In this sense, the members of a "living generation" will continue to evolve and often redefine themselves within a predefined time parameter with limited borders. Generational theory, therefore, provides a conceptual framework that allows marketers and brand managers to explore the dimensions of digital native generations and understand the entire youth market beyond the traditional age segmentation.

Ideas about "generations" and "generational gaps" derived from genera-tional theory are not new but date back to the early 1950s. The sociological approach of Karl Mannheim (1952), as Namer (2006) and Donnison (2007) recall, emphasizes the link that builds a generation (being born within the same period) and the unity of each generation. Mannheim also underscores the acceleration in the rate of appearance of different generations, attributed to the ever-faster succession of changes that characterizes the contemporary era.

Lately, generational theory has found a central place and growing interest in the study of the consumption practices of younger generations (Batat, 2017b; Kjeldgaard and Askegaard, 2006). Considered today as a classic in sociology, Mannheim's work criticizes conventional generational theory, such as the French positivistic and quantitative approach, and highlights the benefits of using a historical and qualitative approach that has German origins. As a result, generational theory has contributed to the definition of youth generations, especially digital natives, who belong to Generation Z by identifying four key definitional approaches:

- A *demographic approach* that gathers all individuals who belong to the same age group;
- A *genealogical and family approach* that includes parents and their children;
- A *historical approach* that refers to the average time needed for a person to become autonomous and integrated into social and professional life;
- A *sociological approach* that defines a generational cohort or group of individuals sharing a certain number of practices and representations because they approximately have the same age and thus grew up at the same time.

In addition to these four approaches, Mannheim revolutionized the field of studies on generations by making a major contribution, that consisted in defining three key concepts: the situation of the generation, the generational whole, and the unit of generation (see Table 1.2). These concepts can help scholars and practitioners to better define the sociological dimension of Gen Z consumption practices and behaviors.

Table 1.2   *The three major concepts of Generation Z*

Concept	Definition
The situation of the generation	Refers to a "class situation," which puts forward the principle of belonging to the same historical and social space that goes beyond the chronological aspect.
The generational whole	Can be defined as the participation in the common destiny of a historic and social unity through the creation of real social bonds between the individuals of the same generation, who share similar social and intellectual content and interests.
The unit of generation	Refers to a concrete link that reflects the appropriation by individuals of common experiences within a generational whole. By giving meaning to their common experiences, individuals from a generational group assert their specificity and differentiate themselves from other entities.

2.3.2   What are the differences among generations?

Members of a generation share the same interests, beliefs, and values, as well as the same consumption behaviors, regardless of the culture or geographic area. Pendergast (2009) provided a synthesis of the set of values and beliefs that distinguishes each generation, as illustrated in Table 1.3. The classification brings together four main elements:

- Regular trends based on the type of generation (idealistic, reactive, heroic, and artistic);
- The recognition that the formative years of childhood – where there is exposure to a specific set of factors – determine the basic moral values and the belief system of the generation;
- The recognition of the stages of the lifecycle (childhood, young adult, adult, and senior) and consequently the characteristics of each generation at these stages;
- A birth generation is defined by its attributes, which are unique to any given period (e.g., Baby Boomers, Generation X, Generation Y, Generation Z).

2.3.3   Contributions and limits of generational theory

Generational theory contributed to the definition of youth cohorts by emphasizing the idea that individuals belong to the same generation not only because they are the same age but also because they have shared experiences that have shaped their lifestyles, consumption patterns, and way of thinking (e.g., the members of a generation who shared the economic crisis in 1929, the subprime mortgage crisis in 2008, or the coronavirus crisis in 2019). In sharing similar experiences, individuals belonging to the same generation define themselves in terms of the characteristics of their timespans and are aware of what differentiates them from previous generations. However, whereas generational theory has been of great use to sociologists and demographers, there are some limitations related to the generational segmentation that make it difficult to analyze the behaviors of young consumers as part of a homogeneous digital native generation:

- The first limitation is related to the issue of "generational localization," which reflects the lack of an absolute definition of the year to which each generation belongs and may differ from one researcher to another;
- The second limitation refers to the American origins and cultural influence of the generational concept. For instance, the G.I. generation does not exist in Europe;
- The third limitation concerns the lack of consideration for the social realities of youth cultures.

Table 1.3   The differences between generations

Factors	Generation X	Generation Y	Generation Z
Beliefs and values	Work ethic, safety	Diversity, freedom	Lifestyle and hedonism
Motivations	Progress and responsibility	Individuality and selfhood	Self-discovery, relationship
Decision making	Authority, brand loyalty	Experts, informed, zappers	Friends, less loyalty to brands
Spending and saving	Pay in advance and save	Credit-savvy, confident, investors	Uncertain spending, short-term needs, depends on the credit
Types of learning	Oral, focused on content and monologue	Oral, visual dialogue	Visual and multisensorial
Marketing and communication	Mass	Descriptive, direct	Participatory, viral, and via friends and peers
School education	In-class, formal, a calm context	Roundtables, planning, relaxed atmosphere	Unstructured and interactive
Management and leadership	Control, authority, and analytical skills	Cooperation, skills, actor-makers	Consensual, creativity, and trial and error

Source: Adapted from Pendergast (2009).

3.   AGE SEGMENTATION MYOPIA

Questioning the traditional age segmentation of young consumers is an essential step before defining a suitable and effective marketing strategy targeting the youth segment. Although several youth segmentation methods, which include age as a key criterion, have been proposed by authors in different disciplines and from diverse perspectives (see Table 1.4), the youth segment remains very complex and difficult to determine due to young consumers' paradoxical behaviors.

Table 1.4   Segmentation approaches of youth populations

Segmentation	Period	Features
Segmentation in the Middle Ages	Early childhood stage "infants": 0–6 years old Great childhood stage "pueritia": 7–14 years old Stage of first adult life: 15–21 years old	The teenage and youth phases did not exist. Individuals evolved from childhood to adulthood.
Piagetian segmentation	Sensorimotor stage: 0–2 years old Preparatory stage: 2–8 years old Concrete operative stage: 8–12 years old Formal stage of operation: 12 years and over	Developed by the Swiss psychologist Piaget in 1975, this approach is based on the stages of cognitive development from childhood to adulthood.
Segmentation by stage of socialization	Perceptual stage: 3–7 years old Analytical stage: 7–11 years old Reflection stage: 11–16 years old	Developed in 1999 by Roedder-John, a researcher specializing in youth and child marketing. She identified the developmental stages in the process of children gradually acquiring knowledge about consumption.
Institutional segmentation	No schooling: 0–3 years old Kindergarten phase: 3–6 years old Primary phase: 7–11 years old College: 11–15 years old High school: 16–18 years old University/graduate studies, apprenticeship/work phase: 18 years old and over	This approach is based on a segmentation method in a local context, namely, the French school system, which proposes a breakdown of the young population according to the school attended. This segmentation has the advantage of helping marketers segment the youth market based on their knowledge and skills.
American segmentation	Pre-school: 0–3 years old Kids: 3–8 years old Tweens: 8–12 years old Teenager: 12–17 years old College students: 18–23 years old Young adults: 23–35 years old	This segmentation is based on the identification of the social realities of young consumers and their consumption behaviors that result from these realities.

By relying on traditional criteria such as age or socioeconomic status (SES) to segment the youth market, marketing and brand managers risk a *myopic segmentation*, which can make their positioning strategy obsolete. To define an effective marketing strategy aimed at attracting the youth segment, professionals should not only propose an adapted offering and analyze the competition; it is also important for them to develop an in-depth and holistic understanding of the consumption youth culture these young people belong to and assess the norms and codes that shape their behaviors and attitudes towards the adoption or rejection of brands. Indeed, the youth segment is very heterogeneous, and significant differences may exist between different youth cultures and subcultures.

A new segmentation method that takes into consideration the criterion of *youth cultures* should be implemented by practitioners to avoid myopic segmentation. Instead, the youth market should be segmented following the idea according to which the consumption and purchasing practices of young people are anchored in cultures and subcultures characterized by common codes, symbolic dimensions, meanings, norms, and values shared by the members in each youth consumption culture.

This new segmentation proposal allows us to rethink the relationship that brands and companies have with their young customers by placing more emphasis on the symbolic, emotional, experiential, ideological, sociocultural, hedonic, digital, and functional aspects of their consumption practices. Unlike traditional segmentation by age and other objective criteria, segmentation by consumer "culture" and "subculture" helps companies understand the different meanings young people assign to products, brands, and services.

Therefore, understanding the meaning that young consumers associate with a product or brand will help marketing directors to target youth audiences with suitable offerings, but above all to build loyalty by sharing strong values with them. So how can we define youth cultures? And what are the main youth subcultures companies can consider to adapt their offerings? The next section answers these two questions and provides examples that illustrate the differences among different youth consumption subcultures.

4.   CONSIDERING YOUTH CULTURE: A NEW RULE OF MARKETING TO YOUTH

Young people nowadays have a great deal of autonomy and are involved in a large number of social and consumption activities. Young people's consumption practices begin at an early age and increase with time. This trend contributes to the individualization of certain consumption practices among young people and the development of different youth cultures and subcultures of consumption. The following discussion will introduce and explain the rise of youth culture in the field of consumption.

4.1   Defining Youth Culture

Youth culture or juvenile culture appeared in the 1950s; for the first time an age group of individuals who were "young" massively expressed their interest in products within the marketplace, especially cultural products, such as music. These young people displayed distinctive behaviors and exhibited different tastes from those of other generations.

The forms of musical practices were an entire departure from the dominant forms at that time. Thus, cultural activities such as music and movie consumption witnessed the emergence of a specific youth culture. This later opened up the paths to several youthful subcultures, namely the punk, rock, jazz, and rap subcultures. The phenomenon contributed to the consolidation and legitimation of an emerging youth culture by providing it with credibility in terms of purchasing power and the growing influence of these young people in defining future consumption trends within society.

BACKGROUND BOX 1.4 SEVEN COMMON CONSUMPTION FEATURES AMONG FRENCH YOUTH

Based on the analysis of several studies that examined the lives of young people and their cultural and daily consumption practices, I have identified seven major pillars that characterize common and shared activities and practices among young French people:

1. Listening to music is an essential, even vital, activity in youth cultures;
2. The bedroom culture is a perimeter of freedom for the practice of leisure activities, such as television, video games, surfing the Internet, etc.;
3. Young people attach particular importance to images as well as the visual and aesthetic aspects of their consumption practices;
4. Two modes of travel are important: physical, through the discovery of tourism destinations, and virtual, via the Internet and other cultural activities, such as cinema and reading;
5. In terms of the mode of transport, two-wheel vehicles are a symbol of emancipation from the family home and independence;
6. Creativity, curiosity, and thirst for learning characterize the different youth consumption cultures in France;
7. The rejection of authority. Young people need to assert themselves in a society dominated by rules defined by adults.

Many studies conducted in the 1960s were devoted to analyzing the practices of young people according to the different youth cultures to which they belonged. The examination by different scholars of the concept of youth cultures has helped to broaden the existing sociological models by further exploring consumption practices and purchase behaviors within youth cultures and the meanings young people assign to their consumption practices and behaviors according to different youth cultural settings (Batat, 2014, 2017a).

Furthermore, the concept of youth cultures captures the idea that young people not only consume; they also ensure the production of meanings and future trends that are likely to influence other people, for instance, their parents and other individuals.

The common definition of youth culture refers to a form of opposition to the adult world, which produces a dominant culture that young people tend to reject. The British sociologist George P. Murdock, in his examination of the concept of youth cultures in 1965, argues that the opposition of youth to the dominant adult culture can be explained by the desire of young people to get together around a common and shared culture, which offers them a collective solution to the issues linked to the contradictions of a society managed by the rules created by adults.

Youth culture, therefore, provides a social and cultural setting for the development and strengthening of one's self-esteem among young people. In other words, these youthful cultures provide a set of symbols and signs of recognition that youth can use to develop a personal and social identity by adopting consumption practices stemming from their youth culture, such as adopting certain types of music, clothing styles, and eating behaviors. To sum up, youth cultures are mainly described in relation to their capacity to produce meanings and symbols through the acquisition, reinterpretation, manipulation, and especially the reinvention of products' usages and consumption practices.

BACKGROUND BOX 1.5 THE EVOLUTION OF YOUTH CULTURE: A SOCIOHISTORICAL PERSPECTIVE

The idea of the uniqueness of youth goes hand in hand with the assertion of common consumption practices specific to this population, which evolved rapidly during the twentieth century. We can distinguish three major phases in the development of the global youth culture:

- Post-war youth culture. After the Second World War, young people, and especially those who were students, made their voices heard by engaging in civic youth actions and joining social movements. It is at this moment that societies became aware of the existence of young people who were no longer considered to be children – and their demands. Thus, the image conveyed by the media in the early 1960s portrays youth as a more autonomous, rebellious, and disturbing population.

- Youth culture, a mimicry of Anglo-Saxon youth. The spread of Anglo-American musical tastes, such as rock music in the early 1960s, influenced youth populations in different countries, especially in European countries. Music has always been part of the identity of young people. They adopt musical styles to express their opinions and identities. The Anglo-Saxon musical style has been acculturated and incorporated into the musical culture of, for example, French young people in the form of yé-yé, which is a style of pop music that emerged from Southern Europe in the early 1960s.

It is, therefore, a culture from elsewhere that distinguishes young people not only from adults and children but also from the rest of society. This culture becomes a generational phenomenon and the youth population is seen as a target market that deserves special attention from cultural industries. At that time, youth culture was regarded as a media culture, which found its origins and inspiration in media content such as radio and television.

- Globalized youth culture. Today, youth culture has become international and globally spread. It is now a question of the Americanization of young people across countries due to the rise of a global economy and the democratization of digital technologies and Internet usages that contribute to creating mass youth cultures, a consequence of the "McDonaldization" of societies. The McDonaldization of society concept was introduced and conceptualized for the first time in 1993 by the American sociologist George Ritzer (1993/1996). Ritzer identified factors for the homogenization of society and the youth culture that is part of it. These factors include fast food, media content, leisure activities, and so on. According to his definition, McDonaldization not only affects the restaurant industry but also education, work, health, travel, leisure, food, politics, and family among other things. Thus, today's young people form a global youth culture comprising a "McWorld" homogenized culture delivered by modern means of communication, information, marketing, and entertainment.

4.2   From Youth Culture to Youth Subculture

Youth subcultures bring together individuals who, through their consumption practices, define themselves as distinct from the dominant social norms in the consumption field. The subcultures emerge in collective movements as an action to deal with the lack of necessary resources. These resources are used to achieve objectives defined by the dominant criteria of the social system of

the middle and upper classes. To illustrate this definition, Table 1.5 presents
the characteristics of two youth subcultures in the field of music consumption.
The concept of a youth subculture finds its origin in the work carried out by
researchers at the Birmingham Centre for Contemporary Cultural Studies
(CCCS) located in Birmingham, England. The CCCS developed an approach
centered on the emergence of a juvenile subculture and its resistance to capitalist values. CCCS's studies aim to understand the youthful collective behaviors
that appear in different subcultures as well as the form of resistance associated
with these behaviors.

The definition of the notion of youth subcultures has evolved over time,
shifting from a "form of deviance" to a "symbolic and marketing" approach
to youth. Table 1.6 provides a summary of the existing definitions of youth
subcultures, their forms, their characteristics, and the main authors who contributed to enriching the concept.

Table 1.5   Youth subculture features: rap versus pop rock

Elements	Rap subculture	Pop-rock subculture
Year of appearance	The 1970s in North America and the United States; the 1980s in Europe and France.	The 1960s in the United States, the United Kingdom, and parts of Europe, and the 1990s in France.
Values	Challenges the elite culture and promotes street and popular culture.	Rejects traditional values defined by parents and adults. Emphasizes youth emancipation.
Social dimension	Consists of lower social classes and often young people with immigrant backgrounds. In the United States, it is more about a racial protest movement against the white music culture.	Considered as a mainstream and commercial version of real rock, mixing pop and rock. It is a representation of popular culture in the middle and upper classes.
Subculture norms	The predominance of masculine values and the separation of genders. Tribal and community functioning. The recent emergence of street rappers.	Challenging institutions, authority, and dominant norms that govern society to make young people exist as legitimate actors in the adult world.
Physical territory	American ghettos and poor neighborhoods. French suburbs.	Urban neighborhoods and peri-urban areas.
Clothing style	Sportswear and comfortable outfits inspired by the sports market: tracksuits, caps, sneakers, etc.	A reworked classical BCBG (*bon chic bon genre*) style with touches of eccentricity.
Brands	La Coste, LVMH, Adidas, Nike, etc.	All Saints, Levi's, etc.

For companies targeting young consumers, understanding youth subcultures
enables them to define effective segmentation strategies and marketing actions
that integrate the different forms of consumption subcultures. This requires

more sophisticated analytical tools to study the significance of both the explicit and implicit characteristics of the consumption practices of young people within different youth subcultures.

Table 1.6   *The forms of youth subcultures*

Youth subculture forms	Characteristics	Main authors	Example
Deviance and transgression	Considered a form of unconventionality and mental delay. The behaviors of young people, often from the working class, are considered as offending acts, which allow them to reach a high social position.	Burt (1925), Bowlby (1946), and Cohen (1956)	Gang culture
Subdivision of a national culture	An assembly of several social realities that are representative of ethnic background, class, residence, and religious affiliation forming a homogeneous unit allowing the segmentation of the youth population into subsegments.	Gordon (1947) and Irwin (1970)	Italo-American youth or Indian-British youth
Opposition and resistance	Interdependent subcultures representing a set of small structures located in a larger cultural network, and in opposition to the adult culture, the dominant culture, and the elitist culture.	Hall and Jefferson (1976) and Hoggart (1957/1970)	British poor youth in post-war Britain
Identity construction	An expression of youthful identity through the same style. Youth subcultures are agents of socialization that replace families and educational institutions.	Cohen (1972)	Youth punks in the UK

MINI-CASE BOX 1.1   TIKTOKERS VERSUS INSTAGRAMMERS: DIFFERENT DIGITAL YOUTH CULTURES?

TikTok is a video-based social media platform owned by the Chinese company ByteDance. The users on TikTok showcase their creativity by producing short videos and setting trends for other users to follow. These trends could be beauty- or fashion-related or include cooking tips and recipes, funny videos, or anything a person might think of.

In contrast, Instagram is both a photo and video-streaming social media platform owned by Facebook and is much more practical than TikTok. It gives its users more options to surf around the platform, especially through sharing photos. The platform is more emotional and personal than trend-setting TikTok. Why? Because people on Instagram normally share their digital photo albums of their favorite personal moments.

In terms of each platform's user profile, TikTok's users are mainly members of Gen Z who are, on average, less than 18 years old. For example, TikTok's influencers include Charli D'Amelio, who had 15 million followers at the age of 15 and now has 105.7 million followers. Its users are attracted to content that is popular, fun, and dynamic, as well as produced by teens for teens.

In contrast, Instagram's users are roughly between 18 and 34 years of age. Millennials, who are in their early twenties and entering adulthood, and Generation Y, the tech-savvy individuals who are always busy are the main users of Instagram. They share photos of their kids, dogs, or whatever they are doing at the moment. The user-friendliness of Instagram, where users merely swipe to see the next post and can tap twice to "like" a post, attracts these busy generations since it is a fast-driven application, and they do not like to wait. This is also similar to TikTok's user-friendliness, where each video posted has its own interface (along with "comments," "likes," and "share" buttons); users also swipe up to see the next post on a different interface.

To conclude, we can see that Instagram's competitiveness in the social media market is growing by the day, locking in all types of users by providing every perk that a social media platform has to offer. Nonetheless, due to TikTok's intensive growth in such a short period (it now has over 1 billion users), Instagram has to up its game.

To analyze the tacit meaning linked to youth behaviors in consumer subcultures, marketing and communication managers should combine several methodological tools. For example, to understand the clothing practices of young people and the link with their subcultures, companies can use a set of qualitative techniques to explore the meanings young people assign to their consumption choices and practices according to the youth subculture's dominant norms and values. These qualitative tools include immersive and exploratory techniques such as:

*   Ethnographic tools to understand the codes and norms shared by young people in their consumption subcultures;
*   Semiotic tools to analyze the various youth subcultures and the dominant practices that comprise them;
*   Historical analysis approaches to understand the evolution of practices, their cyclical dimensions, and the important changes within youth subcultures over time;

- Phenomenological examination through participant observation of places and areas of consumption that connect, unify, and bring together young people.

Exploratory and immersive studies of youth consumption subcultures are, therefore, vital to fully understand young people and their consumption patterns, and be in tune with them. Young consumers are often skeptical of certain brands and companies and are more likely to mistrust them if they adopt their "own" ways of viewing and defining young people, their values, and what their leisure and consumption practices should be.

Young people's deviation from certain consumption items and brands is a dominant practice in youth subcultures to resist individuals and the entire society and thus affirm their uniqueness and difference within the marketplace; this practice involves the seizure of power by young people, who impose their youth standards, ethical values, and symbolic interpretation on the commercial offer. It is thus a symbolic and creative challenge that leads young people to reject the existing and preconceived offer for them. Deviation practices in youth subcultures represent a social reality as seen and defined by young people that managers must integrate into their offerings and marketing and communication strategies targeting the youth market.

MINI-CASE BOX 1.2   E.L.F.: A VEGAN BEAUTY BRAND THAT FITS WITH ETHICAL VALUES OF YOUTH

e.l.f. cosmetics is a beauty brand that launched in 2004. The brand consists of a wide range of beauty products and cosmetics accessible to all types of people, regardless of what they look like. It is known to be a cruelty-free, vegan beauty brand, attracting consumers from all over the world. It was also one of the first beauty brands to go entirely online, distributing its products to various retailers such as Target, Walmart, Ulta Beauty, and other international retailers.

e.l.f. fulfills the needs of every young individual because it produces cosmetics for any eye shape, lip shape, skin tone, and face. No discrimination is implemented in this brand, making it even more attractive for young beauty fanatics who belong to Gen Z. Gen Z-ers love inclusivity. The fact that the brand is 100 percent vegan scores it more bonus points.

To create a better customer experience for young consumers, e.l.f. has adopted a personalization strategy for its consumers. Ever since the brand closed all 22 of its standalone stores and focused more on distributing its products to retailers such as Target and Walmart, as well as put more effort into having a steady online presence, its e-commerce sales have doubled. e.l.f. has personalized the shopping experience of its online customers by carefully studying their behaviors on the website and adjusting the pages they see accordingly. For example, if the user is a new customer, e.l.f. will display all of its products on the homepage; however, if he or she accesses the website again, the site will mainly display similar products to the ones the user clicked on the first time, be it skincare or makeup.

Veganism is the new black, not just in the food and fashion industry, but also in the beauty and cosmetics industry, and Gen Z is ready for it. e.l.f. has pretty much dominated the vegan drugstore makeup community. No animal ingredients or any animal testing are used to produce e.l.f.'s cosmetics. Animal kindness is considered to be "chic," which is one of the reasons why Gen Z-ers are very interested in this brand. Young people have become more mindful when choosing products. They now focus on how products are made. Just as plant-based foods have been growing in the marketplace, so have plant-based cosmetics in the beauty industry. e.l.f. was one of the beauty brands mentioned by Boots, the UK's leading pharmacy and beauty retailer, in its vegan-friendly statements when explaining its expansion of vegan, plant-based products. This beauty trend is not only growing but it is almost dominating. In fact, Gen Z beauty consumers have put many luxury beauty brands to shame for not joining the vegan beauty revolution.

KEY TAKEAWAYS

This chapter shows that developing a relevant segmentation approach targeting young people (children, adolescents, pre-adolescents, and young adults) requires an in-depth understanding of their consumption youth cultures and the codes and norms that govern their purchasing behaviors. Effectively segmenting young people also requires a deep understanding of the differences between various youth consumption subcultures. For companies targeting young consumers, a relevant youth marketing should not be based on age, SES, or gender but rather on the key features of youth cultures that capture both the hidden and explicit meanings young people assign to brands, their consumption activities, and thus, allow firms to decode the paradoxes behind their purchases.

2. From age segmentation to "segmenculture": introducing a new segmentation method based on the youth culture criterion

CHAPTER OVERVIEW

In this chapter, I outline the different definitions and conceptualizations of the concept of youth culture by questioning the conventional segmentation of young people and propose a new method of youth segmentation: segmenculture. I aim to identify the typologies of youth consumption culture that marketing and brand managers should take into account when segmenting the youth market. Thus, the reader will discover and learn about four major segmencultures, namely childescence, adonascence, adolescence, and adulescence. These segmencultures are discussed and illustrated through different examples of brands in the next section.

1. SEGMENCULTURE: AN EFFECTIVE APPROACH TO SEGMENTING DIGITAL NATIVES

Segmenculture is a method based on the idea of a marketing segmentation of the youth market that incorporates the criterion of the youth cultures and subcultures of consumption. Why is it more relevant for marketers and brands to target the youth market with a segmenculture technique instead of the conventional segmentation by age group? Also, what are the aspects that distinguish "segmenculture" from "age segmentation", with its limitations that I explained in the first chapter?

First, the difference between a traditional segmentation by age and segmenculture exists essentially at the level of the method and the techniques used upstream because, at the level of their purpose, the two approaches aim to reveal homogeneous groups of young consumers. Figure 2.1 introduces a synthesis of the elements of differentiation that distinguish the new method, namely segmenculture, from the traditional dominant one that refers to the segmentation of young consumers by age group.

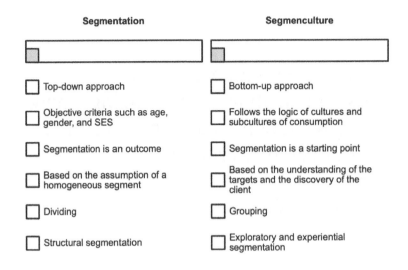

Figure 2.1   Segmentation versus segmenculture

Age segmentation consists of taking a population of young people and break-ing it down more and more finely using a succession of multiple criteria, such as age, gender, social class, and geographical zone, among others. In this case, age segmentation is guided by a top-down logic from companies to market-places and consumers. This segmentation is considered by marketing and brand managers to be an easy method in terms of implementation and is often used when the marketplace already exists. It is identified as a place bringing together different profiles of youth populations with more or less similar needs and attitudes.

By relying on objective criteria (e.g., age, gender), it is, therefore, more practical for businesses targeting young consumers to highlight their differ-ences and similarities related to consumption activities and practices. This helps businesses divide the market into supposedly homogeneous groups and subgroups of young consumers.

However, consider the market of young people who have paradoxical behaviors, and in which brand consumption plays a vital role in the definition of youth identity, their symbolic and emotional needs as well as their needs in terms of socialization: it is obvious that the age segmentation approach becomes irrelevant in this case. Hence there is the need to apply another approach, namely "segmenculture." Segmenculture allows businesses to adopt a more ascending thinking and consideration of the youth market through a "bottom-up" logic centered on the perceptions and meanings young people assign to their practices – that is, the perceptions and meanings embedded within different youth consumption cultures.

Therefore, segmenculture is not only recommended for brands and companies that target young consumers, but it is also the only reliable segmentation method for an effective and successful marketing and communication strategy. The importance of the implementation of segmenculture instead of age segmentation can be explained by five main purposes:

- **Purpose 1**. Segmenculture is the only methodological solution based on the idea that young people, although considered a homogeneous group, develop heterogeneous consumption behaviors. To gain in-depth insights, companies should not consider the youth market segmentation as an outcome, but rather as a starting point. Businesses targeting youth should not start by dividing young consumers into different age groups, but rather they have to first identify the features related to youth consumption cultures and subcultures through a longitudinal immersion in the world of young people so as to decode the hidden meanings that explain their consumption practices and their paradoxes;
- **Purpose 2**. In the traditional segmentation, assessing the relevance of the criteria to divide youth populations is very complex as the criteria selected are not always appropriate. The complexity related to the choice of a criterion in the top-down process raises different questions: is it more relevant to segment by age or gender? What justifies this choice? Thus, several possibilities can exist. One can retain several criteria to segment the youth population, but for which desired outcome? When traditional segmentation is used, marketing and brand managers can combine several criteria and end up with an infinite number of segments without being sure of the correct criteria in the list. Marketing and brand managers may choose more than a hundred segmentation criteria without knowing which ones to use to define an appropriate segmentation and targeting strategy;
- **Purpose 3**. Unlike traditional segmentation used to divide the youth population into groups, segmenculture aims to reassemble individuals according to their common and shared consumption experiences, their perceptions and meanings, their attitudes towards the brands, their consumption cultures and subcultures. Thus, the goal is to identify themes of convergence among young people with diverse psychographic and sociodemographic profiles;
- **Purpose 4**. Segmenculture is an exploratory approach that allows marketing and brand managers to prevent "segmentation myopia" since it identifies the features of youth consumption cultures and subcultures young consumers belong to. Unlike segmentation, segmenculture makes it possible for businesses targeting the youth market to orientate and adjust

their offerings and their communication policies to better match the norms and codes dominant within these youth cultures and subcultures and thus share common values with them;

- **Purpose 5**. The benefit of segmenculture compared to a traditional segmentation technique is that this method helps companies strengthen their connection and bonds with young consumers, which enhances their brand loyalty; this way, youth become interested in "brands that understand them" instead of "brands made for them."

Segmenculture, therefore, responds to the complexity related to segmenting the youth market that companies do not know very well. The market is quite difficult to segment because it stems from a youthful logic anchored in different consumption cultures and subcultures in which emotional, paradoxical, and subjective behaviors replace the rational and objective ones defined by companies.

Moreover, young consumers who are also digital natives belong nowadays to a postmodern consumer society in which consumption practices cover, beyond the tangible and functional aspect, ideological, sociocultural, symbolic, and experiential dimensions. These dimensions are shaped and defined by the norms and codes of a particular consumption culture that companies have to consider in their marketing and communication strategies aimed at youth populations.

To sum up, segmenculture is based on a very strong idea: the discovery of young consumers and the cultures and subcultures of consumption they belong to. Young consumers should be considered to be credible and relevant sources of smart insights. Why? Because they are the only individuals capable of informing companies about their values and ways of consuming, the roles brands play in their daily lives, how they see the world, and the way they see themselves in today's consumer society.

Unlike traditional marketing techniques, which focuses on three stages – segmentation, targeting, and positioning – segmenculture aims to identify segments of young people who share the same values with a brand. The brand, in turn, must integrate these people into its strategic thinking and marketing actions.

MINI-CASE BOX 2.1   THE PUNK SEGMENCULTURE IN THE MUSIC INDUSTRY IN THE UK

In the UK, various British cultural influences can explain the meaning and the norms and codes structuring the youth punk consumption culture as a unique segment to be targeted by the music industry. This can be done by considering four major forms that are specific to this group's practices:

- Their modes of communication. Young people who belong to the punk segmenculture communicate their values through consumption practices loaded with meanings and so-called "punk" values. The members of this segmenculture can be distinguished, beyond their musical tastes, by attributes such as particular hairstyles and colors, and a particular dress code, among others;
- The style. This refers to a production process that combines several objects to build a new, unique, and specific style that distinguishes this segmenculture from others. The style in this youth culture is a bricolage process that aims at collecting and recycling what already exists within society. For example, British flags are sewn onto the backs of parkas that members of the punk segmenculture proudly flaunt to show their belonging;
- The punk segmenculture is made up of heterogeneous elements. However, their organization as a common entity gives this youth culture a homogeneous meaning ensuring consistency between members, consumer objects, and values. These elements are intended to promote a belief or a strong conviction communicated in defiance of the social order established by adults. The use of drugs and illegal substances is an example;
- The punk segmenculture is a means of recognition for these young people. It also allows these youths to differentiate themselves from the dominant values of society.

2. THE FOUR SEGMENTS BASED ON YOUTH CONSUMPTION CULTURES

In this section, I introduce four youth segmencultures that marketing and brand managers, as well as businesses marketing to youth, should consider when it comes to their segmentation strategies. These segmencultures bring together cohorts of young consumers that I have grouped under four major youth segments: childescence, adonascence, adolescence, and adulescence (see Figure 2.2). I explain each of these segmencultures and illustrate the main strategies brands can implement to target them, share value with them, and enhance their loyalty.

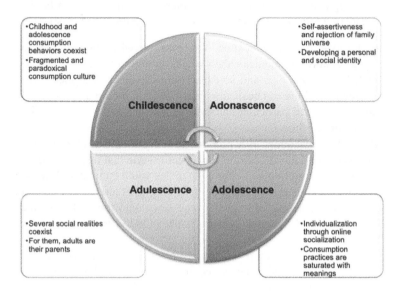

Figure 2.2   Four major youth segmencultures

2.1   Childescence: Amid Childhood and Adolescence

Understanding the universe and the consumer culture of children is an essential step that allows businesses targeting the youth market, especially at an early age, to consider children's perspective by putting themselves in the kids' shoes. This thinking leads brands to be in tune with a world of consumption in which numerous behaviors are related not only to the childhood phase but also to the adolescence stage, which coexist within the same individual. It is, in fact, a consumption culture that encompasses both child and adolescent behaviors and consumption practices.

During childescence, older kids coexist with pre-adolescents, thus contributing to the emergence of fragmented consumption behaviors characterized by paradoxical and opposing practices in the logic of the traditional age segmentation – segmentation that is supposed to harmonize this group of young consumers.

The childescence phase is a complex and difficult phase for parents to go through because children are demanding, often oppose their parents, and want everything immediately. To achieve their goals, childescents often use strategies to make their parents feel guilty. For example, childescents often claim that the parents of their friends provide *them* with certain products or claim that unlike their friends, *they* are deprived. In this youth segmenculture, consumption lies at the center of the relations and exchanges among parents and their children. Marketing and promoting products and brands to this target market should be, above all, emotional but not reflect the same emotions when it comes to the start of the childescence phase, in which marketing discourses should center on the values of socialization and belonging instead of maternal emotions and mothering products.

In this phase, childescents are characterized by a strong prescriptive power and do influence the purchasing decisions within their families. Likewise, childescents gradually acquire relative freedom in terms of their consumer choices and imitating their peers. They also begin to develop financial autonomy as a result of having pocket money, which weekly does not exceed, on average, 10 or 20 euros in European families (Batat, 2014) and $30 in American families, according to the *New York Times* (2019, see https://www.nytimes.com/2019/10/04/your-money/weekly-allowance-average.html).

The childescence consumption culture is based on the idea of using childhood references and their transformation as a landmark of emancipation – one where childescents learn to become consumers. For instance, licensed products, such as the characters seen in cartoons on television, help maintain and create a strong emotional bond with these young consumers. For companies, creating a strong connection with childescents can also be achieved by being part of an event-driven logic that arouses a latent desire via activities orchestrated around a popular product or brand among childescents, as they are also great collectors of consumer goods.

However, it should be noted that as these young consumers approach the end of the childescence phase, their purchases of confectioneries decrease sharply, and the emergence of cultural and digital practices, such as listening to music and using social media (e.g., Instagram, Facebook) begins.

These practices help young consumers in this stage of childescence to forge their personality and identity. Consequently, unlike self-centered consumption practices during the onset of the childescence phase (e.g., buying candy and toys), the end of this phase is characterized by social behaviors oriented towards others. Moreover, this population is a significant youth segmenculture since it nowadays represents a major economic stake for companies.

Childescents are characterized very early on by purchasing power that increases rapidly with age. They are seen as vital prescribers within the household and should, therefore, be considered in marketing and communication strategies (Batat, 2017a).

MINI-CASE BOX 2.2 DIDDL, THE CUTE MOUSE: A CHARACTER THAT APPEALS TO CHILDESCENTS

Diddl is a mouse character. It was created in the 1990s by the German entrepreneur Thomas Goletz. Goletz runs the company Depesche Vertrieb GmbH & Co. KG, which owns Diddl's brand rights. Originally the mouse was the hero of a series of postcards. From there Diddl rapidly became a mascot among schoolchildren and childescents in Europe (e.g., France). Diddl has also evolved from being a kangaroo (the first design) to a big-legged mouse that is so ugly it's cute.

The success was immediate. Depesche immediately entrusted a team of designers with the task of imagining a range of products related to Diddl: from stationery and pajamas to wall clocks and mugs. This diversification contributed to the expansion of the Diddl lineup of characters, with the arrival of the bear Pimboli, the horse Galupy, the mouse Diddlina, and so on.

The success of Diddl is due to the passion and fascination of childescents, both girls and boys, for the mouse, its universe, friends, and what it represents in the childescence consumption culture. The Diddl games that these young consumers play at school and the collections that they share with others play a vital role in the socialization of childescents. For example, a fairly common scene in families with childescents immersed in the Diddl culture is described as follows: "Every morning, ten-year-old Fanny is impatient to go to school, a rather unusual behavior. Her parents wonder about her sudden interest in school, but they don't know that their daughter knows that before the first ring of the school bell, the Diddl exhibition of the day is being prepared in the playground. There, she can proudly exhibit her notebooks with the effigy of the mouse from her personal collection and other licensed products that she attempts to exchange for other rare or coveted collector's items." This consumption can generate multiple situations:

Diddl makes childescents happy and becomes their parents' worst nightmare. For several years now, the little mouse has been considered the enemy of parents because of the expenses incurred related to it given the addiction of their children to the character. The amount European families spend on the franchise continues to increase as parents purchase related products such as pencil sharpeners, photo frames, secret notebooks, and more. For parents, it is difficult to resist the demands of their children. Besides, the mouse has attracted the sympathy of parents because it makes their children happy. The mouse is cute and soft, with a round belly and big ears, which captivates the little ones and inevitably makes parents reluctant to delay the entry of their children into the adonascence stage.

The success of Diddl is based on a marketing strategy targeting both childescents and their parents. Diddl is a perfect example of youth marketing backed by a strong viral phenomenon within the youth consumption culture. Diddl's marketing is based on three chief principles that create and reinforce a rewarding closeness with childescents and the two key socialization agents in this stage: a child's friends and parents. The main elements of Diddl's marketing strategy are rarity, secrecy (or the "between-us" effect), and word-of-mouth. First, rarity pushes childescents to trade their Diddl items to obtain original ones. This practice even becomes a significant moment in the day of childescents, which makes it possible for the brand to expand its market and acquire new fans. Second, the company that owns Diddl wants to keep this practice secret, so it never advertises, and refuses interviews and any partnerships so as to cultivate secrecy. This feeds discussions within families as well as at school. Third, advertising is replaced by word-of-mouth promotion, a technique favored by advertisers. Indeed, collection experiences among childescents are important. That is why the brand's stores organize group games to enhance the commitment of childescents to Diddl. For example, in 2004, the brand's flagship store organized a competition inviting its young customers to draw the Diddl mouse. The creations were exhibited for a month in the store's windows, which elicited comments from customers and thus made childescents feel proud.

Diddl has become part of the childescence culture. Diddl is considered a cute and kind buddy that is protective and reassuring for childescents. In a youth culture where the idea of pleasure prevails, school is often seen as a constraint. Diddl products are the perfect antidote. They allow childescents to take part in their childhood and share it with their friends at school. The mouse has created a strong sense of friendship, complicity, and optimism among this segmenculture.

To sum up, businesses targeting the childescence segmenculture should integrate the codes and norms of this youth consumption culture with their marketing and communication strategies to attract and enhance their connection with these young consumers. Thus, a marketing strategy that incorporates three major pillars, connivance, complicity, and proximity (CCP), should be implemented because it guarantees an effective targeting of childescents.

For example, Ikea's "Say it while cooking" marketing and ad campaign, which focuses on a modern family structure, cooking, and sharing, features a child who uses his parents' divorce to manipulate them by lying to them to obtain favors. The campaign creates connivance with the childescents targeted by establishing complicity with them. Thus, Ikea's approval of this behavior enhances its connections with the target.

2.2   Adonascence: Before Entering the Adolescence Phase

Adonascence is a youth segmenculture characterized by a self-possession phase. Young people belonging to this segmenculture – namely adonascents – do not yet define themselves as teenagers but don't see themselves as kids anymore. Thus, adonascents are an "in-between" group of young people who are attending middle or high school. They are in a pivotal phase full of paradoxes in terms of social and consumption practices. The adonascence segment should, therefore, not be confused with the adolescence stage.

During the adonascence phase, young people are far from the carelessness of the childhood stage but have not yet developed a particular need or an interest in self-assertion by rejecting the family sphere. This is the time for adonascents to search and adopt brands that help them define their personal and social identities, which should be recognized by both their peers and families. In the adonascence youth consumption culture, young people learn to:

• Assert themselves as autonomous individuals and become demanding in terms of consumption items because they use them as signs to enhance their personal and social expression;
• Strengthen their social belonging to a peer group or to a particular youth culture that features similar codes and norms;
• Replace their family identity with a new youth identity;
• Negotiate parental authority to achieve their objectives (e.g., negotiate their bedtime or allowance);
• Take power over themselves and develop the ability to engage in decision-making processes;
• Shift from the individualist thinking "I" to the community mindset "we young people";
• Claim and reveal their personal and social identities through their consumption practices, which convey meanings and symbolic values.

Furthermore, the adonascent segment encompasses various social realities linked to a person's moments of life and personal experiences embedded within diverse family structures (e.g., a nuclear family, large family, single-parent family, blended family, family with same-sex parents, etc.) in which youth consumption practices are heterogeneous. Batat (2017a) states that adonascents living in upper-class families and working-class ones do not have the same consumption practices, and thus their behaviors are different in two major ways:

• In upper-class families, the adonascent's identity covers three meanings defined by his or her filiation, family relationship, and personal identity. In the upper-class context, the identity of the adonascent is constructed in two main ways. On the one hand, a part of his or her life is free of parental control, allowing the young person to experience and experiment with his or her own identity. On the other hand, the person's life is under the control of others, especially when it comes to his or her studies and schooling. This model highlights a significant issue related to intergenerational socialization and common activities adonascents can share with their parents. These activities are common to the whole family and often overlooked by parents yet rejected by their kids.

- In working-class families, the construction of the adonascence identity is part of a continuous process whereby the adonascent has a single identity, that of the "son of" or the "daughter of." The adonascent is, therefore, seen as a member of the family living under the control and authority of adults or parents.

Adonascence is a new phase in the young consumer's life, which despite the heterogeneity of profiles and family structures, can represent a homogeneous adonascent consumer culture because it is based on common markers and shared values among adonascents. In addition, this youth consumer culture is embedded within a much larger national culture that gives it some particular features. The following elements need to be considered by marketing and brand managers targeting the adonascence youth culture:

- It is a culture characterized by consumption practices where adonascents act as social actors and play a social role within institutional contexts, such as middle or high schools;
- It is a culture of consumption that covers diverse social situations characterizing these young consumers according to the family structures to which they belong;
- It is a state of mind rather than a simple stage with a beginning and an end in the youth lifecycle;
- Adonascent social practices often belong to cultural, media, and leisure domains;
- It brings together two intermediate periods of life: pre-adolescence and early adolescence;
- The institutional anchoring specific to each cultural context is a common marker of the adonascence phase. For example, in the French context, schooling is compulsory until the age of 16 years old; a 14-year-old in other countries may not have any obligation to attend school and will likely be directly projected into an adult world of work or assume responsibilities towards his or her family unit.

Adonascence does not reflect an age group but rather social constructs that change over time and space. Also, the adonascence consumption culture involves three main socialization agents, family, school, and peer groups, who have direct or indirect impacts on the consumption practices and behaviors of adonascents. Within the adonascent youth culture, adonascents engage in individual or shared consumption activities, which help them shape their identity as legitimate consumers. Consequently, marketing and brand managers should consider the following characteristics of the adonascent segmenculture:

- These young consumers are seen as "immature" and legally incapable of making decisions;
- Adonascents change physically and develop autonomy towards their parents while adopting parental consumption patterns and behaviors;
- These young consumers belong to peer groups and thus have to learn to become themselves by interacting with others and comparing their needs and behaviors;
- Adonascents are entering a phase where they must continue the journey of developing their personal and social identities;
- The judgment and feedback of their peers, especially when it comes to gender feedback, is vital in the construction process of an adonascent's identity;
- The adonascent youth culture is characterized by a strong need for seduction, whether it is among friends or among the opposite gender. Seduction allows both adonascent girls and boys to feel like accepted members of the community.

These common features, therefore, support the central idea in this book, namely a new segmentation of young consumers based on the principle of youth culture. This youth consumption culture brings together heterogeneous profiles, but at first glance, it seems to homogenize all young consumers who are neither children nor adolescents, by opposing them to their elders and their younger siblings. Consequently, adonascents share an identical attraction for leisure practices and consumer activities and thus the latter contribute to the construction and development of common consumer behavior references.

For brands targeting youth, considering an adonascent consumer culture instead of an age group represents a new essential benchmark that they must take into account to target and adapt their offerings and communication strategies for an effective targeting method for the youth market.

Although the adonascent culture encompasses a multitude of small groups and subgroups distinguished by their tastes for divergent consumption practices, it represents an effective solution to segment the hybrid youth populations. This method allows marketing and brand managers to understand the relationship adonascents develop with the consumption world and how they define consumption from their own perspectives. For instance, these adonascents belong to the same Western consumption culture in which:

- New technologies are an integral part of their world of consumption;
- The purpose of their consumption is above all symbolic and not purely utilitarian;
- Consumption allows them to belong and conform to peer groups;
- Via consumption practices and leisure activities, adonascents build their identities as consumers by adopting brands;
- Adonascents use consumption items to define a social role and status in their peer groups. They can, therefore, be among leaders in the group or among those who are inclined to conform to the codes and standards dictated by the members of the group;
- In the adonascent youth consumption culture, young consumers use brands to impress and develop consumption knowledge daily in order to be considered by their peers as experts and thus attain a special, social role in the group;
- Adonascents develop consumption skills that allow them to position themselves in their peer groups and be recognized by the members of the groups.

MINI-CASE BOX 2.3   HOW THE BRAND ALWAYS SUPPORTED ADONASCENT GIRLS IN THEIR PUBERTY WITH THE "LIKE A GIRL" CAMPAIGN

Always, the American brand of menstrual hygiene products, has understood the importance of focusing on the closeness with adonascent girls by anchoring its discourse within the adonascence youth culture. In 2014, the brand launched a feminist ad that fights stereotypes and restores confidence among adonascent girls in a phase of puberty characterized by lower self-confidence and self-esteem. During puberty, adonascent girls' self-confidence collapses, notes the brand.

Always also launched the social media campaign "Like a Girl." The campaign was a great success and the ad campaign went viral among adonascents and overall among youth and adults with the hashtag #LIKEAGIRL. On Twitter, the hashtag and a corresponding video were shared by many users, including parents. In the video, Always chose to question stereotypes. In front of a camera, young women are asked to "run like a girl," "fight like a girl," or "throw a ball like a girl." One by one, they mimic ridiculous runs, weak shots, and caricatured soft throws. In turn, adonascent girls were invited to do the same. Unlike their older counterparts, they run at full speed, fight aggressively, and imitate an athletic throw.

Thus, businesses targeting the adonascent segmenculture should consider a strategy incorporating three major pillars, support, empathy, and understanding (SEU), to effectively connect with adonascents and develop their loyalty. For example, the Always brand supported adonascent girls in the discovery of their puberty with its campaign "Like a Girl," which put empathy at the heart of its strategy.

By so doing, the brand demonstrated that it understood the importance of building understanding and empathy with adonascent girls facing a difficult moment in their lives. With its communication, the brand fought against stereotypes and restored the confidence of adonascent girls.

MINI-CASE BOX 2.4   HOW THE BRAND DOVE EMPOWERED ADONASCENT GIRLS THROUGH ITS SELF-ESTEEM PROJECT

The Dove Self-Esteem Project is a program that targets adonascent girls 8–16 years old. Research shows that nine out of ten adonascents girls suffer from low self-esteem, which negatively affects their health. For that reason, Dove came up with this project to help these girls gain more self-confidence and heighten their self-esteem. Dove's ultimate goal is to reach a quarter of a billion adonascent girls worldwide by 2030 by building their self-esteem and reminding them of their self-worth.

The Dove Self-Esteem Project consists of its own guide, which is a digital tool called "Uniquely Me." It is a collection of articles written by professionals and experts that tackle certain sensitive touchpoints of female adonascents suffering from low self-esteem. The platform also includes activities to boost their self-confidence and ignite their self-worth. For example, checklists help these girls make significant yet constructive changes by initiating conversations with psychology experts about the subjects that bother them the most. Topics such as being cyberbullied, social media pressure, and appearance-related topics are also included.

This effective marketing campaign boosted the brand image of Dove both online and offline. Adonascent girls nowadays take extra care of themselves, especially when it comes to their mental health. Everything that was once stigmatized, such as depression and anxiety, is now no longer a taboo topic. Adonascents speak more openly about such topics yet are still vulnerable to bullying and social media pressure. What they need to get out of these "episodes" is someone whom they can trust, which is why brands such as Dove are creating these campaigns to understand adonascents better. The goal is to make them feel like the brand is their "safe place" and that beauty should not be a negative or pressure-laden topic for adonascent girls. Instead, it should be celebrated as a positive experience for girls of every color, race, and shape.

Beauty is confidence at its utmost, rather than appearance, according to Dove. For this reason, the company developed its Real Beauty Pledge, which consists of several vows Dove makes to girls to maintain and increase their self-confidence and self-esteem. Some examples of these vows are: (a) "We vow to portray women as they are in real life"; and (b) "We help girls build body confidence and self-esteem." The brand also established the #ShowUs campaign in partnership with Getty Images to create a stock photo album of diverse women and how they look naturally. The album was licensed over 28,000 times by over 2,500 companies in 60 countries worldwide.

2.3   Adolescence: Becoming an Adolescent

The physiological adolescence phase begins around the age of 12–13 years (Batat, 2008), marking the onset of puberty. Adolescence definitional issues are mainly related to the entry and exit of the adolescence stage and its distinction, upstream of adonascence and downstream of the adulescence period.

For marketing and brand managers, segmenting the adolescent target according to the age criterion is thus very restrictive. The segmentation assumes the homogenization of consumption practices, which are in reality diverse. They also depend on the meaning and the purpose that an adolescent belonging to the same age group but more in the "early adolescence" phase, and another adolescent belonging to the same age range but situated in the "late adolescence" phase, will assign to his or her consumption practices.

Thus, two questions arise before examining the consumption practices in the adolescence segmenculture: does the adolescence stage constitute a disruption or a continuity with the adonascent segmenculture? How is the adolescent consumption culture unique and different from the adonascence and childescence segmencultures described previously?

2.3.1   Adolescence: an ambiguous definition

In today's consumer society, the adolescence phase extends between 8 and 15 years old and can last until the age of 40 years (Batat, 2017a). This extension is partly due to two factors: (1) the extending of the average duration of schooling, which delays leaving the family unit, and (2) the fact that adolescence, in Western societies, is seen as a phase of experimentation, or an "interlude" before entering adulthood. Some authors have attempted to define the age of exit from adolescence by distinguishing between post-adolescence after high school, which is characterized by economic dependence but residential independence, and youthhood, which is characterized by residential and economic independence, but not yet stable employment and family formation. Other authors characterize the exit as occurring during the age range of 12–25 years old.

Although the social and cultural reality of adolescence is widely acknowledged in today's societies, its features refer to a more artificial fabrication, standardizing the physical characteristics of the adolescence phase. Indeed, the age of maturation and the standards related to children's empowerment and autonomy differ from one century to another and from one culture to another. As a result, the boundary between adolescence and adulthood fluctuates over the course of history, according to eras, social contexts, and cultural foundations. To be convinced of this, we merely need to historically examine, even briefly, the evolution of the meaning of the concept of adolescence within different cultures and its related perceptions and representations.

A historical perspective is provided in the following background box. Studies on adolescence show that the development of youth as a unified age group reached its peak during the 1960s in the Western context. As we understand it today, adolescence is a relatively recent phenomenon that in certain aspects is still evolving; for example, adolescents in the 1950s did not live in the same way as those in the 1970s, 1980s, or 1990s did. However, it is in terms of the psychosocial and consumption aspects of adolescence that historical changes are the most marked.

BACKGROUND BOX 2.1 A HISTORICAL PERSPECTIVE ON THE CONCEPT OF ADOLESCENCE

Most studies trace adolescence, whether explicitly or implicitly, to literature existing in ancient times. Since then, the concept has continued to evolve with the changes within society. If the term already existed in the Roman period, the analogy ends there. Etymologically, adolescence means "the one who is in the process of growing" and does not refer to any particular age group.

In Rome, only young men between 17 and 30 years old were so named, and they were by no means pre-adults or post-adolescents. Citizenship was acquired at the age of 17, alongside the right to marry starting at puberty. Women, for their part, could directly become "*uxor*" (that is, a wife) without having to go through an adolescence phase. The use of the term adolescence then disappears.

Later, throughout the Middle Ages, the population was divided into children and adults around the natural age of puberty. The terms used to designate young people were, therefore, more frequently linked to belonging to a group or a social condition than to an age group. This clearly shows that adolescence is a vague concept that is difficult to define from a physiological point of view.

While the physical changes that accompany puberty still mark the onset of adolescence and pre-adolescence, the same is not true for its upper limit, signaling the transition to adulthood. On the one hand, puberty is universal and is found in all times; on the other hand, adolescence is a recent phenomenon specific to Western societies. Gradually, the structuring of education increased the isolation of youth. This isolation facilitated the development of a particular culture for each age which, in turn, has strengthened the current idea of the particularity of each youth group in Western society.

2.3.2   The characteristics of the adolescent consumption culture

The adolescent consumption culture is defined less by its uniqueness linked to an age group than by its relative standardization of consumption practices, regardless of sociocultural affiliation. The consumption practices of adolescents are nowadays part of an intra- and extra-school culture in which adolescents show great autonomy that increases with age, both in terms of their schooling and families as well as their peers.

The major characteristics of this consumption culture are related to the rise in individualization reinforced by digital practices and online socialization. Examining this youth culture closely, we can see that the adolescents' consumption practices are saturated with meanings and loaded with emotions and symbolism, giving rise to different "self-experiments." Companies should, therefore, distinguish and analyze these self-experiments in a dynamic between the "singular" and "collective" self-adolescent before incorporating them in their communication and marketing strategies. Moreover, adolescent consumer culture can take many forms:

Standardized adolescent consumption culture. The idea according to which a youth culture becomes uniform under the influence of the global consumer culture is often debated and contradicted. However, when it comes to adolescent culture, standardization is explained by two factors of homogenization: the consumer society and the membership group. In the consumer society, adolescents are confronted with uniform consumption patterns that lead them to create a unique consumption culture in which norms and codes are different from those shaping the dominant adult culture.

Thus, the standardization of adolescent culture is a social construct (in the context of Western consumer society), cultural construct (rooted in youth culture), institutional construct (educational institutions such as high school are the theater where this adolescent consumer culture is exposed and shaped), and marketing construct (a culture driven by the marketplace and the brands aimed at young people). When it comes to adolescent consumer behavior, consumption practices in adolescent culture are characterized by the following:

- Production of the normative discourse of "us" and "others";
- A commitment to be unique and to be oneself;
- Self-actualization that occurs by engaging in a consumption learning process;
- Recognition by peer groups;
- Expertise construction and development;
- Transgression and deviation from the consumption norms established by adults.

Adolescent consumer culture is, therefore, organized within a community of young consumers that supports these individuals in their quest for a singular self but that follows the standards established by the members.

Adolescent consumption culture, a uniform fabric. The adolescent consumer culture can be seen as a homogenization that relies on institutional norms. Compulsory schooling is part of young people's learning and a practice of common and shared consumption activities contributing to the emergence of a high school consumption "subculture." This subculture is a variant of a more inclusive adolescent culture. Thus, these high school students place brands at the center of their consumption practices to differentiate themselves. These teens are the first to recognize the importance of consumption items, digital technologies, and brands in their lives. As a result, "material culture" – the possession and accumulation of digital objects such as tablets, smartphones, and headphones – has become an obsession within adolescent consumer culture. Indeed, these items are both similar and different as adolescents customize them and consider them extensions of their identities. This, in turn, reinforces the idea of a singularity in a community where consumption practices are identical.

Adolescent consumption culture, a practice of singularity. The practice of singularity is related to the cultural autonomy that adolescents acquire at this stage of life. This singularity is conditioned by the "other's" perception and exists in relation to the "other." Adolescents referring to their membership group consider others to be "all the same." For example, twelfth graders feel that the second graders have a uniform dress style; the third graders find the sixth graders funny in their group mimicry.

However, when it comes to adolescents themselves, they find it more complicated to define themselves in a reflexive way without comparison with others, such as their parents and other adolescents. In the field of consumption, adolescents very often introduce themselves with self-mockery, self-deprecation, and humor, both as easy targets of industrialists and as more informed and critical consumers.

Professionals and adults may consider the adolescent culture to be homogeneous and believe young people react and act in the same way and have a similar way of thinking. However, it is relevant for marketing and brand managers to note that there are five major strategies of differentiation implemented by adolescents in their quest for singularity, during which they are faced with difficulties but also failures. These strategies are as follows:

Singularity achieved by standing out from the masses. Among adolescents, the distinction must be embedded within the adolescent consumer culture. It aims to redefine the position and the social status of the adolescent in his or her group through the adoption of new consumption practices. These practices will help either "reaffirm" the position through conspicuous consumption, or "improve" it by embracing elitist consumption practices through cultural products "higher" than the current position of the adolescent.

The two differentiation strategies can help to reinforce the gap between the adolescent and his or her group of belonging, and thus lead to marginalization and sanction the singularity. Indeed, standing out carries risks and exposes the young people to teasing from their peers. Thus, this adolescent demarcation strategy reflects an assortment of practices in a consumer culture in which members follow different movements within the same group. The adolescent's experience of different consumption practices allows the person to forge unique tastes and practices that define him or her in an individual and personal manner.

As a result, these singular practices will subsequently be disseminated and standardized within the group. For adolescents, the line starts on the verbal and conversational level, which can influence a peer's purchase behaviors (e.g., the way adolescents talk about movies, their musical tastes and styles, recounting their vacations, etc.). Distinction and demarcation as well as empathy are strong elements that brands must integrate into their thinking to connect with this adolescent segmenculture because they contribute to the emergence of several hybrid subcultures in which adolescents show fragility alongside contradictory and paradoxical consumer behaviors.

MINI-CASE BOX 2.5   RIVER ISLAND ACHIEVES
AN EMPATHIC CONNECTION WITH
ADOLESCENT SEGMENCULTURE VIA AN
ANTI-BULLYING PROGRAM

The clothing maker River Island is famous for being the brand that "ditches the labels" as part of its anti-bullying campaign. The brand assumes that labels are made for clothes and not human beings. Adolescent consumption culture is mostly exposed to cyberbullying in general, mainly due to adolescents' excessive exposure to social media in the digital age and the freedom of expression of individuals, who may not be the kindest on the Web. For that reason, River Island chose to take a stand on bullying by engaging in a "Ditch the Label" campaign. It is a marketing campaign that cheers inclusivity and takes a stand against discrimination, hate speech, and bullying.

The campaign has its own website where adolescents identify themselves as participating in a global youth charity helping other adolescents aged 12–15 years old through highly affective issues in their lives. This "bond" between River Island and adolescents creates a foundation that attracts more individuals to join the community and build a better brand relationship. River Island, in collaboration with the "Ditch the Label" campaign, designed a whole line of sweatshirts and t-shirts exclusively for this cause. The shirts all have printed empowerment speeches such as "#LabelsAreForClothes" and "Pure Original, Do Not Judge," which are discourses and values that the adolescent segmenculture usually preaches when spreading awareness about anti-hatred and anti-bullying on social media. River Island makes 3 GBP per shirt sold; 1 GBP is donated to the charity "Ditch the Label" if people share their shirts on social media.

Other than this collaboration, River Island has also reached out to several adolescents, who have been the victims of bullying, and incorporated this initiative on its website, calling the platform "Troll Talks." Internet trolls are people who intentionally post on social media to upset people with their negativity. River Island invites adolescents to read about the victims and how they deal with hatred online by interviewing them about their negative experiences. For example, one of the victims, Callie, compared the number of positive comments she got on her photos to the few negative ones, which helped her move on. Another, Skirmy, learned to focus on content creation, which is his passion, rather than dealing with the negative comments by not taking them personally. Thus, the platform created by River Island can help adolescents learn how to handle cyberbullying by reading about the past experiences of people who were unfortunate enough to be exposed to this hatred.

Another brand also taking action against bullying and hatred is Hollister, a global teen retail brand owned by Abercrombie & Fitch Co. Hollister created an anti-bullying campaign in the back-to-school season. The campaign encourages adolescents to print anti-hatred and anti-bullying speeches and paste them on their schools' bulletin boards to spread positive vibes. Hollister also designed a limited-edition collection exclusively for the cause. Proceeds go to DoSomething.org to further the cause. Likewise,

Capri Sun, a German juice concentrated drink brand, created "The Together Table" campaign to spread more awareness about bullying. The campaign was inspired by the fact that more than 160,000 adolescents skip school because they fear being bullied. The Together Table is a long, wave-shaped table that is an alternative to regular separated tables. The idea is to encourage adolescents to sit together at lunchtime so as to promote more inclusion among them.

Singularity achieved through authenticity. Adolescents' search for authenticity results in their rejection of the "fake" or "artificial" world constructed by their communities or societies. In their quest for authenticity, adolescents do not seek originality or self-delineation to think outside the box. Their primary objective is to give meaning to their lives and above all to consume according to their own tastes; that is, they want "to be themselves" and "to have pleasure while being in tune with their desires."

In this case, authenticity and consumption are linked and allow the fulfillment of the real and authentic identity featured in peer groups following their own definition: "These outfits reflect my personality. It's really me," or "This style or brand is more me." Unlike adonascents, who are eager to talk about their styles, adolescents have a much harder time defining their styles. Their assessments often boil down to something like the following: "That's all me. That's how it is. I don't know how to explain it." Within the adolescent consumer culture, young consumers find that authenticity is nonexistent in the digital sphere, especially when it comes to their social media practices. These consumers display a fabricated representation of themselves: "The best of me."

Singularity achieved through expression and creation. Adolescence is also defined by the need for creation and innovation. This phase goes together with the development of creative activities, which can be expressed through consumer objects as well as cultural practices and leisure. Adolescents have creative faculties and great spontaneity. Inspiration and improvisation are two important elements for expressing their creativity. Creativity gives adolescents great satisfaction and self-confidence and is one of the pleasant moments that they can experience on their own in harmony with themselves or shared with family members and peers.

Singularity achieved through competition. As another way to show their uniqueness, adolescents are capable of developing a winning and competitive spirit to be the best. Singularity through competition must be recognized as such by one's peers; its existence depends on it. Socialization and relationships between individuals belonging to the same group, or the same adolescent consumption culture, are then modified under the influence of competition and the cult of performance. Competition in the adolescent culture manifests itself in areas of consumption such as video games, sports, music and artistic activities, new technologies, clothing, and so on. In the competitive singularity, adolescents do not seek demarcation or authenticity; they simply want to achieve their personal goals and have their performance recognized by their peers. To do this, adolescents must improve themselves and develop skills in their chosen field and work hard while remaining focused on the outcome. This, in turn, translates into "winning." Yet regression or failure is a painful experience for adolescents.

Singularity achieved through imitation. This singularization strategy may appear to contradict the very obvious definition of the adolescent culture and the dominant logic of assertiveness. Furthermore, imitation is often confused with the effects of conformism that characterize the adolescent culture and obeisance to an adult or dominant figure. However, singularity by imitation is related to the admiration expressed and assumed by adolescents of a figure or a role model because of the person's style, activities, speech, personality, or performance.

In the adolescent culture, where the concept of a "different self" is seen as an obligation to arouse the interest and consideration of one's peers, singularity by imitation of a model appears to be liberating. Why? Because it allows the adolescent to feel relieved of the pressure of becoming oneself.

The imitated model is consciously chosen by the adolescent, who takes it as a reliable and recognized benchmark to build a personal and unique identity in his or her peer group. Thus, adolescents adopt the dress styles of their favorite athletes, for example, imitate the language of their favorite singers and actors, dance like their favorite hip hop groups, and so forth.

MINI-CASE BOX 2.6   BRANDS THAT ARE PART OF THE ADOLESCENT CONSUMER CULTURE

For brands, adolescents are more assertive, know better how to handle the codes of look and fashion, and seek to express their personalities through consumption items, fashion, and music. However, belonging to "tribes" and conforming to tribal codes is strongly linked to adolescents' selection of the brands they purchase. There are more brands targeting adolescents today than there were ten years ago. For example, in the retail sector, we can find the French high-end retailer, the Galeries Lafayette, which opened a dedicated spinoff retail store targeting adolescents, called Lafayette VO. The store is located in the basement of a big shopping mall on Boulevard Haussmann in Paris, bringing together 150 brands of sports, jeans, lingerie, t-shirts, and shoes, among other items.

Another brand, H&M, has decided to occupy specific junior "spaces." The brand features the "lolita style" for girls and streetwear for boys. In the sportswear sector, Quiksilver launched Beach Attack, a brand dedicated to beachwear for girls. On the boys' side, the brand is betting on multi-use clothing that incorporates headphones in hoods. Dim, an underwear brand, has chosen a hidden approach to launch its junior underwear line. The line targets adolescents via an ephemeral site called "detail that kills." The line has no logo, and the site generated traffic (50,000 subscribers) thanks to an online game launched at the same time as the opening of the line's popup store.

To sum up, companies targeting adolescents should implement marketing and communication strategies based on three pillars, namely: uniformity, singularity, and standardization (USS). For example, SFR, a French mobile communications company that serves millions of French households, parodies in its ad campaign the problems that many parents have already experienced with their Internet service provider.

The company has done so by staging an adolescent crisis in its advertisement called "Inspired by real stories: Adolescence crisis." The ad is about presenting a standardized form of adolescence via the crisis while highlighting the paradoxical character, both singular and standardized, of this period of life.

2.4   Adulescence: Towards Adult Status

The adulescent segmenculture consists of young people with heterogeneous consumption practices and purchase behaviors. Numerous profiles of adults coexist in this culture: post-adolescents still living with their parents, students, young workers, young people who are unemployed, young parents, newlyweds, and young couples, among others. Also, several social realities within this segmenculture exist, leading marketers to question the relevance of segmenting the youth market by age group.

To define this segmenculture, we can state that the adulescence stage refers to young people, who are in their post-adolescence because they are still in the phase of rectifying their personalities, as well as the phase before entering adulthood. Adulescents seek to integrate the learning and skills they have acquired in the first two previous phases, namely, adonascence and adolescence.

By incorporating prior learning, knowledge, and social experiences, adulescents redefine their own identities, their relationships to their families and others, and their consumption practices. In other words, adulescents enter a phase of life where they call on the resources they have acquired to develop a strong self-concept, interpersonal skills, know-how to act, as well as serenity and respect towards oneself.

Adulescence is also defined as the interminable phase of adolescence that has persisted since the 1960s. It denotes adults who, in terms of their lifestyles, identify with adolescents but fail to reach adulthood. Such adolescent norms and practices have invaded the contemporary consumer society in the West and are even becoming dominant. Among the dominant adolescent consumer culture, the following values can be identified:

- The importance of self-image and aesthetics is emphasized;
- Imagination and subjectivity lie at the heart of one's consumption practices;
- Emotions replace rationality;
- Symbolism, youth culture, and hedonism are the main components of the commercial offering and advertising;
- Media and entertainment are cultural references;
- The juxtaposition of formal elements, mainly informational and infor-mal, is replaced with entertaining elements to achieve edutainment and infotainment;
- Reality TV shows and their relationship to ephemeral time have become a significant phenomenon;
- Consumer tribes have arisen;
- A person's virtual self and online socialization occurs through social media.

Why adulescents remain in the adolescence phase can be explained by two key factors: the enhanced immaturity of these young people and the expansion of the self-experimentation phase.

Maintaining adulescents' immaturity. Social structures and families nurture the immaturity of young people and contribute to the prolongation of the adulescence phase. Contemporary education in the Western system gratifies childhood and pays special attention to adolescents (a phase considered to be problematic because of the adolescent crisis). This situation contributes to people stuck in the phase being dependent.

During their childhood years, they were able to meet their demands. Therefore, once these people attain adult status, they believe their personal goals will be easy to achieve. Adulescence is characterized by an emotionally charged young culture dominated by an economy that marks the shift from attachment to one's parents to the emotional attachment to social and profes-sional relationships.

Despite being married and parents, some people do not see themselves as adults. From an age perspective, these young people are perceived by society as adults. However, they feel that adults are their parents and that they do not belong to adulthood (Batat, 2017a).

Adulescents, therefore, have trouble seizing the adult dimension as it is defined within the sociocultural context they belong to where standards are set for them, in contradiction with the claims and the way of being themselves. In other words, these people are in between three stages: childhood, adulthood, and adolescence. This situation means that these youth see themselves as:

- Children in need of protection;
- Adolescents expressing fears and anxieties related to low self-esteem and the need to belong to a group of "adulescent" peers with whom they can share similar values and apprehensions;
- Adults because society perceives them as such and also in their work they are considered to be full and emancipated adults.

Adulescents believe that it is their parents and not themselves, who are part of the adult world. They have, therefore, not learned to become empowered adults aware of their adult status. This raises the question of the responsibility society bears for not helping them become emancipated adults. The world of consumption has adapted to the adulescent culture, offering international events such as Comic-Con, for example, which bring adults together around practices and brands that are part of their childhood and current consumption world.

MINI-CASE BOX 2.7   COMIC-CON: A POP-CULTURE FESTIVAL AS PART OF THE ADULESCENT CONSUMPTION CULTURE

Comic-Con is a popular cultural event where geek culture, cartoon characters, and superheroes are celebrated. Originally known as the comic convention, the event has become one of the unmissable and must-do festivals "dedicated to pop culture" among today's adulescents, who grew up with these characters.

Created in 1970 in the city of San Diego, in the United States, the event has spread over the years to all areas of cultural entertainment (e.g., cinema, video games, TV series) without putting aside its major pillar, the comic strip. For several days, visitors, who are mainly fans and young adults, discover exclusive content on their favorite programs, including Marvel, DC Comics, and Disney-related content. They meet authors, cartoonists, and screenwriters, and attend film sessions and workshop. In an adulescent youth culture, the fans feel united; they can express themselves fully and without any fear of judgment; they can reveal the adolescent identity they keep hidden in their workplaces and from their families.

Expanding the self-experimentation phase. Life extension emphasizes the idea that young people have more time to prepare and engage in the adulthood phase. Today's longer life expectancies contribute to the youthfulness of society and to people feeling indifferent towards their future selves. This indifference is quite acceptable in the adolescence phase but can become worrying when it persists in the post-adolescence stage. Nonetheless, many adults prefer to delay their entry into adulthood and live in the moment because they are unsure they will feel fulfilled as adults.

Some adulescents, who do not particularly want to become adults, do not experience their youth as a period of learning and reflection before entering adulthood, but rather as a time to focus on oneself and one's desires to engage in cultural and hedonic experiences. Given the transfer of values due to almost quasi- or nonexistent relationships with their parents, adolescents who are seen by society as individuals, who do not know anything about life, take advantage of the adolescence stage.

They use the stage to discover new things and live new experiences by experimenting with diverse fields of consumption to reinvent their world and define themselves. As such, they take on a flexible, hybrid, and fragmented youth consumer identity.

BACKGROUND BOX 2.2 GAP YEAR: THE ENCHANTED BREAK IN THE ADULESCENT CULTURE

A rather American and British tendency is globally pushing more young people to interrupt their studies for a year to travel and reflect on themselves and their purpose in life. A gap year is a break prior to going to college and/or starting a career. Common in Anglo-Saxon youth cultures and even in the Nordic countries, this sabbatical year is frowned upon in Europe, mainly by parents and schools.

However, many students consider gap years to be rewarding experiences. As a result, the image of the gap year has evolved into a life project. They can select, for example, an exchange semester or the Erasmus program. Indeed, taking a trip on one's own requires a huge amount of determination and courage. Adulescents can get engaged in a gap year for multiple purposes, including the following:

- Forge their identities by exposing themselves to other cultures and adapting to them;

- Carry out volunteering missions;
- Dedicate their time to humanitarian or ecological causes;
- Test a profession before starting an extensive training experience;
- Expand and enhance their resumes to improve their chances of being accepted into prestigious universities or top companies;
- Improve their language skills by practicing them in a native context.

To sum up, businesses targeting the adulescent segmenculture should implement marketing and communication strategies that focus on three key pillars, or the 3F strategy: fun, free, and for us. Haribo, a German confectionery brand, has implemented this strategy by incorporating the 3Fs alongside humor, transgression, and self-mockery. The goal is to target adulescents by valuing the their childish side.

KEY TAKEAWAYS

To implement effective marketing and communication strategies aimed at young consumers, businesses should take into account four main segmencultures: childescence, adonascence, adolescence, and adulescence. These four youth cultures provide a set of symbols and signs of recognition young consumers can adopt and share to construct and enhance their personal and social identities by adopting certain consumption practices and brands.

3. How do youth become consumers? Exploring consumer socialization from childhood to youthhood

CHAPTER OVERVIEW

This chapter describes the socialization process of young consumers by explaining the role played by the main socialization agents involved in consumption learning in different youth cultures. I introduce different stages of youth socialization, namely: (1) primary socialization typical of childescence and adonascence youth cultures; and (2) secondary socialization, which concerns adolescents and adulescents. This chapter aims to present the major socialization agents that companies and brands targeting the youth market should consider in their communication and marketing actions aimed at each segmenculture. The socialization and learning processes of young consumers across different youth cultures are discussed in this chapter. The processes are also illustrated by different examples.

1. THE MAKING OF THE YOUNG CONSUMER: YOUTH ARE NOT BORN CONSUMERS; THEY BECOME THEM

Becoming a young consumer can be achieved through an intense socialization and learning process, which involves various stakeholders and differs according to multiple youth cultures and segmencultures ranging from childescence to adulescence. The social actors involved in youth consumption socialization can affect a brand's adoption or rejection as well as the development of certain consumer behaviors among young consumers. This section examines the socialization and the learning process among different youth cultures. The goal is to help brands and businesses targeting the youth market understand and capture the mechanisms related to the making of the young consumer.

1.1 The Socialization Process among Youth Consumption Cultures

The term "socialization," which is borrowed from sociology, is defined differently by various scholars. Two marketing scholars, Secord and Backman (1964), define socialization as a learning process throughout the life of a person. Although the definition may appear interesting because of its timeless dimension, this conceptualization is, nevertheless, limited for the following reasons:

* Its general nature;
* A lack of insights about what is learned by the individual;
* The purpose for which the knowledge is learned;
* By what means learning takes place;
* The person or people who generate the learning.

By defining socialization as the process by which individuals acquire various patterns of cognition and behavior, Brim (1966) clarified the concept of socialization by indicating what is learned by the individual. However, he does not mention either the purpose of this learning or how it is carried out, or even who the socializing agents are. I thus use the definition of Ward et al. (1977), who define socialization as the process by which young people acquire the knowledge, skills, and attitudes necessary for their functioning as consumers in the marketplace.

This definition is accurate as it explicitly refers to the logic according to which consumption among young people is an internalization of the codes and norms of their youth cultures. The definition captures a process by which young people, during the different stages of their lives, will adopt multiple social rules and modes of consumption linked to the youth cultures to which they belong. Table 3.1 presents a summary of the perspectives and theories of socialization according to three major approaches: cognitive (psychology), social (sociology), and cultural (anthropology).

Thus, consumer socialization, as a process in the field of consumption, allows young people to build their own identities and to conform to the norms and codes prevailing in their peer groups. Beyond the acquisition of knowledge about consumption, socialization is understood as interactive learning anchored in a defined sociocultural context, which begins in childhood and continues into youthhood and adulthood.

From an early age, children are in contact with the world of consumption, the world of adults, and with other children with whom their interactions take place. Thus, we can question the functioning of these interactions within the marketplace: how do these interactions unfold? What elements are transmitted to young consumers during the process of socialization? What are the typologies of socialization in youth consumption cultures? Who teaches young people about consumption? How do external social actors affect how they learn about consumption? And what is the outcome?

To answer these questions, I define young consumer socialization from an anthropological point of view as a process by which a young person incorporates surrounding social elements to build his or her identity as a consumer. Thus, the experiences lived in different youth cultures during the lifecycle constitute many elements of transformation. These elements must be taken into account when examining the socialization process of young consumers. The following section will present the two typologies of young consumer socialization: primary and secondary.

Table 3.1   Three approaches to young consumers' socialization

Discipline	Theory	Type of socialization	Characteristics
Psychology	Cognitive theory	Cognitive learning	The approach integrates the cognitive dimension as well as the accumulation of knowledge and their impact on individuals' learning processes about consumption.
Sociology	Social theory	Social bonds construction	Socialization is a lifelong learning process. The social perspective emphasizes the importance of one's relationships with others.
Anthropology	Cultural theory	The personal and social construction of the self	It is a process of the incorporation of habits by individuals. Socialization is seen as a social construction of reality. The individual's mind is formed from the following:
			• Knowledge and mutual recognition of identity;
			• Symbolic representation and appropriation of the object;
			• The work generated by the process of identity construction.

1.2   The Typologies of Young Consumer Socialization

Drawing on the works of the American anthropologist Margaret Mead (1935/1963), two types of youth socialization approaches, primary and secondary, that take place from childhood to adulthood should be considered by marketing and brand managers. The idea is to examine the consumption practices of young consumers within various youth cultures and subcultures.

Figure 3.1 illustrates how brands can participate, through the various socialization agents, in the lives of young consumers and support them becoming full, legitimate consumers during the primary and secondary phase of their socialization. The two types of youth socialization and the youth consumption culture in which they are expressed are discussed and illustrated through examples from the marketplace in the next section.

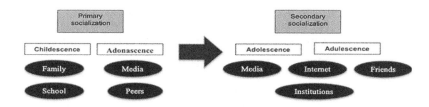

Figure 3.1   *Primary and secondary socialization in youth consumption cultures*

1.2.1   Primary socialization in the childescent and adonascent consumption cultures

Primary socialization manifests itself in the early stages of the lifecycle of a person and belongs to two segmencultures, namely childescence and adonascence. Primary socialization refers to an intense period of life that allows young people to absorb the universe of consumption in which they live. This world of consumption is perceived in the absolute as the only existing universe of consumption; no other world exists.

In these two consumption segmencultures, both childescents and adonascents acquire fundamental know-how and knowledge in terms of their consumption, which subsequently enables them to consolidate their social roles within the youth cultures to which they belong. Family, school, media, and peers are the main agents that influence the consumption learning process of childescents and adonascents. Thus, primary socialization aims at:

- Allowing childescents and adonascents to build their identities as consumers;
- Facilitating the adaptation of young consumers and their integration into social life by sharing the meanings and values related to consumption objects and practices;
- Ensuring both cohesion and harmony within each group of young consumers.

For marketing and brand managers, several avenues for reflection can be considered during the experimental phase of the primary socialization. The learning process childescents and adonascents are engaged in within this phase is intense. However, they easily accumulate and remember information about consumption. Consequently, companies targeting these youth should adopt a more engaging discourse with them. The discourse should incorporate the values and norms that are part of their consumer cultures and also their families while supporting these youths in their efforts to become legitimate consumers.

MINI-CASE BOX 3.1   TOOFRUIT, A BRAND DEDICATED TO CHILDESCENTS AND ADONASCENTS DURING THEIR PRIMARY SOCIALIZATIONS STAGES

Toofruit is a French brand. It was the first dermatological and organic hygiene skincare brand dedicated to both childescents and adonascents. The brand is sold in France in 600 outlets and pharmacies as well as in other countries, such as Austria, Switzerland, China, and Thailand. The brand offers organic deodorant and facial treatments for young consumers 7–12 years old.

Toofruit is one of a number of brands that have adapted adult products to childescents and adonascents. The brand connects with these youth by entering their world of personal hygiene and communicating directly with them, especially in the primary stage of their socialization process. By selling organic deodorants to these young consumers, the brand offers them solutions to problems that allow these youth to behave like little adults. By studying the skin of people in this age group, Toofruit was able to develop products specifically formulated to build a protective shield for children's skin. The products are ecofriendly, produced ethically, and come in gourmet scents. Toofruit treatments are adapted to young consumers' lifestyles and their desires so that they take care of their skin independently.

In its communication, the brand directly speaks to childescents and adonascents with messages such as the following: "My First Deodorant Toofruit helps to fight against bad smells and perspiration. Alcohol and aluminum-free, it is designed for the sensitive skin of children. Bacterial agents fight against the appearance of bad odors, while bamboo absorbs excess moisture. Mint and grapefruit extracts give a feeling of long-lasting freshness." The brand also addresses parents via messages about how the products should be applied: for example, "After showering, apply deodorant to your children's armpits."

To be adopted by these young consumers, a brand has to consider the values of childescents and adonascents as an integral part of their universe. The brand can do so by integrating playfulness, a value that increases the youths' desire for the brand. Brands can also revisit the culture of families (e.g., the youths' parents, grandparents, and relationships with siblings) to find a common ground and propose new ways of consuming by focusing on intergenerational or family consumption practices. This approach is recommended as it helps companies strengthen the presence of their brands within the sociocultural and family spheres of young consumers.

MINI-CASE BOX 3.2   COCA-COLA: "BROTHERLY LOVE" CAMPAIGN CREATES A SOCIALIZATION PRESENCE BY EMPHASIZING LOVE AND CONFLICT IN THE FAMILY

"Brotherly Love," an advertising campaign launched by Coca-Cola in early 2016 and featured on the brand's website, tells the story of love and conflict among family members, specifically, the difficult relationship between two brothers. One advertisement shows the older brother dominating the younger brother by engaging in aggressive and inappropriate behaviors towards him. However, when one day, a group of young people steal the little brother's bottle of Coke, his brother comes to his rescue and intervenes to defend him and recover the bottle of Coca-Cola. This shows the solidarity and love between the brothers despite their conflicts. These values, along with the Coca-Cola brand are, therefore, seen as the glue that holds the relationship together.

This campaign is also designed to show that Coca-Cola cares about family bonds and friendships, and how its product is made for friends and family to gather around, whether it is at the dinner table, standing up against bullies, or any other scenario. Coca-Cola wants to position itself as a beverage brand that drives people closer to one another instead of apart; the brand wants to build an emotional connection with its customers through the campaign rather than merely delivering a product. Coca-Cola is relying on this strategy to lead customers to buy the product, to an extent where they might think, "There is no gathering without Coca-Cola."

Usually targeting the youth market, Coca-Cola aims to project an image of people sharing their happiness with family and friends over a thirst-quenching drink: Coke. Naturally, when youth plan to meet up, it is often over lunch or drinks. Moreover, since a cola is a somewhat "universal" drink for most people, Coca-Cola aims to be the drink to which these friends form strong connections. The same is true with families; when they meet up for lunch dates and celebrations, or are merely catching up, you can almost always find a Coca-Cola on the table being poured.

Similarly, in 2019, Coca-Cola sought to increase family bonds and intensify friendships with its "Taste the Feeling" campaign, which ran in Thailand and targeted millennials. Coca-Cola organized a food event and invited Thai families to have meals with their children, in addition to having a coke, of course. Food plays an important role in Thai culture. Coca-Cola wanted to join in with the culture by having its brand feature where families and friends share their cherished moments and make memories.

Another Coca-Cola campaign utilized a "friendship machine" to celebrate Friend's Day in Latin America. The company did so by putting Coca-Cola vending machines 3.5 meters tall in the streets. No person could reach the machines to get a Coke without the help of others, who provided them with chairs, or even let them to stand on their backs, to reach the machines. People reacted positively to the campaign; 800 plus cans of Coca-Cola were sold every 9 hours, and sales increased by more than 1,000 percent.

All these campaigns show how much Coca-Cola not only values its mission statement of bringing people together but also comes up with creative campaigns that ensure people bond with each other.

Primary socialization is, therefore, seen as the first process of building the identity of the young consumer in which brands can participate in a context where childescents and adonascents learn to become consumers through multiple relationships and interactions within the family sphere. In this primary socialization stage, the consumption learning process is achieved through three types of interactions: with one's family members (e.g., parents and siblings), peers and school (e.g., cultural and other sports activities), and media (e.g., ads).

Interactions among family. The brand's presence in the interactions among childescents and adonascents and their families helps to strengthen the bond between the family members following different types of relationships, such as parents and their children, children and their grandparents, and between siblings. Sharing consumption practices is considered as a moment of complicity and thus leads to pleasure and positive emotions if the moment is appreciated by those who share it. For example, a candy can represent a bonding moment between a father and his child, who is keen to share the candy with his father and compare tastes while having fun.

This mode of consumption becomes a means of building an emotional bond by helping to re-establish privileged communication represented by a particular consumption practice or a specific brand. The learning process is then achieved through transmission and sharing consumption experiences, which generate among children a form of nostalgia for the product or brand once they become adults.

MINI-CASE BOX 3.3   COMPTOIR DES
COTONNIERS, AN INTERGENERATIONAL
BRAND THAT RELIES ON THE BOND
BETWEEN MOTHERS AND DAUGHTERS

The relationship and closeness between mothers and daughters are honored by the French clothing brand Comptoir des Cotonniers. Comptoir des Cotonniers has succeeded in building strong relationships with young customers by emphasizing the bonds among the generations. The brand was founded in the early 1990s with the opening of the retailer's first two stores: one in Paris and one in Toulouse.

Comptoir des Cotonniers targets both young and adult women aged 13–50 with simple and understated fashions. The brand positions itself in the high-end midrange of the women's ready-to-wear market. The company's products are also of good quality and made sustainably.

For two years, Comptoir des Cotonniers remained a hidden brand. But in 1997, Georgette Elicha, the creator's wife, had a revolutionary idea that would forever change the future of the brand: after observing a mother and a daughter window shopping, she proposed to develop additional collections likely to appeal to *both* mothers and daughters.

The brand relies on the unique bond shared by mothers and daughters around the world. All of the brand's communications are oriented in this direction, and its advertisements feature real mothers and their daughters. The public adopted the brand and it developed rapidly. Comptoir des Cotonniers stores first flourished in France and then abroad as sales exploded.

Interaction among peers. In primary socialization, the peer group, school friends, the reference group, and the membership group are among the socialization agents who play a significant role in the consumption learning process in youth cultures. Brands can then target both childescents and adonascents by leveraging the values of their peer groups. Outside of the family, the social dynamics are different. Young consumers in the primary socialization phase are often left alone to experiment and define themselves. They have to make a place for themselves on their own.

Hence, brands need to be part of this youth experience by supporting these young people in their process of becoming consumers, which involves experimentation by developing friendships and interacting with one's peers. The peer group thus plays a central role in this phase; it is to their friends that childescents and adonascents turn when they separate themselves from their parents. They seek to move away from family consumption practices by shifting more towards consumption patterns and brands popular among their peers, based on the norms and values prevailing in their consumption culture.

Brands can be integrated into games or through interactions with peers. This, in turn, helps to structure the development of their knowledge, allowing these young consumers to engage in satisfactory social interactions, thanks to sharing interests, concerns, and feelings with their peers.

MINI-CASE BOX 3.4   NIKE, THE TOP BRAND AMONG PEERS IN SCHOOLS

Nike is a popular brand among young consumers and their parents. When questioned, almost all parents state that their children prefer to wear designer clothes. Although more boys than girls say they want to wear Nike sneakers and outfits because they are attractive and good-looking, most parents think their children do so mainly to be more easily accepted by their peers.

The question of clothing is indeed essential in the harsh world of playgrounds. It can lead to popularity and respect as well as mockery and rejection. Young consumers, who want to fit in, therefore do everything they can to convince their parents to buy them designer clothes. As for the favorite brands among elementary and high-school youths, the majority of these young consumers favor Nike shoes. In terms of accessories, Nike also dominates the field of caps, having a 21 percent greater market share than Lacoste and Von Dutch.

Media interaction. Media is an impersonal socialization agent that exerts a major influence when it comes to a young consumer's learning process in terms of developing consumption knowledge. No longer little children and not yet adolescents, childescents and adonascents are beginning to develop their identity and to place more importance on the image they project. Brands can integrate the world of these young consumers by treating them as adolescents or in some cases as adults.

By considering these young consumers to be independent and mature consumers, brands can succeed in warding off the influence of their parents, who will be replaced by advertising. This leaves young people vulnerable to potentially unhealthy messages about their body image, sexuality, relationships, and violence. Integrating the consumption culture of childescents and adonascents in the primary socialization phase leads brands to develop a "cool" image and thus encourages these young consumers to share them with their peers.

The cool image of the brand is then endorsed and promoted by these young consumers within their consumption cultures. However, assessing the evolution of the "coolness" of the brand is necessary because it can be an ephemeral trend in youth culture, and young people may turn to something else without warning. Media, through advertising, capture the specificities of childescents and adonascents and recycle them into products or discourse.

This action leads to marking the transition from a youth consumption culture built by young consumers via incorporating personal, sociocultural, and symbolic aspects towards a fabricated youth culture.

MINI-CASE BOX 3.5   OASIS, A "COOL" SOFT DRINK BRAND AMONG YOUNG CONSUMERS

The success of the drink brand Oasis is due to its "cool" image featured in ads and on social media sites as well as through exclusive content produced by the brand. The brand regularly disseminates two to three messages per week, and their content is humorous and laden with puns and current events.

Oasis became the first French brand on Facebook and now has more than 2 million youth fans on the site. The brand's third best-selling drink in France, P'tit Oasis, was pitched to the youngest group. It was positioned to be enjoyed by childescents with the same nutritional content (fruit, spring water, and no preservatives or artificial coloring) and the same format (20 cl, with a straw).

Oasis is one of the brands that features a cool attitude to enhance its attractiveness and connect with the youth segment, both younger and older consumers. For several years now, the brand has succeeded in creating a real youth community around its products, and especially its fruity "mascots" and its image in the online and offline media, thanks to its creative and funny advertisements.

In 2008, the brand's "Only Doo" ad revealed the drink maker's quirky side. The ad easily reached its young target (people 8–24 years old) with a tag line that has become a cult: "Only youuuuu … No no, no, Doo!!!!" The ad changed the brand from a drink for children to a drink for different youth cultures. At the end of 2011, the superfruits arrived, with fruity superheroes each protecting their own bottles. With the character of the valiant Wonder Papaya created for the launch of a new flavor – Pineapple Papaya – Oasis made use of its fans for its choice of advertising. The drink maker's collaborative and participatory campaign was based on sympathy, humor, and emotional capital.

Likewise, Oasis's social media campaigns aim to strengthen the brand's interactivity with young consumers. For example, they can scan QR codes to view the brand's ads, discover its parodies in viral videos, and participate in contests. Oasis's latest app allows people to take a picture of someone and then photoshop a small fruit on the person's back, face, or eyes before posting it on the web.

1.2.2   Secondary socialization in adolescent and adulescent consumption cultures

Secondary socialization is related to the two segmencultures adolescence and adulescence. These two youth consumption cultures are linked to two main stages in the life of young consumers: (1) their entry into the physiological adolescence phase and the discovery of their bodies, and (2) the end of the adolescence phase and becoming an adult by getting their first jobs or becoming parents. Secondary socialization refers to the integration of these young people into social groups through professional belonging, marriage formation, higher education, or childbirth.

Unlike primary socialization, which emphasizes young consumers' interactions with the family circle, secondary socialization is more oriented towards social exchanges with others. It is, therefore, a matter of much more unstable socialization and more a source of transformation of social reality from a subjective to an objective vision. For example, a young employee who adopts a certain formal dress code during his or her first professional experience may easily give it up if he or she notices his or her colleagues are wearing a rather casual style.

Thus, while primary socialization conveys general standards defined in a family context and based on socially acceptable rules, secondary socialization relates to specific and local standards that may vary according to the person's phase of life or the place of work. Yet it should be noted that the primary and secondary socialization are linked. Secondary socialization never completely erases consumer identity and brand preferences developed during a person's primary socialization phase. However, secondary socialization can change and transform the consumption practices of young people who, with age, are more inclined to multiply their sources of socialization.

MINI-CASE BOX 3.6   CRUNCH, A CHOCOLATE BRAND THAT IS PART OF THE SECONDARY SOCIALIZATION OF ADOLESCENTS AND ADULESCENTS

Crunch (Nestlé) is one of the brands that have evolved with the evolution of the youth market and young consumers. The brand took up this challenge by moving its marketing and communication strategy from a childish and family universe to a more adolescent and adulescent youth culture sphere.

To do this, Crunch relied on the Internet, social media, and participatory campaigns by involving young consumers in a co-creative process. Since 2012, the chocolate brand has implemented a digital strategy in which young users are invited to participate in the creation of its next ad.

Several situations have been proposed to guide young consumers in the co-creation of advertising. For example, offering them the possibility to decide on the brand's influencers' destinations for a world tour organized by the brand or co-writing the screenplay for the brand's next ad by submitting their ideas on the company's Facebook's page. In addition, the brand gives these young consumers the possibility to vote for their favorite flavors launched by the brand. By so doing, the chocolate brand has succeeded in entering the secondary socialization phase by seducing both adolescents and adulescents and engaging them to better retain them and collaborate for the long term. They are perceived as a source of innovation with great creative potential.

2.   HOW DOES CONSUMER SOCIALIZATION WORK IN YOUTH CULTURES?

Young consumer socialization is based on the idea of learning to consume in a particular sociocultural context. This means that young people's learning approach is not only limited to the process of acquiring consumption knowledge about the products and brands they purchase but also integrates the social actors that are part of the marketplace and the social environment of these young consumers. These actors are called "socialization agents" and they can have a significant influence on the consumer behavior of young people. Socialization agents are also actors with whom young consumers create two-way interactions and social exchanges throughout their lives, as shown in Figure 3.2.

Following this perspective, the influence of youth cultures on the behavior of young consumers remains essential. However, unlike the classical learning theories that focus on the cognitive aspect of knowledge, in consumer socialization theory, significant emphasis is given to sociocultural and symbolic factors that can influence young consumers' behaviors and perceptions of their environments.

These people's perceptions are often more important than the real conditions in which they find themselves. Indeed, young consumers do not respond only to stimuli; they interpret them according to their perceptions formed by elements of their youth cultures. However, the model presented in Figure 3.2 represents triadic and reciprocal causality. It does not imply that each of the three factors intervenes with the same force in a given situation, or that all three factors are involved at the same time.

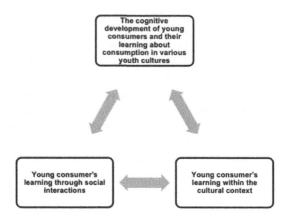

Figure 3.2   A social and cognitive approach to youth socialization

The bidirectional nature of influence also means that young people are both the producers and the product of their cultural environments because they are interacting with social agents belonging to both their youth cultures and environments. In the marketing field, studies highlight the impact of the three major socialization agents, namely a person's parents, peers, and the media.

The conclusions of these studies underscore the important role parents play in terms of the formation of youths' attitudes towards brands or product categories; the same is true for price sensitivity. Serval studies have been conducted by scholars to examine the influence of socialization agents on young people's consumption learning. These studies mostly adopted a "top-down" approach; in other words, the socialization process operates through a top-down logic based on the interaction between agents such as parents or media towards young consumers.

These studies were supported by other works integrating a bottom-up approach that examined the influence young consumers have on the attitudes of their parents. The results of these studies highlighted the growing influence of children on their parents in terms of their clothing, leisure activities, home décor, and so forth. In the same vein as these studies, the concept of "reverse socialization," which refers to the growing influence of girls on the dress style of their mothers for example, has been established in the marketing field (Batat, 2008, 2014).

Table 3.2 summarizes the contributions of three main types of socializing agents that are equally important for young consumers: traditional, professional, and virtual agents. These agents can be assessed according to their formal, informal, and symbolic aspects, and whether or not they are perceived by young consumers as essential socialization agents within their consumption youth cultures.

Table 3.2   The main socialization agents in youth consumption cultures

Socialization agents	Socialization stage	Youth segmenculture	Agent's role in the socialization process
Traditional agents	Primary socialization	Childescence	The childescents' socialization is influenced by traditional agents such as family, peers, and school. These agents are involved in the consumption learning process during the primary phase of socialization.
Professional agents	Primary and secondary socialization	Childescence and adonascence	Professional agents are represented by the actions of brands targeting both childescents and adonascents via traditional media (e.g., TV, press, youth magazines, etc.).
Virtual agents	Secondary socialization	Adolescence and adulescence	Virtual agents are essential players in the socialization and learning of consumption practices among adolescents and adulescents. They include online communities and groups on social media platforms.

2.1   The Role the Family Plays in Young People's Consumption Learning

From a sociological perspective, the family is an institution that brings together a set of people united by family ties. Understanding new family structures and interactions among members allows brands to appreciate how parents convey potential consumption knowledge and learning. Put another way, parents influence their children's knowledge which, in turn, contributes to the development of their consumption skills.

In terms of socialization, the role of the family was first described from a functional perspective: to teach children a set of reasoning skills linked to the rational aspects of consumption. In marketing studies, almost all authors agree on the fact that parents primarily teach the most rational aspects of consumption, leaving it to peers or the media to introduce its symbolic value (Batat,

2008; Ward et al., 1977). For example, mothers would be more interested in teaching their kids the value of money. Thus, parents play an important role in the education of their children, such as helping them to develop the skills related to consumption and encouraging them to make purchasing decisions, visit places where products are sold and deal with salespeople, and be exposed to a large range of products with increasingly varied prices.

The interaction between parents and children in the field of consumption has a long-term effect on the development of their preferences for a brand and the ability of these young consumers to distinguish its real nature from the exaggerated claims of brands and products featured in advertisements. Family communication, as a vehicle for learning and skills development among young consumers, lies at the center of socialization and the acquisition of a person's knowledge about consumption.

MINI-CASE BOX 3.7   GOYA FOODS: AN "ALLY" BRAND THAT ENHANCES FOOD WELL-BEING AMONG US HISPANIC FAMILIES AND THEIR KIDS

Founded back in 1936, Goya Foods is now the largest US Hispanic-owned food company. Goya offers a wide variety of ethnic foods with an American twist, providing recipes and flavors that suit every taste. The company has long been considered as an "ally" to families, as it teaches children in Hispanic families about their cultural roots while still being inclusive of different American cultures. Goya Foods also teaches non-Hispanic Americans to include more culinary choices in their diets. This has proven that cultural diversity and welcoming traditions are not something to be ashamed of. Rather, they are something to be proud of. Based on what has been mentioned before, we can conclude that Goya Foods aims to position itself as a "family" brand that by selling ethnic foods supports cultural diversity and traditions among Hispanics.

When it comes to health and well-being, Goya Foods assumes its fair share of corporate social responsibility. First and foremost, the company considers its employees to be "*la gran familia Goya*," or "the great Goya family." The food maker has a family-oriented management style and organizational culture. Goya also joined with the bank Wells Fargo to serve the community by creating Goya Gives. Goya Gives supports more than 250 organizations and events that help with disaster relief. By giving back to the community, Goya Foods shows that it is not merely a business run for profit; rather, it is a company that shares relationships with both its employees and communities.

Moreover, during the COVID-19 pandemic, Goya encouraged families to stay safe and be prepared for any natural disasters that might occur. The company asked families to make a plan and build a supply kit to instill the importance of preparedness among their children. Also, via Goya Gives, Goya Foods has donated more than 4 million pounds of food to families all around the United States, Venezuela, and Mexico since the beginning of the pandemic. The company donated 400,000 pounds worth of food to families around New York and New Jersey alone, with the help of more than 4,000 hardworking employees.

Bob Unanue, the president of Goya Foods, says the donations have brought people together during critical times. Unanue thanked organizations that helped with the effort. Food donations were distributed to churches, local food banks, community centers, soup kitchens, and programs for people in need. Goya Foods also donated 500,000 pounds of food and 20,000 masks to healthcare providers around the country.

The role of the family is vital in the lives of both childescents and adonascents, although it significantly decreases as they approach the adolescence and adulescence stages. In addition, marketing scholars have examined the impact of the family structure – e.g., whether it is nuclear or single-parent – on the behavior of young consumers and their learning processes in terms of their consumption and purchase behaviors. The results of studies that involved single-parent family structures revealed that:

- Children living in single-parent families are more often involved in their families' purchasing decisions;
- In this family structure, the first field of spending refers to leisure activities, depending on what children choose.

These results show that the role a person's family plays as a socialization agent varies depending on one's family structure. The reason is that in single-parent families, parents communicate and discuss more with their children while involving them in various "co-shopping" consumer activities. Other studies underscore the differences in the consumption practices of children from broken, or divorced, families versus nuclear families.

The results show that children whose parents are divorced use consumption items and brands as a substitute for "family happiness," which otherwise is supposed to be achieved by the presence of both parents. In broken families, parents feel guilty about causing their children to suffer following a separation or divorce and feel compelled to buy them more products, including clothes and video games, to make them feel happy. Other variables have been studied, such as social class and family size, which appear to play an important role in these young consumers' learning process.

Furthermore, it can be noted that the influence of children is usually more significant in large families because such families are more used to considering group goals than smaller families are. Family structures have been the subject of several consumer research studies, including the consumption of leisure, music, holidays, and clothing. In his study of the impact of family structure on the construction of children's musical tastes, Nuttall (2007) examined the impact family structure has on the consumption and musical choices of British adonascents in nuclear, single-parent, and blended families. His conclusions revealed three typologies of music consumption among young consumers, which are strongly related to the family structure:

- Experiential. This profile reflects the characteristics of children in "nuclear" family structures:
    - They have eclectic musical choices;
    - They represent an easy category to define and target;
    - Their peers are the main sources of information;
    - They are not affected by conflicts.
- Chameleon. This profile reflects the characteristics of children in "blended" family structures:
    - They have highly selective musical choices;
    - Different methods are used to target them;
    - They tend to avoid conflicts and use music to form extra-family ties.
- Defender. This profile describes the characteristics of children in single-parent family structures:
    - They make deliberate musical choices;
    - They are an interesting target market for the music industry;
    - They are influenced by their peers;
    - Music allows them to defend their values.

The family is a constantly changing social institution. Blended, single-parent, traditional/nuclear, or homosexual, new types of families are now part of our contemporary societies. The definitions of the concept of the family depend on its founding. It is the articulation of the bonds of kinship. This definition of the family by the function it fulfills does not necessarily originate in marriage; it can also bring together people of the same gender and includes blended families.

MINI-CASE BOX 3.8   COCA-COLA FEATURES
                      DIVERSE FAMILY STRUCTURES IN
                      A SPANISH AD

In 2015, Coca-Cola Spain broadcast for the first time a new commercial highlighting new family models, including a family headed by homosexuals. With the change in society and the emergence of new family structures, it is now becoming more frequent to reach all kinds of families: couples with children, couples without children, single parents with children, couples formed by people of the opposite sex or same-sex, couples with people of different ethnicities, and so forth. That is why the brand launched a new ad titled "Happiness Is Always the Answer" in which parents ask their children what they have heard in school.

The ad shows several types of families. The goal is to send the message that there is "no single formula to be happy." Thus, in the commercial, we find, among other things, a single mother and adoptive parents. The ad is in tune with today's social reality: new family models and structures are all legitimate and should be considered by brands in their communication strategies and offerings.

2.2 The Role Peers Play in Young People's Consumption Learning

Outside of the family, the social dynamics are different. Young consumers are more on their own. They must define their own social roles and personal identities. The independent world of consumerism for this youth group is built and experienced as a result of developing friendships and bonds. Thus, the peer group plays a central role, especially in the age range 8–18 years, a phase in which children become detached from their parents or from "made in family" consumption. The start of a socialized life is the discovery of the symbolic function of consumer objects and self-acceptance within the peer group. This is a determining factor in the consumption preferences of young people.

Beyond consumption, the peer group provides young people with security that replaces parental authority because they know that their values are shared by others. A study by McCandless in 1969, which analyzed the impact of peers according to the social status of their parents, showed that the group to which they belong is more important for children in low-income families than children in high-income families. Also, social relationships among peer groups can change among different segmencultures ranging from childescence to adulescence (see Figure 3.3).

As Figure 3.3 shows, the role peer groups play among young consumers can evolve:

- During the childescence stage, the relationships among young consumers are based on activities and games shared within the peer group. The peer group responds to needs related to the hedonic and playful dimensions of consumption activities;

- In the adonascence and adolescence phases, the young consumer develops expectations in terms of sincerity, loyalty, and trust. Rejection by the group is experienced as betrayal and can be a source of suffering that scars young people until adulthood;
- During the adulescence phase, the search for common experiences and interests lies at the center of the exchanges in peer groups. The values sought in the groups correspond to the tolerance for individual differences. Each individual has the right to exist and can claim a different identity or engage in different consumer behaviors.

Furthermore, a peer group's consumption culture can also be affected by brands, marketers, and the media, which are all an integral part of the socialization process of young consumers. A marketer's aim is to create a commercial offer adapted to young people according to the peer groups to which they belong. For example, at the beginning of the 2000s, Nike and Reebok financed the construction of playgrounds in suburban cities, organized tournaments, and offered the winners their latest products. The aim was to take market share from Adidas. Therefore, support for ordinary sports practices is above all support for the sociability that underlies these practices.

Although parents and family remain the key socialization agents in terms of consumption learning, it is more a youth's peer group that becomes predominant among young consumers. This leads to situations of tension or conflict between the consumption style of the youth's family and the consumption style of his or her peer groups.

Figure 3.3   *The evolution of relationships from childescence to adulescence*

2.3   The Role Virtual Communities Play in a Youth's Consumption Learning

Social media especially marks the daily lives of young people, who are going through a period of intense online socialization. Online communities allow young consumers to form other social bonds, youth cultures, and consumption practices. On social media, young people express themselves and reveal more of their emotions and passions.

In virtual communities, the connections between young people are publicly visible. Moreover, a person's reputation is based on the number of contacts he or she has or comments he or she receives. Friends, relatives, and acquaintances are a person's primary audience on social media. Connections with other Internet users can take place afterwards, depending on whether these users have common tastes or relationships.

For today's young consumers, using digital technologies has become as natural as watching television. To communicate with younger and older people alike, brands use virtual communities that extend far beyond a youth's network of physical contacts with his or her peers at school. Unlike adolescents and adulescents, who use popular social networks like Facebook, Twitter, and Instagram, to connect with childescents and adonascents, brands should use alternative virtual communities and social media platforms more adapted for the youngest consumers, who are still under parental control.

MINI-CASE BOX 3.9   THE BARBIEGIRLS.COM WEBSITE, A DIGITAL SPACE TARGETING THE CHILDESCENT YOUTH CULTURE

Presence on social media and the use of emails, chats, blogs, and forums are no longer reserved for adults. From an early age, the use of digital technologies and different platforms by youths has become a common practice. This has been a boon for toy brands like Mattel, which wants to use the Internet to attract and retain its targets, mostly childescents, for as long as possible.

To appeal to childescents, who are also digital natives and familiar with the Internet and virtual socialization, Mattel launched its new Barbiegirls. com website to recreate and enhance the link online with its youth targets. To create the site, Mattel was inspired by online video games as well as social media platforms and the instant messaging popular with childescents, adonascents, and adolescents.

Barbiegirls.com is intended for childescents and adonascents between the ages of 7 and 14. It allows them to create characters, which they can dress and make up. The characters created by little girls can be personalized from their skin tones to hair colors and facial expressions. To access the virtual community, all kids have to do is connect to the site and then plug into a computer, via a docking station and a USB port, a kind of connected toy.

On Barbiegirls.com, these childescents and adonascents can chat with other kids and, of course, buy clothes and furniture in a virtual shopping center using B-dollars (earned by playing on the site). The site has rapidly become popular, gaining more than 20 million members. The site also responds to a very real trend: the desire of young girls to grow up and replicate the adult experience. The virtual world of Barbiegirls.com is filled with everything a girl could want.

Barbiegirls.com aims to turn visits into revenue by providing the opportunity for children and devotees to join a brand community. Other toy brands have already launched their virtual community sites, with brands for both girls and boys. In the United States, two virtual worlds, dubbed GoLive2 (one for girls, the other for boys), have been launched by the Play Hut brand. In France, the site dedicated to Bradz dolls, a style different to Barbie, was set up after the launch of Barbiegirls.fr. Mattel also launched an online community site for boys in 2008. Lego launched its virtual world in 2010.

Unlike childescents and adonascents, young consumers entering the phase of adolescence and adulthood are hyper-connected. These youth spend more than 10 hours on average per week on social media. Thus, several trends can be identified, such as the widespread use of instant applications like Facebook Messenger, Snapchat, Instagram, and WhatsApp. Nearly all adolescents and adulescents watch videos on the Internet, mainly on YouTube, and play online games. These youth also participate more and more online by writing comments, articles, and reviews about products and brands.

MINI-CASE BOX 3.10   INSTAGRAM, A SOCIAL MEDIA PLATFORM POPULAR AMONG ADOLESCENTS AND ADULESCENTS

According to social media studies published by Facebook, young people aged 10–24 in Australia, Brazil, Canada, Germany, United Kingdom, the United States, and France use visual language in general, and more specifically, photographs on social media. The results of these studies show that:

- 72 percent post photos every month;
- 53 percent say Instagram helps them define who they are;
- 63 percent use Instagram to help them in their lives;
- 56 percent feel more connected with people they know;
- 52 percent say social media helps them feel part of a community;
- 33 percent go to Instagram when they wake up in the morning;
- 39 percent connect to Instagram just before going to sleep;
- 68 percent interact regularly with brands, mainly viewing and liking photos but also visiting websites.

The studies revealed that the most popular topics on Instagram among teens and adults are fashion and beauty, food and restaurants, television and films, hobbies, and music.

Source: http://insights.fb.com.

The presence of brands in online communities is essential to support young consumers as they discover and learn about consumption with their peers online and offline. The question that arises is this: in what form and with what type of content can brands target adolescents and adulescents on the social networks they favor?

To target these young consumers on social media, brands should take three approaches. First, they should provide communicational content based on youth storytelling by creating engaging stories with content inspired by the life of adolescents and adulescents and their consumption practices – practices that are shaped by the codes and norms in their youth cultures. Storytelling inspired by the youth consumption culture is popular among adolescents and adulescents if they can identify with a story and the characters featured by the brand.

MINI-CASE BOX 3.11   HOW LACOSTE ENGAGES ADOLESCENTS AND ADULESCENTS BY DEPLOYING STORYTELLING ON INSTAGRAM

Telling short, engaging, and emotional stories is the most suitable technique for communicating with adolescents and adulescents on Instagram. For example, consider the case of the Lacoste brand, which used Instagram to launch a new product, its "LT12" tennis racket. The particular communication strategy focused on the authentic and technical side of the brand. The seven ads in the campaign played on the visual and emotional impact of the racket's encounter with other objects, people, and so forth. Lacoste made it clear with the campaign that it is not about telling a big story; it is about engaging the community.

Second, brands can offer fun and interactive content with innovative contests to meet the hedonistic needs that emerge in the adolescent and adulescent youth cultures, where playfulness and meanings are two critical traits of young consumers' behaviors.

MINI-CASE BOX 3.12   COOKIE BRAND BISKREM TARGETS ADOLESCENTS AND ADULESCENTS VIA FUN AND ENGAGING GAMES ON INSTAGRAM

Turkish cookie brand Biskrem has created an engaging game to retain adolescents and adulescents alike. They are encouraged to reinvent Biskrem's famous cookie recipe by switching between Instagram accounts. The brand offers puzzles presented via a treasure hunt with photos and videos to find other Instagram accounts of the brand corresponding to higher levels.

Third, brands should focus on creativity as a core value to connect with adolescents and adulescents. These people live in a consumer society where marketing and advertising are omnipresent; thus, they are accepted, but creativity and compelling images are important.

Catchy ads are a popular form of expression, especially because they instantly convey meaning and grab the attention of young people. Social media and digital socialization mixed with reality are arguably the best places for a brand's creativity when it comes to this type of expression. Besides, when the advertising is creative, it is perceived by young people as less disturbing than that of most other media; in other words, it is less affected, unlike TV.

MINI-CASE BOX 3.13   PEPSICO RELIES ON CREATIVITY AND PHYGITAL: AN AUGMENTED REALITY BUS SHELTER IS DESIGNED TO APPEAL TO ADOLESCENTS AND ADULECENTS

The advertising agency AMV BBDO has put together a surprising bus shelter in London to promote Pepsi Max via the drink's "Unbelievable" campaign. Glass in the shelter has been replaced by a screen that broadcasts images of the street in real-time as if the screen were a transparent window. However, a few events add to the augmented reality and make people react to the bus stop. For example, using a hidden camera, people in the shelter can discover extraterrestrial saucers in the sky, a falling meteorite, a giant robot that shoots lasers through its eyes, and a tiger in the middle of the city.

The digital campaign associates the real with the virtual. It does so by highlighting Pepsi Max's "unbelievable" slogan. The slogan evokes the taste of Pepsi Max, which is "unbelievable" because when you are drinking it, you forget it has no sugar.

3. THE CONSUMPTION LEARNING JOURNEY: HOW DO YOUTH LEARN TO BECOME CONSUMERS?

The consumption learning process in youth cultures takes many forms. Young consumers learn to become consumers by following four major paths: trial-and-error, vicarious learning, experiential learning, and multitasking learning. These types of learning should be taken into account by companies as they implement their marketing and communication strategies targeting the youth market.

3.1   Learning to be a Consumer through Trial-and-Error

This mode of consumption learning is a way for young consumers to acquire knowledge by engaging in experimentation. The American psychologist Thorndike (1932) was the first to explain how trial-and-error learning works. Thorndike did so after getting inspired by works on animal psychology. Thorndike's book *Animal Intelligence* was vital not only for animal psychology but also for human psychology. His theory showed that human behavior could be studied by the same procedures as animal behavior, thereby shifting psychology from the study of mental activity to the study of behavior, its acquisition, and evolution. Thorndike believed that learning is ineffective if it is not accompanied by punishment or failure. This view of linking learning to motivation and failure has greatly contributed to studies of how young people learn to become consumers.

In this type of learning, young consumers proceed through a series of unsuccessful attempts. Thereafter, their behaviors are refined to gradually eliminate the less effective options and arrive more and more quickly at a solution. Hence, the error fully participates in learning by reducing the probability of the occurrence of the behavior it engenders. It is important to allow young learners the opportunity to make mistakes, not only to teach them to avoid them, but also to allow the adaptation of learning strategies to individual differences. Thus, the principle of trial-and-error is based on a learning model that works well for young consumers belonging to the youth cultures that include adonascents and adolescents.

Progressively, young consumers, both adonascents and adolescents, will build rules "for them" applied in their consumption cultures. These rules will guide them in the organization of the relations between themselves and the rest of society, other groups, as well as intra-group relations, which means between members of the same youth culture. By developing this form of learning, both adonascent and adolescent consumers set up a complex and often implicit process. The lack of awareness of this process does not prevent its effectiveness.

Therefore, the essence of trial-and-error learning in these two youth cultures lies in the progressive construction of the operational forms, which will then provide the necessary elements to allow them to construct their identity as consumers. The success of trial-and-error learning is linked to the ability of learners, both adonascents and adolescents, to complete quick and effective trials.

3.2   Vicarious Learning

Vicarious learning refers to an observational learning process whereby young consumers learn to replicate a behavior presented by a model they value, such as their parents, idols, or peers. The concept of vicarious learning was introduced by the sociologist Bandura in 1977. According to Bandura, vicarious learning could correspond, in a school context, to what a child can learn from a teacher's speech, for example. This can be done by watching and listening to those who know or, by extension, analyzing the production of those who know how to do. We should, however, distinguish social learning by reference to the model from mimicry because vicarious learning consists of observing and analyzing the steps in the performance of an action by someone before copying it. Thus, vicarious learning promotes the emergence of new creative behaviors.

This form of learning allows young consumers to integrate behaviors without going through research or repetition. Taking advantage of the experiences of others is an extremely common way of learning. Young people can use the successes and failures of consumers they observe to adjust their behaviors.

3.3   Experiential Learning

Experiential learning refers to the lived consumption experience as a source of learning and knowledge development among young consumers. The experiential learning theory is different from cognitive theories of learning based on the accumulation of knowledge as well as behavioral theories of learning that neglect the role of its subjective dimension in the learning process. Grounded in the works of Piaget (1975) and Kolb (1984), the concept of experiential learning reflects the process during which young consumers shape their consumption knowledge and their conceptions of brands and products through affective and cognitive transactions shaped by the codes and the norms of different youth consumption cultures.

Experiential learning enables a young consumer to think about his or her consumption activity, feel it, perceive it, and then experience it by purchasing or using products and brands. Some of the benefits of experiential learning for young consumers include:

- Increased self-esteem and interest in a brand or consumer area;
- Growth of youth autonomy and moral reasoning by developing an increased awareness of one's own values and the values conveyed by the brand;
- The social and intellectual development of young people as a result of experiencing certain areas of consumption, such as art, opera, or gastronomy;
- A sense of responsibility and social intelligence;
- A positive attitude towards peers and adults;
- The desire for social involvement;
- The feeling of having learned more;
- A better problem-solving ability.

3.4   Multitasking Learning

This type of learning means that today's young consumers, who are also digital natives, engage in multiple activities simultaneously while on the Internet or watching TV. It is an essential aspect of their modern consumer culture and life, something that can help them master the use of digital technologies and use them to learn to consume and develop knowledge in a specific area of consumption. Thus, brands and marketers should take into consideration the learning process of these young consumers according to the stages of their socialization and the different agents of socialization involved in their consumption learning, which may vary from one stage of socialization to another.

KEY TAKEAWAYS

The key takeaways from this chapter underscore the idea that the consumer socialization process in youth cultures helps young people acquire varied patterns, knowledge, and behaviors in the consumption field. Socialization allows young consumers to build their identities and to conform to the dominant norms and codes in their youth cultures. There are two phases of young consumer socialization: primary socialization occurs among childescence and adonascence; secondary socialization concerns adolescents and adulescents. Also, the main agents involved in primary socialization are a person's peers, family, school, and media. In terms of secondary socialization, virtual agents, friends, and institutions are most important among adolescents and adulescents. Finally, the chapter presents four forms of young consumer learning across youth cultures: trial-and-error, vicarious learning, experiential learning, and multitasking.

4. Are digital natives competent or vulnerable consumers? A challenge for brands targeting the youth market

CHAPTER OVERVIEW

Chapter 4 attempts to answer two main questions: are young consumers, who are part of a digital native generation, competent or vulnerable consumers? Do young consumer competencies differ across different youth consumption cultures? This chapter provides answers to these questions by exploring the specificities of consumption practices and risky behaviors that can emerge and evolve from childhood to adulthood. The exploration should advance the debate regarding business actions and policy programs targeting both the dark and light sides of young consumer behaviors.

1. WHAT DOES CONSUMPTION COMPETENCE MEAN?

Young consumers might be perceived by marketers and society as competent or vulnerable consumers, depending on the areas of consumption and their experiences. Thus, brands need to question the competency and/or the incompetency of young consumers while targeting them with suitable offerings. In the marketing field, studies on the consumption competencies of young consumers follow two opposing approaches:

- On the one hand, studies in the European research stream called "Competent Childhood" were conducted by researchers such as Tufte (2004) in Denmark, Buckingham (2004) in England, and Ekström (2005) in Sweden. These authors highlighted, through their studies, the idea that young people are competent consumers. They acquire and develop knowledge and capacities that enable them to navigate the marketplace, decode advertising messages, and satisfy their functional and symbolic needs;
- On the other hand, North American scholars proposed the "Vulnerable Childhood" approach represented by Cook (2005, 2008), Pechmann et al. (2005), and Kline (2006). This approach emphasized the vulnerability

of these young consumers and their inability to cope with market actors because of their lack of consumer experiences and their inability to consume independently. These researchers examined the vulnerability of young consumers in areas such as alcohol and tobacco use and their sexual behaviors.

Consequently, the issue of whether young consumers are competent or vulnerable consumers is debatable. The discussion starts first with questioning what consumption competence means. The notion of competence in the consumption field is a fairly recent concept in marketing that was introduced by Batat in 2008 and then developed in her recent works examining the competency and the vulnerability of young consumers. Unlike the concept of "consumer expertise," which is linked to the ability of young consumers to optimize their information search process to make satisfactory purchase decision-making, in the context of youth cultures, satisfaction is multiple and encompasses several intangible aspects.

They include the symbolic, hedonic, experiential, and ideological aspects sought by young consumers through a multiplicity of consumption situations experienced in the youth cultures they belong to. Thus, young consumers will gradually develop several types of competencies, whether they are social, symbolic, cultural, or functional, which are considered to be either an outcome or driver of their experiences within a particular field of consumption.

Defining young consumer competence is a difficult task due to the proliferation of the use of the term in human resources management and among sociologists or specialists in other disciplines. In sociology, competence is defined as the implementation and use of knowledge by the individual for a given action while being capable of implementing broad actions such as integrating, transferring, learning, and adapting to the context.

The process of knowledge transfer or competence building is a central element. It is not enough to demonstrate an individual's capacity and knowledge; it should be made operational and actionable. To be useful and usable, knowledge about consumption by young consumers should then be transferable and integrable in decisions and actions according to the complex situations these youth have to face.

Most of the definitions of the notion of "competence" underscore its multidisciplinary nature. To better understand this multidisciplinary dimension, Batat (2014) provided a synthesis of studies carried out in the human sciences: psychology, sociology, educational science, and management science.

The analysis of the definitions of competence revealed five main dimensions that characterize the construct of competence: technical, social, cultural, ethical, and existential (see Table 4.1).

Table 4.1   *Five typologies of human competencies*

Type	Definition
Technical	Refers to know-how as well as instrumental and behavioral capacities to derive the maximum benefit from these skills
Social	Inscribes the competence in an environment where it has a certain value as it allows a person to create social bonds through interactions with others
Cultural	Reflects the domain of meaning where any skill is supposed to give meaning to the world around us
Ethical	Refers to judging individuals negatively in relation to the intellectual and moral elements associated with their skills
Existential	Denotes the construction of the individual as a subject capable of developing and enriching his or her personal identity

Studies focusing on "consumer competence" can be divided into two main categories. On the one hand, there are studies that examine the expertise of the adult consumer, and, on the other hand, those that focus on consumer socialization and the consumption learning process among young consumers from childhood to the adulthood stage. However, the concept of "competence" has not appeared explicitly in marketing and consumer behavior studies but rather has been studied through a multitude of perspectives.

Most of the works published between the 1980s and 1990s that examined the notion of competence were limited to the study of how consumers process information about consumption during the process of purchasing. From the 2000s, marketing and consumer behavior scholars began to study the mechanisms for creating new knowledge by examining consumption practices within their cultural and experiential contexts.

Then, towards the end of the 2000s, the concept of consumer competence appeared in the field of youth marketing through studies carried out by Batat (2014, 2008), who proposed an effective definition of "consumer competence" allowing its distinction from the notion of "consumer expertise" and highlighting its interest for both scholars as well as marketing and brand managers targeting the youth market.

BACKGROUND BOX 4.1 THE CONCEPTUALIZING OF CONSUMER COMPETENCE

Consumer competence can be defined as a practical skill, as it requires time and multiple experiences for a consumer to acquire it. Blasius and Friedrichs (2003) consider practical skills to be part of the cultural capital defined by the sociologist Bourdieu (1986) and that they can be transformed into either social or economic capital.

According to Belk and Costa (1998), skills and knowledge can also be defined by the norms, meanings, symbols, and values that group members share in a particular consumer culture. Thus, consumer competence should be differentiated from the notion of consumer expertise, which according to the two American researchers Alba and Hutchinson (2000), reflects the consumer's cognitive capacity to perform tasks related to the product so as to gain knowledge.

Consumer competence is then used and recreated in varying consumption settings. Thus, the young "competent" consumer will be the one who, having acquired knowledge through his or her own experiences in a specific field of consumption, will be able to reuse it in other consumption situations, implementing them to obtain and create meaning and satisfactory value. Consequently, the young competent consumer combines knowledge, know-how, and interpersonal skills without which he or she cannot give meaning to the collected information and make a value judgment.

2. TYPES OF CONSUMPTION COMPETENCIES ACROSS YOUTH CULTURES

Are there specific consumption competencies in each segmenculture? In youth cultures, the consumption practices of young people are characterized by aspects such as the do-it-yourself (DIY) culture, usage deviation, and a high level of personalization and customization, which allow them to build their personal and social identities.

Young people invent their own consumption cultures and define their own outcomes. They do not buy products for the sole purpose of satisfying their functional needs or displaying their statuses; instead, young people strive to make sense of the purchases according to the youth cultures to which they belong. Products and brands, therefore, allow them to organize their social relations and define themselves in a social role within their consumer cultures.

These aspects highlight the importance of the creative potential and the capacity to innovate that young people use to divert offers and consumption experiences targeting them – consumption experiences that are predefined, supervised, and controlled by companies. This observation leads brands to question the creative potential and the types of consumption competencies that young consumers including childescents, adonascents, adolescents, and adulescents are capable of developing in their youth cultures to play particular social roles. These competencies can also differ according to different segmencultures and areas of consumption, and should then be assessed and considered by companies to better understand young people's consumer behaviors, attitudes, and expectations.

Drawing on my prior research (Batat, 2008, 2014) on how young consumers develop consumption competencies, I have identified three main categories of consumption competencies that young consumers build and develop throughout their life course within the different consumer youth cultures, ranging from childescence to adulescence. The examination of the scholarship confirms the existence of consumption competencies among young consumers. These competencies are built during a composite socialization process and are shaped by the norms and the codes in youth cultures.

Consumption competencies bring together cognitive, technical, symbolic, experiential, institutional, and ideological dimensions. These dimensions help youths build their identities as consumers, play social roles, disagree with the adult world, innovate, and manifest their values and commitment. In addition, a youth's consumption competencies emerge and evolve from childhood to adulthood following different stages that I illustrate in Figure 4.1 and discuss in the next section.

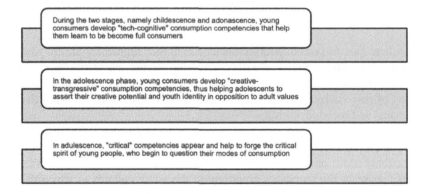

Figure 4.1   Consumption competencies in youth cultures

2.1   Tech-Cognitive Consumption Competencies in Childescence and Adonascence

Among the tech-cognitive competencies often assigned to very young consumers, we can cite their ability to develop an in-depth understanding of the consumption field, analyze commercial discourses, compare offerings, and assess purchase options. In the childescence and adonascence stage, mental processes are engaged in three phases: memorization, internalization, and implementation.

The tech-cognitive consumption competencies allow both childescents and adonascents to become consumers by developing consumption skills related to four main fields, namely saving money, optimized comparison, multiplying sources of information, and developing a bargaining spirit and ability to consume for free.

In the childescence and adonascence consumption cultures, to become a competent consumer, the young person should acquire and develop the skills and knowledge related to these four fields. They are essential when it comes to the performance of consumer activities, as stated in the following quotes from some young consumers I interviewed:

> I already knew how to create a website, I searched on the Internet for a server to host my Stargate Fusion site. ... That sounds great!!! I'm always looking to go further; now I'm looking for software to make flashing avatars. For my age and without bragging about it, I think I am competent. ... I don't know if many do that. My mom doesn't even know how to turn on a computer (laughs). (Adonascent, male)

> I think that the consumer who calls himself competent must be very careful with how he spends his money; he must not buy anything; he must save money because everything is too expensive in this society. (Childescent, female)

Therefore, the tech-cognitive competencies in youth cultures defined from the perspective of these youth can take four main forms related to the field mentioned above. The competencies can be summarized as follows:

- Know how to save your pocket money. Receiving pocket money is a big step in the life of childescents and adonascents; it is a sign of autonomy. Pocket money allows them to learn how to manage small budgets with an introduction to savings. Managing pocket money well is considered a consumer competency by these youth. According to these young people, competent consumers in their youth cultures should control their spending and take the initiative to save what is left of their pocket money;
- Get products for free. Today's childescents and adonascents belong to a digital generation characterized by the idea of free access to culture, art, information, and also consumer products via downloads. These young consumers would rather not pay for cultural products and other types of consumption items that they can download for free;
- Get information from different sources. Searching for information by multiplying the sources of information is an amusement for childescents and adonascents. Although this activity can sometimes be long and tedious, it is effective according to these young consumers. They can combine multiple online and offline sources, magazines, TV shows, shops, friends, family, and contacts abroad, among others, to optimize their searches. For these

people, having such capacities is a sign of competency and control in the field of consumption;
- Comparing offerings and prices both in different stores and on the Internet. This practice is a very common activity among childescents and ado-nascents looking for the "best deal," which must be attractive and suited to their needs. Comparing offers is seen by these young consumers as a form of taking control over their consumption. Also, they are continually looking for the best quality-to-price ratio.

2.2   Creative-Transgressive Consumption Competencies during Adolescence

In the adolescent consumption culture, transgression and the development of creativity go hand in hand. It is clear that in the adolescence phase, the tendency to break the rules is vital to one's personality formation and learning about consumption. Transgression and values cannot be conceived one without the other. When the adolescent transgresses, it is always about a given value system.

When speaking of adolescents' online activities, it is a question of the transgression of the standards established by adults to the extent that adolescents seek in their online practices to surpass themselves. Therefore, online activities, such as illegally downloading films, music, and video games, are considered an integral part of consumption competencies from the perspective of these young consumers. Thus, rule-breaking is a hallmark of the adolescent youth culture.

Consequently, it is important for brands and companies to provide adolescent consumers with opportunities for transgression that are not dangerous. To build their future adult consumer identities, adolescents need to test the limits of the laws and guidelines imposed by adults and society overall.

MINI-CASE BOX 4.1   VIRGIN RADIO "LOUDER IS BETTER": TRANSGRESSION AND INSOLENCE IN THE WORLD OF CHILDREN AND PARENTS

Virgin Radio's 2011 "Louder Is Better" ad campaign favored a communication style that highlights the rebellion and the refusal of the rules imposed by parents on their kids. Such a phenomenon often lies at the center of the conflictual relations between parents and children in the phases of adolescence and adulescence.

The advertising campaign shows a teenage boy and his mother. The boy is going to see his friends, but as soon as he gets in the car, his mother arrives to yell at him. Not wanting to hear it, the boy challenges his mother's authority and turns up the volume on Virgin Radio to drown out the sound of her screams. Interestingly, the loud music gives the impression that the mother is singing on the backtrack to the sound of the radio!

Virgin made a name for itself with the catchy video on its YouTube channel and also managed to differentiate itself in a very competitive market as a result.

The creativity of brands and the possibility offered to adolescents to collaborate with them are also seen by these young consumers as a kind of consumption competence. For adolescents, they should possess and develop innovative consumption practices to be considered competent consumers. In this youth culture, adolescents see themselves as creative and innovative consumers. Their creative process in the consumption field can be defined according to three main stages:

*   *Incubation and illumination.* In the first phase of the process, the adolescent consumer interprets the consumer universe that surrounds him/her and the first ideas emerge from his or her observations;
*   *Elaboration.* In the second stage, adolescents enter a process of organizing their ideas related to a particular consumption field or a product around a specific meaning or vision;
*   *Fertilization.* The third and final stage of the creative process refers to the development of new competencies that help adolescents forge their creative potential, which will shape their consumer behaviors as well as their attitudes towards brands and products.

MINI-CASE BOX 4.2   THE TIPP-EX EXPERIENCE:
A CREATIVE AND INTERACTIVE DIGITAL
CAMPAIGN TARGETING ADOLESCENTS
AND ADULESCENTS

In 2010, the corrective products brand Tipp-Ex (Bic group) launched a viral campaign targeting adolescents and adulescents with an interactive video on YouTube titled "A hunter shoots a bear." The hunter, not wanting to kill the bear, proposed to rewrite the story using Tipp-Ex correction tape. The brand featured a hunter and bear imagined by the agency Buzzman, which was the subject of a quiz game, the Big Tipp-Ex Quiz. Thanks to this game, fans of the two famous characters are able to test their knowledge and prove that they are experts on bears and hunting by answering 50 questions. The campaign generated more than 50 million views on YouTube. The goal of this viral and participatory campaign was to urge Internet users to participate in the games and to develop their creative potential through the proposals they make.

In the online video "A hunter shoots a bear," the Internet user can use Tipp-Ex's corrective tool to change the action verb contained in the title and thus modify the course of the story. Dozens of scenarios had been imagined by Buzzman. A second video posted in 2012 on YouTube used the same strategy. It was a birthday party threatened by a meteorite. To avoid it, it was enough to correct the date for the story to continue. About 20 million people collaborated.

With this viral, creative, and participatory campaign, the brand has seen a real impact on its sales of corrective products, which was almost immediate. Between 2010 and 2013, Tipp-Ex's market share in corrective products increased by 4.3 percentage points in France, even though the first two campaigns were broadcast only in English and did not target French consumers directly. But the Internet has no borders and, in the end, even the brand's French customers got caught up in the game. Thanks to these collaborative campaigns, the brand has broadened its market by targeting and retaining young people between 15 and 25 years old, including school children and their parents.

2.3 Critical Consumption Competencies during the Adulescence Stage

Adulescents have gradually become aware of the challenges of sustainable development. Thus, questioning their consumption practices is an indicator of consumer competence for these young market actors. They are becoming more and more critical towards the consumer society and its hyper-consumption practices.

Overall, adulescents are conscious of the impact their consumption activities have on the environment. For them, the competent consumer should be morally, socially, and politically engaged. This ideological dimension of consumption is often infused (1) by parents who convey their own values to their children, and (2) by the media and the dominant discourses related to eco-friendly and responsible consumer behaviors. In the adulescence youth culture, ethical consumption can take many forms:

• Autonomous and free consumption in terms of purchasing decisions;

- Solidary consumption that integrates how individuals develop capacities to protect the environment and reduce the negative impact of their consumption activities;
- Fair consumption that supports vulnerable populations;
- Consumption centered on the well-being of both the individual and community.

The act of consumption among adulescents is then an act of activism or claim and expression of one's values. To adapt to the responsible behavior of these engaged and responsible young consumers, companies should develop eco-friendly products and promote responsible consumption practices, such as recycling and secondhand shopping.

MINI-CASE BOX 4.3   H&M, A RESPONSIBLE CLOTHING BRAND THAT APPEALS TO ADULESCENTS

H&M is a very popular clothing brand among young people who want fashionable outfits for accessible prices. To be in line with sustainability and eco-friendly values as well as enhance its commitment among young people, the brand has decided to implement ethical actions in its European market by taking back a used piece of clothing in return for 5 euros. H&M was a pioneer clothing brand that launched this initiative.

H&M's approach consists of offering a service that meets the new expectations of adulescents, who can now drop off their old worn-out clothing from the brand or other brands for recycling. Beyond this responsible action, H&M's objective is above all to improve its image with these young customers but also to position itself as an environmental defender. Other brands have followed suit.

3.   UNVEILING (IN)VULNERABILITY AMONG DIGITAL NATIVE CONSUMERS

The concept of *consumer vulnerability* has been defined in various ways by authors in consumer research and other human science disciplines. Achieving a consensus on the definition may be difficult due to the complexity of vulnerability and the perspective followed by researchers within their works.

Overall, though, researchers have distinguished between vulnerability and risk. Cardona (2004) did so by showing that vulnerability is considered to be an outcome of the exposure to risk. Baker (2009, p. 118) proposed that the materialization of risk is related to the "objective probability that security will be lost."

The most thorough examination of vulnerability within the field of marketing and consumer research to date synthesized the literature, providing an exhaustive definition of the concept (Baker et al., 2005). In this work, consumer vulnerability was defined as "a state of powerlessness that arises from an imbalance in marketplace interactions or the consumption of marketing messages and products" (Baker et al., 2005, p. 134). The related model portrays consumer vulnerability as a flexible concept that depends on external (e.g., marketers) and internal (e.g., consumers' moods) factors, as well as several other elements, such as a consumer's age, race and ethnicity, income, and education. These factors, can, in turn, reflect the interaction between internal and external (e.g., marketers exploiting people's age-related vulnerabilities) factors.

Therefore, consumer vulnerability is multidimensional, context-specific, and does not have to be enduring. Most researchers agree that for the majority of consumers, vulnerability is typically temporary because consumers ultimately develop coping mechanisms to deal with their circumstances. Situationally vulnerable consumers are at risk for a limited time, either due to changing external factors or to increased competency. At the other end of the spectrum are individuals with enduring vulnerabilities or vulnerabilities of a more permanent nature, for example, due to permanent cognitive impairment.

Shultz and Holbrook (2009) expanded the concept of "vulnerability" by adopting a macro perspective. Drawing on Bourdieu's (1979/1984) definition of cultural capital and economic capital, Shultz and Holbrook (2009, p. 124) defined two key consumer characteristics related to vulnerability: (1) knowledge and beneficial means–ends relationships (similar to cultural capital) and (2) access to beneficial means (similar to economic capital).

Therefore, the cross-classification of these two characteristics provides four typologies of consumer vulnerability: economically vulnerable people, culturally vulnerable people, doubly vulnerable people, and invulnerable people (Shultz and Holbrook, 2009). Obviously, the four types of consumer vulnerability are flexible and depend on time, resources, and shifts in abilities or other "circumstances that might affect a person's knowledge of beneficial means–ends relationships and/or access to beneficial means" (Shultz and Holbrook, 2009, p. 125).

To sum up, vulnerability might be seen as relative across multiple areas in which various degrees of vulnerability may occur. Additionally, one person's vulnerability in any given area can be situation-specific and differ from another's according to the context.

All people – even those who are skilled, healthy, rich, and so on – experience vulnerability at one time or another. Although different conceptualizations of consumer vulnerability have been offered, less research has examined the vulnerability of digital natives in the consumption field. As a consequence, a significant gap exists in the literature – a gap that hinders interventions and policies aimed at reducing risky consumption behavior.

3.1   Consumer (In)vulnerability in Youth Consumption Cultures

The paternalistic perspective is common among research that has examined the risky behaviors of youths (Mason et al., 2013). Mainstream researchers have looked at vulnerability among youth in different consumption fields, such as alcohol use and driving, sexting, obesity, sexual activity, video games, Internet addiction, and the influence of advertising.

However, these researchers did not explore how digital natives perceive and define consumer vulnerability from their own point of view by re-embedding it within their youth consumption cultures. Furthermore, scholars suggested that future research on youth risky behaviors should explore youth vulnerabilities via a bottom-up approach by shifting the focus away from a paternalistic adult perspective to a youth perspective.

The recent research by Batat and Tanner (2021) conceptualizes vulnerability within youth consumption cultures by examining the type of vulnerabilities that emerge in the consumption field from the perspective of young consumers. In this research, observational and verbal data were analyzed to create an interpretative youth-centric framework around which the meanings, drivers, and outcomes of consumer vulnerability from a youth perspective are articulated.

This framework shows that consumer vulnerability is a social construction embedded in a particular youth consumption culture where its meanings are constructed. The results show that the meanings of young consumer vulnerability are generated in a context marked by youth consumption culture characteristics such as psychographic and psychological factors related to adolescence stage, transgression, belongingness and socialization, self-esteem and self-concept, self-construction, and digital culture. These markers contribute to shaping the meanings of young consumer vulnerability, which can take two major forms:

• Imposed and deliberate vulnerability. Imposed vulnerability refers to what young consumers, both young and old, define as a vulnerable state in which they feel forced to behave a certain way. There are four main sources of imposed vulnerability: social agents (peers and salespeople), consumption experiences, social class, and perceived parenting styles. These drivers enhance the feeling of vulnerability among both younger and older consumers who feel incapable and unskilled when dealing with market actors, social agents, and consumption situations;

- Deliberate vulnerability. It refers to what young consumers, especially older ones, define as an *invulnerable* state. It is a siutation in which they feel powerful and thus experience risky behaviors for fun. The dark side of invulnerability covers three significant meanings: risky online behaviors, transgressive and socially unacceptable behaviors, and materialism. There are three main drivers to young consumers' vulnerability: the anti-adult culture, risk attractiveness, and expert status.

3.2   Why Are Digital Natives Attracted to Risky Behaviors?

Although society fears risk and can pass the fear of it on to others, digital natives are far from wanting to be risk free. Youthhood is a crucial period in life in which risky behavior is paramount. Young people, who are part of the digital generation, seek to discover the world around them by exploring new experiences. This usually leads to the unpredictable and the uncontrollable, and, therefore, to the adoption of "risky behaviors." The list of these behaviors is endless. For example, young people may:

- Seek to surpass themselves in sports fields by going beyond their limits;
- Have an increased need to be constantly connected to their smartphones, which causes addictive behavior, or even phobia if they do not have their smartphones on hand;
- Endanger their health by consuming psychoactive products (e.g., cigarettes, alcohol, cannabis, or other drugs).

The important thing is not so much to list all the risky behaviors specific to digital natives but above all to understand the motivations that lead these young people to adopt such behaviors. This reflection is all the more important because digital natives are future adult consumers. The risk lies in the repetition of these unsafe behaviors later on to the point where they become addictive and ripple through adulthood.

For example, studies have shown that 90 percent of people who die from tobacco start to smoke before the age of 18. Unlike toddlers, who have a low perception of risk and who gradually learn the limits and rules put in place by those around them such as parents and educators, young people who are digital natives are more aware of the risky behaviors and have sufficient cognitive and social skills to understand the limits and the rules implemented, to question them, discuss them, criticize them, and even transgress them.

Although digital natives have a clearer view of risk, they have an increased need to adopt these behaviors. Risk-taking is also a fundamental part of the adolescence stage because it is a way to build one's identity. Particularly, adolescence is a period that is usually accompanied by a feeling of unease and doubt. During this time, a person's self-esteem, which may have been relatively high during childhood, can decrease (Batat and Tanner, 2021).

Becoming a young adult or an adulescent is also the time in which people assert their personalities by breaking rules and limits while trying to build a positive image of themselves for their friends. In sum, there are three spheres of youth vulnerability: (1) social through peer group pressure; (2) family including parents; and (3) the self (self-esteem, personality). Thus, businesses targeting digital natives should also decipher risky consumption behaviors that characterize different youth cultures. The goal should be to understand the identity mechanisms underlying the adoption of such behaviors but also to understand how to respond to them.

It is important then to ask the following questions: what risky consumption behaviors adopted by digital natives are different from those of adults? And why are young people attracted to these behaviors?

3.2.1 Types of risky behaviors in youth consumption cultures

Digital natives belong to a youth consumption culture in which they engage in multiple risky and transgressive behaviors to construct their personal and social identities and thus become legitimate adult consumers in the society. Among the risky behaviors youth are attracted to, we can cite the following: corporeal, mental, and digital risky behaviors.

Corporeal damaging behaviors. Risks related to roads and sports are twice as high in the youthhood stage as in other periods of life. For instance, one in three deaths of people between the ages of 14 and 18 is due to a road accident. Youth account for one-third of moped riders killed, and nine out of ten victims are boys. Alcohol is the leading cause of these fatal accidents (30 percent), followed by cannabis (10 percent).

When it comes to sport, boys are generally more often the victims of accidents than girls. Eighty percent of young people aged 13–18 years old practice a sport outside of school time, and 50 percent of them play in sports clubs. Motivated by fun, appearance, and health, 25 percent of young people exercise more than eight hours per week. The majority of young people prefer team sports to individual sports. Boys, in particular, look for thrilling sports to assert their freedom, such as board sports and motorsports.

Mental harming behaviors. The consumption of psychoactive products is significant in youthhood, especially in the adolescence stage where the use of these drugs intensifies sharply during the "high-school years." During college, the most frequently tested psychoactive substance is alcohol, far ahead of tobacco and cannabis. The elementary and high-school years are not an initiation phase but rather a phase of generalization of the diffusion of alcohol.

Tobacco use occurs among a little less than a third of elementary school students and increases strongly between the beginning and the end of elementary school, from 12 percent to 52 percent. During the transition to high school, more than 30 percent of adolescents in the second year say they are regular smokers, consuming more than 10 cigarettes per day. Thus, it is during the adolescence stage that the vast majority of long-term smokers learn to smoke. The average age people begin smoking is between 11 and 12 years old.

While initiation to cannabis is marginal in the sixth grade (1.5 percent), it becomes significantly more marked in the third grade, where almost one in four teenagers say they have tried this product. The diffusion of cannabis during the elementary school years is characterized by an increase among those who use it most. Some figures on the consumption of psychoactive products among youth digital natives reveal the following traits:

- Cigarette consumption. 40 percent of high school students smoke occasionally. One in three adolescents smoke regularly, and 40 percent of adolescents vape electronic cigarettes (compared to 9 percent in 2011);
- Alcohol consumption. 40 percent of elementary school students drink alcohol once a month, compared to 80 percent of high school students. One in three teenagers gets drunk once a month; 50 percent of high school students consume a minimum of five drinks in the same evening with friends;
- Cannabis consumption. One in three adolescents regularly uses cannabis. One in eight adolescents is addicted to cannabis. Also, cannabis use has become commonplace among boys and girls: 40 percent of boys have tried cannabis, compared to 25 percent of girls. The brain continues to develop until the age of 25. Therefore, cannabis use can have irreversible consequences on the brains of adolescents.

Furthermore, digital natives' vulnerability has also been demonstrated in terms of new risky drinking practices such as "binge-drinking," a practice that is widespread among today's young people. It involves consuming a very large amount of alcohol in a very short time period.

BACKGROUND BOX 4.2 WHAT IS BINGE DRINKING?

Binge drinking is a common practice among young college and high school students: among young people aged 16–17, 56 percent of boys and 36 percent of girls say they binge drink occasionally. Although the origin of this phenomenon comes from Anglo-Saxon and Scandinavian countries, it is increasing among European adolescents, especially among the 13–15 age group.

The massive consumption of alcohol in a very short time quickly leads to drunkenness. A recent study has shown that the practice of binge drinking has a lasting and visible effect on the white matter of young people's brains, which contains thousands of axons, which are nerve fibers connecting neurons in different regions of the brain. During adolescence, the brain's white matter thickens, helping to accelerate the connection speed of neurons.

Binge drinking, therefore, has very harmful effects on youths' brains. It can result in the loss of memory, and difficulty in learning, reasoning, and reading. Young people who binge drink are often smokers and cannabis users as well. The very harmful effects on the brain are partly due to these consumption choices.

Digital risky behaviors. The overconsumption of digital technology, such as video games, the Internet, smartphones, and tablets, among others, is a source of multiple risks for youths. Unlike previous generations and the generation of their parents, who are referred to as "digital migrants," today's young people are digital natives. Technology and digital devices are part of their daily lives. While younger youth such as childescents and adonascents mostly use the family phones and computers, older youth including adolescents and adulescents have their own devices. These youths can spend more and more time on the Internet and are the biggest users of smartphones.

Compared to the game console or the computer, they spend an average of 6 hours a day on their smartphones; 60 percent of young people send text messages during class hours, in class, and need to consult their smartphones every hour. Moreover, these young people do not know how to measure the time they spend using their smartphones and thus develop obvious symptoms of addiction. Some take their smartphones in the shower, to the bathroom, and to bed.

In fact, many of these youths are terrified of being separated from their phones. The excessive fear of being far from their smartphones has a name: it is called *nomophobia* (Yildirim and Correia, 2015). Digital natives are the most disturbed by the loss of their smartphones: 25 percent are "upset," and 18 percent "panicked."

These phenomena of smartphone addiction and nomophobia have significant consequences:

- Health-related dangers (headaches, hearing problems, eye blinking, memory loss, fatigue, and insomnia);
- Social-life problems (isolation, loneliness, depression, etc.);
- Schooling problems (lower grades, difficulty concentrating in class, dropping out of school, etc.).

The addiction to video games on networked computers also exists among digital natives. Video games are like drugs, complete with online role-playing games such as MMORPGs (massively multiplayer online role-playing games), like "World of Warcraft." This passion can easily become an obsession with a youth playing 10 to 15 hours a day. Some youths get so obsessed with the games they forget to eat, sleep, or wash.

3.2.2 Digital natives' motivations to adopt risky behaviors

Beyond the figures that paint a portrait of young "rebels" adopting various risky behaviors, it is important to understand the reasons leading these young people to adopt such risky and harmful behaviors. What is really at stake is less the fact that digital natives are rebels, but above all the fact that they are in search of an identity.

Risky behaviors (e.g., consuming cigarettes, alcohol, and cannabis, extreme driving on the road, extreme sports, and excessive screen consumption) are a way for young people to assert their need for autonomy by breaking the rules and pushing the limits in order to fit in with a group, and to test themselves against others.

We can distinguish three areas of the affirmation of the identity of digital natives, which affect three dimensions of their lives: biological (the extent of their bodily changes during puberty, which affects their levels of self-esteem), affective (the space for the construction of emotional autonomy towards one's parents, which materializes through a need for transgression), and social (the space of social relations with one's peers, which manifests itself in the search for social approval and the desire to integrate with one's peers). Next, I discuss these three spheres of identity development among digital natives that lead them to adopt risky behaviors.

A new body and a lack of self-esteem. The transition from adolescence to youthhood and adulthood is a critical phase that allows individuals to build their identities amid important physical and psychological changes. These changes produce an upheaval in an individual's image of his or her body: the body is profoundly modified during puberty, so the image that younger and older young people have of themselves is generally questioned. Faced with these physical transformations, young people remain fragile and vulnerable. They cannot recognize and define themselves, especially during adolescence, which often is associated with feelings of unease and doubt. Their self-esteem is low.

Such changes give this period the character of an identity crisis (Erikson, 1968/1972). The fact that a young person is disinterested in his or her body shows that he or she is going through a period of fragility. For example, these youth may be tempted to mask, hide, deny, erase, or show off their bodies. This situation refers to a "bodily break-in," whereby young people harm their own bodies.

It should be noted that gender differences mark these risky behaviors: girls' pain is internalized, whereas boys' distress takes the form of aggression against the outside world. Girls are more likely to self-harm (11 percent of girls versus 6 percent of boys), whereas boys are more likely to demonstrate force, such as violence or speed, or ends up with alcoholism and/or drug addiction. Young people can badly harm their bodies and engage in risky consumption (cigarettes, alcohol, cannabis) to compensate for their low self-esteem.

For digital natives, the smartphone goes beyond the its function of information and expression to become a real space for building identity. Youth identity is forced to constantly adapt to these multiple upheavals, which are the physical and psychological changes of young people. Thus, confiscating a youth's smartphone is like tearing away a part of the person. Doing so puts the person in a position of submission to the adults around them, just like a child.

The weight of the peer group. Young people obviously, and in particular their peer groups and friends, play a key role in initiating social practices, such as the first consumption of cigarettes, cannabis, or alcohol. These young people are indeed vulnerable consumers, who are sensitive to peer group pressure and social conformism. Recent studies on the empowerment process show that the peer group is a social model that helps them to acquire their autonomy. It is not so much a question of the influence of the peer group that is at stake, but rather the desire to acquire and defend a strategic position within the group. Therefore, young people are willing to make many sacrifices so that their needs, wants, thoughts, and actions are compatible with those of their peer groups. Otherwise, they risk being excluded. Society and the tobacco industry play an important role in terms of establishing this social norm and implementing strategies that promote the persistence of these rites of passage and integration.

MINI-CASE BOX 4.4   HOW DOES THE TOBACCO INDUSTRY APPEAL TO DIGITAL NATIVES?

Usually faced with the ban on direct or indirect advertising of a product, the harmfulness of which it knows perfectly well, the tobacco industry is relying on a new medium: consumers themselves, especially if they are young and can serve as role models for others.

A new phenomenon, observed in the United States, is now appearing in Europe on the Internet: "smoking reviews." These are videos made by teenagers and young people to praise the virtues of a particular brand of cigarettes they themselves have experienced. Nowadays, we can see that young people themselves promote smoking via social media and the videos they make are circulating in different languages.

I misbehave, therefore, I am. Digital natives are by nature a contradictory generation of consumers. They claim their freedom while seeking another form of dependence: through the consumption of illicit products as a defensive mechanism against anxiety. We can talk about the paradox between the need for independence as well as dependence, which lie at the heart of youth identity development. These youth need to question parental and social values and break prohibitions to mark their independence.

Consequently, the consumption of psychoactive products (cigarettes, alcohol, cannabis) and the adoption of extreme sports or risky behavior are, for these young people, a means of rebelling against their parents. Risky practices are not seen as the pursuit of pleasure but rather as an initiation rite linked to puberty – that is, a rite of passage into adulthood. In Western society, violent and collective rites have given way to graduated and tempered learning.

Today, the passage from adolescence and youthhood to adulthood has instead transformed into a kind of progressive learning that is prolonged over time and results in back-and-forth kinds of trial-and-error. Thus, risky behaviors are a kind of initiation path to becoming an adult by cutting one's umbilical cord with childhood.

4.   WHAT KIND OF ACTIONS ARE TARGETING YOUNG CONSUMER COMPETENCE OR VULNERABILITY?

What do companies and policymakers think about youth competency or vulnerability? This section presents the results of my various exchanges with companies and brands that target young people. Companies have different views about whether youth are competent or vulnerable consumers:

*   For some companies, young people are seen as fully competent consumers. They are competent enough to know the true value of products and buy them where they are offered;
*   For others, the competence of young consumers has limits when it comes to digital and interactive consumption practices, or areas of consumption reserved for adults (car purchases, bank and financial products, etc.). These companies believe young people are vulnerable and are thus considered an at-risk group of consumers.

4.1   How Can Companies Benefit from Youth Consumption Competence?

When it comes to recognizing the competence of young consumers, some professionals argue that young consumers should be put at the center of a company's marketing and communication strategy. The company should see them not only as a target but also as active partners and a source of innovation.

Among the three consumption competencies (tech-cognitive, creative-transgressive, and critical) identified in different youth consumption cultures, the transgressive and creative capacity of young consumers should be placed at the top of the current concerns of marketing managers. Indeed, young people who transgress are often creative and expert in their use of products. The transgression can be interesting if the brand wants to add other dimensions or functionalities to its products and services targeting the youth market.

Illegal downloading is obviously going to occur because these digital natives' perceptions of consumption have changed. Values are shifting for this free generation. Consequently, companies have to adapt to these new consumption trends among youth cultures.

MINI-CASE BOX 4.5   DANONE ADAPTS THE PRICES OF ITS PRODUCTS TO FIT WITH THE PURCHASING POWER OF YOUNG CONSUMERS

For years, manufacturers of consumer goods have targeted the top of the market. Relying on the power of their brands, brands like Danone, Nestlé, and Unilever sought to distinguish themselves from low-cost products and popular brand labels, even if it meant selling their branded products for a little more.

However, due to the declining purchasing power of some people, especially young consumers, Danone has changed its strategy. The company has started to target young people by proposing attractive offers. For example, Danone began selling for 1 euro an "Ecopack," which is a package of six yogurts. The company promises "Danone quality at a mini price." Danone did so without advertising to reduce costs. Since then, many manufacturers have followed Danone's lead, not by creating new brands, but by extending the range of those that already exist in their lineups.

4.1.1   Youth and brands, a possible dialogue?

Companies can use some of the competencies developed by young consumers to establish a business relationship with them. This can be done through the implementation of creative strategies that incorporate the competencies of young consumers by involving them in co-creation actions.

Companies can also involve these young consumers in the process of sharing, designing, and producing offerings targeting the youth market. The co-creation of the offer in areas of consumption where these digital natives have tech skills, such as the production of online content, can, therefore, generate common and shared values.

Thus, companies can set up actions to support young people in their process of building consumption competencies in areas related to music, social media, and other online platforms. Recognizing the digital skills of young consumers regarding the use of social networks, such as Facebook, YouTube, Instagram, and Twitter, can encourage companies to involve these people directly (creation and production) or indirectly (ideas, suggestions, communication) in the creative process and thus tap their creative potential. Moreover, by involving these digital natives and recognizing their consumer competencies, companies retain them and build long-term bonds with them.

Furthermore, creativity is often sought after by young people and is of increasing interest to brands seeking to innovate and differentiate themselves from their competitors while remaining in harmony with the expectations of youth targets. Young lead-users are, therefore, considered a source of innovation for the brand because they are always seeking new ways to consume and live unique consumer experiences.

They can even go beyond what the company offers to meet their needs. This provides an absolute treasure trove of ideas for marketing and brand managers, who can communicate differently with this target group by focusing on the community value and personalization of the offer. This consumer competence can be reflected in the company's communication strategy and its loyalty policy, or even more upstream by actions aimed at reorganizing the process of co-creation of the offer by involving young people in the co-conception and idea-generation process.

Ecological awareness and moral values expressed among young people and considered as consumption competencies are two other realities, which apply to companies that target young consumers. Brands should take them into account in the process of developing an offer targeting the youth market, especially adulescents.

Today's young people are engaged and more sensitive to the ethical and ecological dimension of their consumption. To take this new trend into account, brands should pay more attention to ecology and get engaged in actions to protect the environment and raise people's awareness of it. Also, companies should rely more on transparency in their commercial actions to attract these ethical and responsible young consumers.

MINI-CASE BOX 4.6 THE FASHION REVOLUTION DAY: AN ETHICAL CAMPAIGN APPRECIATED BY YOUNG CONSUMERS

April 24 is a special date for those who campaign for ethical textile production. On April 24, 2013, a building collapsed in Dhaka, Bangladesh, killing more than 1,130 workers at a low-cost textile factory. As a result, each year on this date, which has become known as Fashion Revolution Day, consumers are encouraged to relay on social networks, through hashtags, their opposition to the bad working conditions the poor workers who produce the clothes face.

As part of this campaign, the Fashion Revolution committee produced an original video: it shows a vending machine installed in the city of Berlin. The vending machine allows people to buy a t-shirt for 2 euros. But when customers put their coins into the vending machine, they are shown a movie explaining by whom and how their discounted garments were produced. The buyers then are given the choice to purchase the t-shirt or to donate their money to fight against the poor working conditions.

Many choose the second option, joining the movement with a central message that is summarized by the following slogan: "People care when they know." The video was shared on social media by many young people, who were very supportive of the action and touched by the issues raised in the video.

These youthful consumption competencies suggest that brands and advertisers must integrate a logic based on multiple types of consumption and usage skills developed by young consumers. Why? Because it can be a source of value and differentiation. Adopting such a perspective makes it possible for companies targeting the youth market to develop a policy centered on young consumers and their creative, transgressive, cognitive, and ethical potential. Youth consumption practices and the resulting competencies can then be seen as sources of inspiration for brands, allowing them to co-create offers with young people.

By involving young consumers and recognizing their consumer skills, companies retain them and build strong and long-term bonds with them. The example of Italian teenage clothing brand Brandy Melville, which has been booming among American teens since its launch, is very revealing. Brandy Melville works with teens who are employed by the brand and are entrusted with final decisions regarding collections, designs, communications, and the production of online content.

Brands must consider digital natives to be an inexhaustible source of inspiration when it comes to creating new products. The Dutch telecom operator

Bliep, was the first telecom brand made by teenagers and for teenagers. The operator initiated the collaborative project with adolescents to benefit from their creative potential. For this operator, teens are seen as innovative thinkers with open minds that allow companies to learn a lot from them, not just learn about them.

4.2   How Can Businesses and Policymakers Deal with the Vulnerabilities of Young Consumers?

What kind of marketing strategies should be adopted in the face of the risky behaviors that are common practices among digital natives? Should limits be imposed and prohibition encouraged? Should we adopt strategies that promote fear or even terror to get their attention? Do we need to protect these youth in the face of risks? Or should we offer them opportunities to take charge of themselves via empowerment? In other words, how should both businesses and policymakers consider digital natives: as fragile or, rather, as responsible and autonomous young consumers? In the next section, I propose different strategies businesses and policymakers can implement to cope with the risky behaviors of youths.

4.2.1   Recognizing youths' needs for autonomy

In a society that recognizes specific rights and emphasizes the protection of children (as evidenced by the adoption of the Declaration of the Rights of the Child in 1989), it may seem natural to want to protect young people from the grip of marketing and commercial advertising and sales. Many markets are regulated by laws in different countries; bans on the sales of alcohol and tobacco to minors in some countries are examples. Moreover, the rules on the sales of these products to minors have been tightened in recent years by the authorities.

Yet do young consumers need to be protected as the tobacco and alcohol laws strive to do? Young consumers nonetheless have acquired rights. The laws on parental authority, for example, recognize that adolescents have a certain amount of authority over their own lives: not only are parents listened to, but so are their children, who are consulted more today when it comes to decisions involving them. In addition, the law has defined a series of acts for which minors have a certain amount of autonomy. For example, they can use means of transportation, practice sports activities, access shows, and so forth.

These laws reflect a positive view of young people. Likewise, in France for instance, at the age of 12, French youth are entitled to have bank withdrawal cards; at the age of 14, young people can have supervised driving lessons; and at the age of 16, they can hold credit cards. To this end, companies should consider these young people as informed and thoughtful consumers who are capable of developing critical thinking of commercial offerings as they develop independent thinking and acquire consumer skills (Batat, 2014).

Recent studies have shown that the assertion of young consumers as autonomous people breaking away from the cocoons of their families is vital. It is a way in which the consumption behaviors of these youth and their motivations are expressed. Young people use consumption to integrate better into society while standing out from the world of childhood and that of adults. It has been indicated in prior studies that many consumer behaviors are acquired from the age of 12, corresponding to the onset of adolescence.

Parents and educators should encourage young consumers to adopt healthy behaviors as early as possible, while their autonomy in terms of their consumption decisions increases considerably. Thus, young consumers' thirst for autonomy should not be developed to the extreme. Hence, marketing scholars highlight the danger of certain ideas, such as the notion that teenagers are "little adults" or that it is up to their parents and not companies to protect children in the marketplace. However, could these excesses lead young consumers to adopt immoral consumer behaviors?

Nowadays, moral values within Western society often seem blurry and everyone uses autonomy as they see fit. Because autonomy has become a founding principle of morality, young people want to live their lives to the fullest and can, in this context, adopt multiple risky behaviors without grasping the consequences of their actions. Let me refer again to the example of illegal downloading of music on the Internet.

The young person who pirates CDs on the Internet and then exchanges them with their friends does not fear the law. The person sees nothing wrong with stealing royalties from producers and authors. But perhaps they could seek to understand why what they are doing is not moral under the principle of "do not do to others what you would not like to be done to you."

Rather than establishing hard-to-control laws and regulations, marketers are encouraged to engage in a strong dialogue with these digital natives. Thus, new relational or participatory marketing strategies should be implemented at the ontological level and not only at the level of the relations between companies and the youth market. Companies must rethink their marketing and communication strategies by recognizing the knowledge and skills acquired by young consumers through their consumption experiences.

Several marketing studies (Batat, 2008, 2014) have shown that young consumers have become full partners, even producers, who actively contribute to the process of consumption and creation of offers. Hence, parents and educators may be worried about this youth empowerment, with youths becoming active players in direct connection with companies.

The importance that youth place on consumption may even raise fears of the advent of materialistic generations, with consumption as their sole value.

This is how we observe a majority of these young consumers, who are digital natives, highly dependent on their smartphones and living in a permanently connected world.

4.2.2   Strategies emphasizing youth empowerment

Among the traditional anti-smoking prevention programs implemented in schools, it is now recognized that the perceived vulnerability used for preventive purposes among young people is not an effective strategy. The perceived vulnerability strategy emphasizes the dangers of consuming psychoactive drugs by causing anxiety.

By emphasizing risk, this strategy has had the opposite effects by causing young people to reject the recommendation given in the communication message to join a group (Batat and Tanner, 2021). As cited previously, vulnerability creates a "boomerang" effect by associating risk-taking with a tool for better social integration. In other words, young people seek to take risks to gain popularity and defend their social positions within their peer groups.

Thus, the most effective anti-smoking campaigns targeting youth are those aimed at adults. Youthhood is a crucial period for identity building. During this period, young people need to be recognized as autonomous beings and consumers, just like "little adults." It is, therefore, important to reveal the truth to these digital natives by portraying the tobacco industry as being manipulative in an effort to get them addicted to tobacco. One way to get the attention of young consumers is to develop a communication message presenting cigarette smoking not as a form of independence or even rebellion, but rather as a manipulative industry.

Several strategies can help de-normalize the use of products such as tobacco in schools, for example, inviting anti-tobacco activists to present strategies to counter attracting young people, thereby enabling them to take charge of themselves ("empowerment") through the implementation of actions during "anti-smoking" days.

4.2.3   The critical role of authenticity

It is necessary to go beyond the stereotypes specific to youth cultures by only seeing these young people as digital natives and tech-savvy. Technology allows them to fulfill not only their functional needs but above all their social expectations. Yet one of the privileged moments for these young people is when they have concrete exchanges with their friends in the real world.

Although the Internet is popular in youth cultures, these digital natives seek the truth from other sources of information. Almost 70 percent of them trust their parents, compared to only 13 percent who trust the Internet when they need answers. Indeed, digital natives are in search of authenticity. As another sign of authenticity, it has been observed that scouting has risen sharply.

Youth who are scouts seek truth in the world and in nature. The idea of taking vacations without the constraints of a smartphone, which is known as taking a "digital detox," is in vogue at the moment.

The concept of taking a "digital detox" was launched first in the United States, from Silicon Valley, in response to this desire to disconnect. It consists of disconnecting from screens (smartphones, tablets, and computers) to better reconnect to yourself. Disconnecting is an invitation to come back to real life to better enjoy your stay. Young people and their families occupy their time with activities, books, board games, sports, and massages for example.

The objective of these "digital detox" vacations is to learn to cut through screens to refocus on concrete activities and create "real" links with others. Digital detoxification is starting to take hold in Europe and across different countries. Therefore, we can note these young consumers are demanding consideration and authenticity. They are looking for communication campaigns that focus on people and transparency.

4.2.4   Transmission as a strategy to connect with youth

Parents have a key role to play in transmitting codes of good and healthy behaviors to their children. Parents are also role models, who should raise their kids' awareness of the risks associated with the consumption of illicit products (tobacco, alcohol, cannabis, and other drugs). Young people are more likely to smoke and be addicted to nicotine if their parents are smokers.

According to a recent study (Kandel et al., 2015), girls are more influenced by the behaviors of their parents. The same is true for behaviors related to alcohol and other drugs. For Kandel and colleagues, most smokers start smoking when they are teenagers. Parents have a strong influence on children. To prevent young people from starting to smoke and becoming addicted to tobacco, we must help their parents quit smoking.

A longitudinal study published in the *American Journal of Public Health*, conducted over a period of 8 years (2004 to 2012) with 35,000 adolescent–parent pairs, highlighted the preponderant role of parents in the initiation of and dependence on smoking among their children (Kandel et al., 2015). This study showed that 13 percent of the adolescents of non-smoking parents say they have never smoked a cigarette.

Conversely, nearly 40 percent of adolescents of nicotine-dependent parents have smoked. Overall, young people are three times more likely to have smoked cigarettes and almost twice as likely to be nicotine-addicted if their parents are as well. Girls are more influenced by parenting behavior than boys. Girls are four times more likely to be addicted to nicotine if their mothers are too.

Parents, therefore, have a duty of transmission and socialization. Parents need to not only inform their children about the risks involved in the consumption of psychoactive products, but above all, make them aware of the process of dependence and addiction with which their children can identify.

Second, school is a significant socialization agent involved in the transmission process. Although school is not the only place where digital natives interact with their peers, it is becoming more and more important in the lives of a growing number of young people today. Much more than a simple institution, school is a place where young people live daily among their peers. Schools also play a major role in the sense that they have the responsibility of transmitting to young generations both knowledge and interpersonal skills, which are vital competencies.

School is a living environment in its own right that plays a key role in promoting healthy behaviors. Studies revealed that bylaws that prohibit smoking on the premises of establishments together with the prohibition of alcohol and other drug use reduce the number of young daily smokers. Nevertheless, many school heads are not in favor of strict regulations to ban tobacco consumption since, according to them, this measure would only "shift the problem" by encouraging young people to smoke right in front of their schools.

Therefore, as noted earlier, the desire for transgression and risk attractiveness are two factors contributing to the dark side of vulnerability, resulting in deliberate behaviors that enhance the feeling of invulnerability among young consumers. To address dark-side vulnerability, policy actions revealed by my previous research encompass four major measures aiming at (1) developing attractive off- and online educational campaigns by (2) co-creating educational campaigns with adolescents, (3) resulting in micro-targeted campaigns, and (4) developing experiential consumption knowledge.

Co-creating educational campaigns with young people through empathetic collaboration and by incorporating adolescents' cultural markers and views in educational discourses and policies can offer numerous advantages over more traditional paternalistic forms of education concerning risky behaviors and vulnerable situations. Empathetic collaboration can allow youth, policymakers, and marketers to develop and share new knowledge within the youth vulnerability management framework. Such participatory educational actions can transform adolescents into active players collaborating with adults and policymakers to co-create more effective educational programs.

For example, when developing anti-smoking campaigns, collaborating with young consumers enables legislators and public health officials to incorporate youth cultural markers that will enhance the campaigns' credibility and adoption. Prior research on youths' impressions of anti-smoking advertisements revealed that advertising geared towards young people is more effective when it addresses their subcultures in a language they understand and appreciate.

Studies have shown that not only should the youth consumption culture become a crucial part of educational policies, but it also should take into account how risky behaviors such as smoking are shaped by the norms of this youth culture. This is the case because young people do not perceive smoking as resulting in a vulnerable state (dark-side vulnerability).

Furthermore, youth are aware of their imposed vulnerability and open to influence if their trust can be gained. Thus, any communication strategy beginning from an adult perspective is likely to fail because of a lack of trust. Continuing with our anti-smoking example, smoking may be viewed as deliberate vulnerability. However, when that vulnerability is changed by a campaign that suggests that tobacco companies are manipulating teens into smoking, then successful behavior change can be achieved. Thus, a communication strategy that is more about recognizing and coping with imposed vulnerability rather than avoiding deliberate vulnerability may prove to be more effective, leveraging adolescents' desire to master their environments.

Besides, there is a need to address risky online behaviors, which are a form of dark-side vulnerability that reflects the feeling of invulnerability among youth. Policy measures can focus on two main aspects: (1) advancing digital well-being and online risk consciousness, and (2) enhancing digital literacy so that youth can recognize attempts to impose vulnerability and respond accordingly. To enhance the digital well-being and online risk consciousness of youths, policymakers should focus on youth use of social media and the Internet.

Furthermore, policymakers should explore and investigate virtual experiences among youth cultures and subcultures. They can create online communities addressing youth issues with the help of experts serving as community managers. However, these experts need to take a youth perspective in their online exchanges, enabling young Internet users to ask very personal and intimate questions (e.g., about one's eating disorders, sexuality, drugs, and puberty) of reactive and empathetic community managers.

Because young consumers are uncomfortable when dealing with adults, online communities allow them to use digital language codes such as emojis to express their feelings, anxieties, and fears, and talk freely in their own words. Enhancing digital literacy can help young people to balance risk with social media opportunities by developing strategies that empower them. Empowering digital strategies can involve different actors ranging from businesses and digital firms, such as Facebook and Google, to educators.

The collaboration between digital firms and educators can encourage youth to think critically about the digital sphere and develop their skills, views, creativity, and interest as users of digital media. Policymakers, social media, and educators should work together to develop guides based on youth cultural markers for educators, youths, their parents, and so forth.

The social media guide could include a focus on digital privacy and safety, social media usages in school to share knowledge (e.g., reflecting on

Wikipedia contributions and the use of Twitter to share new insights), connecting and socializing in an online safe environment, and so on. This can help parents become more engaged with the digital consumption of their kids by making it safer and more relevant, and with responsible choices throughout the online consumption context.

Policymakers and businesses should also address consumption illiteracy, which can increase the likelihood of deliberate vulnerability. The materialistic behaviors of youths may reflect a state of perceived invulnerability as young consumers engage in accumulation and materialism to develop skills and become subject-matter experts (e.g., in video gaming or electronics). This contrasts with adult materialism literature, which relates materialism to a person's emotional and social vulnerability.

Developing consumption literacy programs related to consumption domains such as food issues and one's self-image or money management could be integrated into traditional curricula. Such integration could reduce imposed vulnerability by strengthening adolescents' ability to discern marketing messages more clearly. Creating tools to link novel consumption domains and risk awareness to a person's actions can enable digital natives to experience new and risky situations in a safe context and under adult control, as well as develop consumption literacy skills transferable to other domains. Policymakers and program leaders should also consider building intentional coping versus reflexive coping skills when developing consumer literacy programs.

Youths' social anxieties, pressures, and their identity construction are a dimension related to imposed vulnerability – what young people consider as real and imposed states of vulnerability. Developing school as well as family education programs that focus on positive identity development among youths is an urgent agenda. Young people who can develop positive identities as a result of their struggles during adolescence often transition more easily into adulthood.

The programming should help young people develop coping strategies to avoid being vulnerable to social and emotional factors and to form positive identities. The enhancement of positive identity development in youth culture is important to prepare the next generation of confident and empowered adults; it can be achieved at both the individual level (self-esteem and self-discrepancies) and the social level (social relationships).

By addressing vulnerability from the perspective of youths, marketers can empower every generation of young consumers by developing consumer literacy that fosters their functioning optimally.

KEY TAKEAWAYS

The key takeaways from this chapter reveal the fact that digital natives can be considered competent or vulnerable consumers, depending on three aspects: areas of consumption; their experiences; and economic, sociocultural, and structural criteria. Marketing managers and advertisers should focus more on young consumer competencies and integrate them into their offerings and communication strategies. Among the competencies developed by young people in different youth cultures and which might be of interest for brands, the following should be considered: cognitive, creative, and moral consumer competencies. Also, businesses targeting youth and policymakers should address the vulnerability that emerges in youth cultures and develop effective strategies to help these youths become fully legitimate and competent consumers.

5. Consumption, brands, co-creation, and empowerment in youth cultures: how can businesses capture the creative potential of digital natives?

CHAPTER OVERVIEW

In this chapter, I explore consumption practices among young consumers across different youth cultures and examine their relationships with brands. The objective is then to shed light on the creative potential of digital natives and the incentive for companies to collaborate with them and consider these empowered consumers as active partners who can co-create offerings with them. To fully understand the collaborative process that brands can put in place to build offers with young people across different youth consumption cultures, we must take an interest in consumption traits of young people, their relationships with brands, and the co-creation process stages as well as the activities that can make collaboration possible.

1. WHAT DO WE KNOW ABOUT COMMON PATTERNS IN YOUTH CONSUMPTION CULTURES?

Based on the studies and contributions of several generations of scholars and specialists of youth consumers, we can note many shared traits when it comes to young people's consumption activities and purchase behaviors. These characteristics can be summarized as follows:

- Digital natives have a growing interest in brands, friends, leisure, and digital culture;
- They are confident, relaxed, and committed;
- They represent a youth generation with a high level of education compared to previous generations;
- They display a strong need for security;

- They are impatient and focused on their well-being while appreciating team spirit and collaboration;
- They have been spared from wars but are under great pressure from society to succeed in their professional lives.

One of the main shared behaviors among these digital natives is "multitasking," or the art of combining several tasks at the same time. These multitaskers often work as a team via online social media and are influenced by their friends, people online, and their peers.

These characteristics may evolve or differ under the influence of the interactions between young consumers and the socioeconomic context that exists during their first years of socialization. These influences will then bring in community policies and practices, thus shaping the traits of this digital native generation. For Fields et al. (2008), this generation as a group also has a growing influence on our culture and has a powerful impact on the workplace and new emerging trends in terms of consumption and social interactions.

Thus, these young consumers represent a new cultural phenomenon that is shaping future consumption practices as well as the relationships with brands and the marketplace. Therefore, for advertisers and brands, the only way to create relevant and adapted marketing policies for offers targeting young people (childescents, adonascents, adolescents, and adulescents) is to develop an in-depth understanding of the different consumption cultures these digital natives belong to.

These youth consumption cultures are characterized by codes, symbolic dimensions, meanings, norms, and values that are shared by members of each consumer youth culture. The components of the youth consumption cultures are presented in Figure 5.1.

1.1   Five Major Common Traits among Young Consumers

We can classify the common patterns that characterize and define digital natives as a unique generation and youth consumption culture according to five major themes: attractive market segment, terrorism, economic crisis, hyperconnected, and co-creation. These five shared consumption traits are discussed next.

1.1.1   An attractive market segment

Digital natives are part of a youth culture that represents a high market potential and an attractive segment to target for companies. This generation consist of a very large number of individuals worldwide. According to forecasts by the United States Census Bureau (2006), the world's population by the year 2050 is estimated to consist of more than 9 billion people. This means that by 2050 digital natives will be 45 years old, on average; the average woman will have a life expectancy of 83 years, and the average man will have a life expectancy of 78 years. Together the group will represent half of the world's population and, therefore, half of the consumers on the market and professionals employed by companies.

In the United States, digital natives spend an average of $30 million each visit to the mall. Their purchasing power exceeds $200 billion annually, and their power over family purchases is between $300 and $400 billion annually (Martin and Turley, 2004). Thus, these young consumers spend a large amount of money. Nonetheless, they remain a very complex target to reach, although brands have learned to use different tactics to target them.

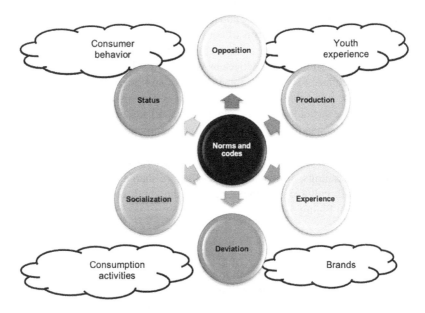

Figure 5.1   The components of youth consumption cultures

1.1.2   A youth culture marked by terrorism

Digital natives are also part of the first generation to have known terrorism during their childhoods. Considered citizens of the world, they form a cohort of individuals marked by terrorism, which is not found in any of the previous generations. These people have experienced a combination of a series of terrorist events that took place during their early years of formulating their values and beliefs. Furthermore, social media platforms and information and communication technologies have enabled the massive exposure of these young people to terrorist events.

The turning point in the lives of this generation compared to previous generations and the generation of their parents was the occurrence of the September 11, 2001, terrorist attacks in the United States. The attacks targeted the Twin Towers of the World Trade Center in New York City and killed nearly 3,000 people.

It is, therefore, not surprising that a study conducted by the New Politics Institute in 2006 found that young people 13–17 years old are particularly concerned about safety because crime and terrorism helped form the background of the first years of their childhood. Terrorist events and their dissemination via social media platforms have contributed to strengthening the safety concerns of members of this digital generation.

1.1.3   The impact of the economic crisis

At the financial and economic level, the behaviors of each generation are different because they are closely linked to the social tendencies of the societies in which they are reared.

Digital natives are familiar with credit and often depend on their parents financially, unlike previous generations, who were characterized as savvy savers. Moreover, the onset of the global economic crisis in 2008 marked the difficult entry of these young consumers into their adult lives. Thus, forecasts of job losses, the closures of businesses, credit restrictions, and rising house prices marked the transition from a stable era, solid with a high level of confidence and favorable economic climate, to an uncertain financial future. These effects taken together relate to factors such as immediacy, short-term satisfaction, risk, security, and communication among today's young consumers.

It is, therefore, not surprising that the values of this generation reflect the need for safety and security and a certain self-confidence due to their mastery of technologies. Frequent change and technological advancements are welcome realities for digital natives but may be troubling for previous generations.

1.1.4   Hyperconnected young consumers

Today's young consumers are referred to as digital natives. They were born with digital technologies and thus have an accelerated and unconventional pace of life compared to earlier generations. Other common features among these young consumers include the fact that they operate randomly rather than in stages; they combine different parallel process treatments rather than a single linear process. Also, for them, it is the graphics first and the text afterwards. They are also connected (not alone) and are exposed to several screens, such as TVs, computers, and mobile phones, simultaneously.

The digital uniqueness of these young consumers has led to the proliferation of technological tools. An American study of more than 7,000 members of this digital hyperconnected generation in the United States shows that 97 percent of these young people have a computer, and 94 percent of them have a cell phone (Reynol and Mastrodicasa, 2007). Furthermore, digital natives use technological devices differently from members of other generations, particularly when it comes to mobile phones (Batat, 2008). A study on the uses of Facebook among these young consumers highlighted the following common characteristics:

- Among the 150 million active users on Facebook, 45 percent are men, and 55 percent are women;
- The demographic is mainly represented by the 18–25 age group;
- A user has on average a group of 100 friends on the site;
- More than 3 billion minutes are spent every day on Facebook worldwide;
- More than 13 million users update their profiles at least once a day;
- More than 800 million photos and 5 million videos are uploaded to the site each month;
- More than 20 million active user groups exist on the site.

In addition, studies on the use of digital tools among digital native students highlight the shared characteristics of digital uses specific to these people. They include the need for information; the need for rapid and immediate access to information (immediacy); multitasking; and the ability to manage multiple aspects of their life by using different digital devices and platforms at the same time.

1.1.5 Co-creation at the center of youth consumption activities
Young consumers naturally feel comfortable using digital devices and online platforms in their daily activities that are directly or indirectly related to consumption. Digital technologies provide these young people with an enduring connection with the digital world while offering them a playful dimension with games, the possibility of socializing via social networks, and the information necessary to accomplish their work.

In this youth culture, information is, therefore, no longer reserved only for professionals and experts. For example, Wikipedia, a free multilingual encyclopedia, is co-produced, thanks to the collaboration of volunteers worldwide. The collaboration often is initiated by digital natives, who then work and collaborate with members of other generations to produce the necessary information.

These practices call into question the expertise of and need for professionals who have been trained for this work, such as journalists. The use of Wikipedia, for example, has become commonplace and spread among all members of youth culture, who are considered by society as experts, early adopters, and lead-users (Von Hippel, 2005). The concept of lead-users highlights the collaboration that manifests itself through the participation of these young consumers in the co-creation of a company's offerings.

1.2 How Can Brands Leverage Youth Cultures to Win Back and Retain Digital Natives?

Digital natives are part of a postmodern consumer society that unites tribes of young consumers whose behaviors are part of youthful consumer culture. Identifying the different youth cultures allows brands to better understand emerging youth consumption trends and the meanings each youth culture assigns to its consumption experiences.

Thus, to better target digital natives, brands should leverage the codes and norms that shape youth consumption cultures and reflect them in their marketing and communication strategies. An effective strategy aiming at the youth market must, therefore, integrate five major elements: hedonism and coolness, generous spirit and volunteerism, symbolism, experiential values, and role models.

1.2.1 Hedonism and coolness

A study by Ferguson (2008) highlights the idea of hedonism and the "cool" consumption of digital natives. This exploratory study shows that the definition of "cool" is largely shared among these young consumers in their youth consumption cultures. Most digital natives distinguish between the "cool" dimension of the activity and the profile of the consumer, who practices it. In this sense, the definition of the "cool" related to consumption activities depends on the meaning that emerges in each youth culture (childescence, adonascence, adolescence, and adulescence) and is shared by members of each segmenculture. In other words, what is considered "cool" for adonascents might not be perceived to be "cool" in the adulescence youth culture.

1.2.2 Generous spirit and volunteerism

The generous and voluntary spirit among digital natives is exhibited by altruistic behaviors such as volunteering and donating. Several studies highlight the importance of donation among digital natives. For instance, Ringer and Garma (2006) conducted a study on the behaviors and motivations of helping others. It compared digital natives and adult generations (e.g., Generation X) and found that there is a difference between young people and adults in terms of how they perceive the need to help others. The need to help others is more present among digital natives. Thus, understanding the altruistic motivations of these young consumers to attract and retain long-term donors would be beneficial for nonprofit organizations as well as companies interested in involving them in charity. Focusing on altruism allows brands to engage and retain digital natives by appealing to their emotions related to social issues.

To connect with them, the brand's communication strategy must focus on the importance of acquiring skills and experiences, which corresponds to the self-centered view of helping (intrinsic motivation) perceived by young people. Thus, the generous spirit and the representation of the gift are consistent with how digital natives describe themselves: turned towards others, free, and little associated with the notions of duty and effort. Their commitment and investment in charitable causes must produce pleasure to attract and motivate them.

1.2.3   Symbolism

The symbolic consumption of brands among digital natives is a critical aspect that needs to be considered by brands while targeting these young consumers. Given the size and influence of the youth market as well as the number of brands like Red Bull that exclusively target this generation (Miller, 2007), brand image has become a strategic pillar for professionals and brand managers.

According to Miller, who examined the image of the brand Red Bull among digital natives, the brand image is closely linked to its symbolic dimension, which means what it represents for young people. The growing interest of brands in attracting digital natives by sharing symbols and signs with them (such as the Red Bull symbol) is explained by the fact that the construction of a youth identity is an issue among digital natives. They are looking for meanings and brands to identify with. Thus, image and aesthetics are essential elements in the daily lives of young consumers, who use brands to express themselves and build their social and personal identities.

1.2.4   Experiential values

Although visiting shopping malls has been a subject of interest for retail professionals for at least 35 years, studies on young consumers and malls have not benefited from the same enthusiasm, except for a study published by Taylor and Cosenza in 2002.

It revealed that young consumers have positive feelings towards shopping malls. They visit the mall in search of exciting experiences. During their adonascence and adolescence, these young consumers visit malls many times a week for socialization and dating purposes: to see and be seen. Some shopping centers have become so overwhelmed by hordes of young people that regulations and restrictions have had to be implemented (Hazel, 2001). Although mall managers sometimes see these young people as a source of problems, they nevertheless do not want to neglect the growth of this market segment.

Other studies show that there are differences between digital natives and previous generations. These studies emphasize the significant role that music and ambience play when it comes to attracting young customers. Thus, those in charge of shopping centers must be particularly careful when using the music variable because, according to Yalch and Spangenberg (1993), the perception of music among digital natives is not universal and varies according to age group.

1.2.5   Role models

According to Minkiewicz and Bridson (2007), heroes and role models are an integral part of the daily lives of digital natives and have a significant impact on their values, attitudes, and consumer behaviors. The results of the study showed that among young people 15–25 years old, sports role models and celebrities are very important in the daily lives of the younger cohort. In contrast, the older cohort tends to view these role models as less influential in their lives. These young people are more independent and interested in role models from those around them (friends, family, and co-workers), not those imposed by the media. The study also highlights the fact that role models can act as anti-heroes or negative role models. When this is the case, their influence can be negative.

2.   LOVED VS. UNLOVED BRANDS: SEEKING THE MISSING BOND

As for the few star brands, things have changed very little over time. Apple, Nike, Adidas, Google, Samsung, and Coca-Cola, for example, have remained the favorite brands among young people for several years, with slight variations in their rankings from year to year. Yet what is arguably the most instructive is to see that the global dominance of these brands may be faltering.

If we now look at the vast majority of brands, we see that young people are particularly selective when it comes to letting commercial messages enter their worlds of consumption. There is sometimes a line between what can generate a warm welcome towards them and what will often lead to a firm and definitive rejection. This is why, as the Forbes 2015 Cassandra report recommends, brands must know how to establish "intimate and honest relations" with these young consumers, who are emotional, pragmatic, and skeptical.

2.1   Becoming a Loved Brand among Digital Natives

Young consumers, who belong to the digital native generation, prioritize their principles to the detriment of brands in the product categories that interest them. Benefiting from a positive reputation thus becomes one of the key elements of the system that will allow brands to win their favor. Furthermore, community management will play an essential role in mastering the brand's e-reputation and ability to successfully approach digital natives: knowing how to listen to them, being able to interact with them, as well as being able to consider and integrate their opinions and feedback on the company's products and brands.

Having always known the Internet and having grown up with the advance of social media platforms, digital natives are anything but passive receivers; they are often the source of the echoes, noise, and information that will make a brand what it is. Whereas previous generations were characterized by tolerance about many societal issues, digital natives fully claim their diversity and subscribe to a more marked logic of solidarity. This is why the differences that can be observed between individuals (e.g., their origins, ethnicities, lifestyles, tastes, and sexual orientations) are not really about them; rather, they reflect the very wide variety of possibilities within what is called humanity; but at the same time, they convey the idea that responsibilities must be shared by all.

The first strong memories these people have of communication were related to September 11 or its consequences. What is sustainable, what respects the environment and, much more broadly, anything that is ethically correct, is not negotiable for this generation. Thus, to gain their trust with such standards, and above all to know how to keep it, authenticity should be the priority sought by brands and marketers. Companies targeting the youth market should not try to move forward in a "mask" or want to project an image far removed from what they really are; instead, the companies should focus on transparency and speak to every young person by personalizing their messages as much as possible.

This statement is in line with recent studies that highlight the fact that the majority of American digital natives want brands to communicate with them by email and on their social media. Brands should, therefore, use data available on social media to provide young consumers with a more individualized dimension when it comes to communication. Thus, to transform youth into brand lovers, companies should know how to increase what we call "the conversational power" of their content to not only attract the attention but also the interest of their young audiences.

Developing an authentic image for a brand means that it deserves the time and money devoted to it by young people because it is in line with their claimed values and truly reflects what the brand's values are. To develop closeness with digital natives, brands must consider them as partners and emphasize this aspect in their communication and commercial messages. Therefore, any display of authority and condescension should be removed from the brand's discourse because young people aspire to achieve equality with brands that engage them with conversational relationships. Digital natives want to have the means to interact with brands and with other consumers at the same time, not from a top-down perspective.

Ten years ago, young people complained about opt-out text messages on their cell phones. Young people today are even less tolerant. If they have the feeling that a brand is attempting to intrude on them online, the brand will pay a price. Thanks to social media, brands may believe they are informed of everything that is trendy and that digital natives are easy targets who can be seduced. Yet being informed does not mean these young people can be seduced. Moreover, overly automated marketing directed toward them can quickly lead to failure.

Digital natives often have a very opportunistic outlook, and they only connect with and like a brand when they can gain some form of advantage (e.g., discounts, prices, contests). To succeed in building real relationships with these young consumers, brands should know how to enrich the conversations that emerge from social media interactions without interrupting young people's online exchanges. This is a very difficult challenge. The brand Dove, with its campaign on self-confidence, has succeeded in achieving this by having the right balance between interaction and noninteraction.

Furthermore, digital natives are creative but they do not seek to be revolutionaries. Thus, they fit quite well in the continuity of what their elders already like to do, namely, not to break brand codes but rather to hijack them. These young people use them with a positional or statutory logic, whether to show their belonging to a group or to stand out from it. Likewise, they greatly appreciate adopting but also playing with the logos from brands they like.

By letting young consumers make this diversion or creating connivance through self-mockery or other forms of humor such as absurdity, the brand benefits from an indisputable capital of sympathy with this youth population through the so-called LOL (laugh-out-loud) culture. Clearly, as humor has a natural tendency to be shared, the Internet and social media platforms represent a fantastic sounding board that helps broadcast everything these young people can find funny about a brand.

2.2   Brands as Drivers of Identity Construction in Youth Cultures

Brands remain a path of identity construction among digital natives. Youth identity can be defined as the result of a balance between a personal dimension, self-esteem, and a social dimension, belonging to a group (Erikson, 1968/1972). Identity construction in youth cultures is a process that lasts throughout a person's lifetime. However, the period of adolescence and youthhood represents a very particular moment of it insofar as the young person lives through a period of destabilization and questioning: the person has lost the bearings he or she had as a child and has not yet found his or her place as an adult.

To help them get through this difficult time in their lives, young people will generally seek out memberships in peer groups. There are usually a lot of similarities between members of the same group; first because they are already grouped at the start according to their proximity (lifestyles, centers of interest), and then because the experiences they will live through together will accentuate the initial similarities and lead to a certain homogenization of the youth culture and its consumption practices.

During the adolescence phase, peer groups help the individual in several ways. They first act as a mirror by allowing the person to see that he or she is not the only one going through this difficult time. They will then act as a support, each ensuring, through the friendly relations that are established, encouragement for the others. Finally, the group can also be an opportunity to test relationships of domination or submission or competition for the leadership of the group.

Nowadays, the Internet and social media communities are changing how relationships between young people are formed and practiced and how brands should be present. Indeed, brands are a necessary support for the construction of the identities of youths by allowing them to highlight their personalities and express themselves in the group. Of course, young people can, through their personal identities, compare themselves to others in an interpersonal relationship, but it is clear that it is most often through their social identities that these people gain rewarding self-esteem.

Though brands play an important social role in the lives of young consumers, they are used to belonging to a certain group and gaining recognition through a perpetual tension between a desire for assimilation and differentiation. It is, therefore, of great importance for these digital natives to wear brands synonymous with "the right style" and the brands adopted by the peer group. Indeed, young people seek material solutions to their identity problems (Holt and Thompson, 2004) by using resources to strive for an ideal ego that engenders respect in others (in relation to their social identities) and inspires a love for the self (personal identities).

During the youthhood phase, the symbolic benefits of the product are more important than the functional ones and are considered to be a reflection of a youth's identity. In other words, young people prefer products that look like them. Therefore, possessions, due to their reassuring and emotional quality, their ability to strengthen the self-images of youths and their sense of belonging, are very important to digital natives (Voss et al., 2003). Possessions become a visible extension and allow young consumers to convey a certain image, to distinguish themselves from others while being linked to a reference group.

What is new with digital natives is the heavy use of social media. Compared to previous generations, social media offer them both a capacity to considerably multiply the number of people with whom they will be able to interact and the possibility of managing the level and nature of these interactions with each person. There is, therefore, as compared to their elders, a new opportunity to manage different "selves" through digital identities. It is still too early to know whether a digital identity can have lasting effects when a young person leaves the virtual world. Sharing one's activities on social networks is obvious to a youth insofar as the activity is used for self-invention and the expression of the person's individuality. Social media platforms allow young people to come together around sociocultural affinities with their peers, in a space where the youths can express their consumption practices and adopted brands.

3.   THE POWER OF CO-CREATION TO ENGAGE DIGITAL NATIVES

The co-creation practices present in different youth cultures reflect the changing role of young consumers, who become more active and involved in their consumption and purchase experiences. They then develop cognitive and social competencies as well as a creative potential, which are of interest to brands that can use them to establish a strong connection with digital natives. Thus, today's young consumers can collaborate with brands on different levels, ranging from the conception of products and services aimed at them to the products' manufacturing.

The co-creation process in youth cultures is also made possible thanks to the development of digital devices and social media communities. Young consumers, who are comfortable with digital technologies and social media usage, can post their ideas and discuss them with other consumers or with brands. To fully understand the collaborative process that brands can implement to connect with digital natives, adapt their offers (products and services) to their tangible and symbolic needs, and thus build a strong competitive advantage, it is critical to understand how the co-creation process works and what its drivers, types, and stages across different youth cultures are.

This section responds to these questions by first addressing the typologies and characteristics of co-creation among digital natives in different youth cultures. Second, I introduce Youth Collaborative Marketing (YCM), an effective strategy to engage, connect, and retain young consumers in the highly competitive youth market.

3.1   How Does Co-creation with Youth Work?

Co-creation in the different youth consumption cultures is an active, creative, collaborative, and social process generated by multiple exchanges between brands and companies and their youth targets. Thus, young consumers are actively involved through the tools and exchange platforms made available to them by companies to facilitate and engage them in an enduring co-creation process. The interest for brands is to use young consumers' knowledge, creativity, and competencies in their innovation strategies and communication campaigns. Yet engaging digital natives co-creating with brands is influenced by four major factors:

• The culture of the consumer society;
• The codes and standards of consumption shaped by different youth cultures;
• The marketplace, which involves various stakeholders such as the media, businesses, institutions, and government, among others;
• Online and virtual communities including online peers.

Consequently, young consumers are not alone in the co-creative process; they are directly or indirectly influenced and inspired by these four elements that constitute their environment. The practices of co-creation between young consumers and companies can also take several forms (e.g., sharing opinions, contests, votes, personalization, promotion, suggestion boxes, etc.).

To examine the co-creation model embedded in youth consumption cultures, I propose a classification of the levels of young consumers' involvement according to three main categories: bricolage, collaboration, and co-innovation. Each level calls for specific knowledge of the field of consumption, competencies, and tools that make the co-creation of value between brands and digital natives conceivable.

As Figure 5.2 shows, the three levels (bricolage, collaboration, and co-innovation) suppose a creative potential and a more or less strong commitment on the part of young consumers, who will participate in the collaborative project. For example, while product personalization can be seen as a fairly accessible form of co-creation, co-innovation requires technical skills and a very high creative potential. Understanding these three levels is critical for brands that want to set up a collaborative process with digital natives and thus engage them in a long-term collaboration.

The three levels identified suggest that the brand must apply a strategy of prioritizing co-creation practices that will facilitate young consumers' choices according to the degree of their commitment and competencies. These levels require a young consumer to acquire a certain degree of commitment and competency that is different according to the type of the co-creation the person is engaged in. Thus, a simple action such as personalization through bricolage supposes a lower level of commitment and skills than collaboration or co-innovation, which both necessitate in-depth knowledge and skills to engage in real product and service innovations:

- Co-creation through bricolage is characterized by simple tasks, such as personalizing objects based on the options available and proposed by the brand. It is an effective way to help young consumers take ownership of a product or service by transforming its appearance or function. These digital natives view co-creation consumption activities through bricolage as an extension of their identity as consumers;
- Co-creation through collaboration refers to young consumers' collaboration with brands. The collaboration can take two forms: passive or active. The passive collaboration of young consumers is a form of co-creation that consists of them providing their feedback and opinions. Active collaboration includes practices that aim to involve digital natives in the design or the promotion of a product or service. The project is defined and framed by the company. It then gives instructions that young consumers have to follow in the collaborative process.

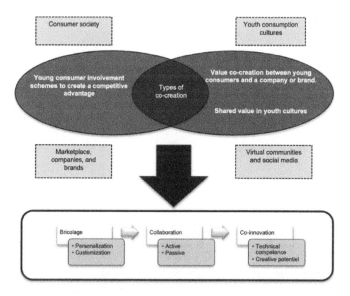

Figure 5.2   The co-creation model in youth consumption cultures

3.2   Types and Characteristics of Co-creation Approaches among Youth

Young consumers' involvement in a co-creation process requires favorable conditions that allow the transformation of their ideas into innovations and thus marketable products. Businesses should then be capable of integrating the creative potential of young people to improve and adjust their offerings targeting the youth market.

However, before embarking on co-creation with digital natives, companies should ask the following questions: at what stage should young consumers be involved? For what type of task? And what is the purpose of the company? Young consumers can be involved at all levels of the co-creation process, including idea generation and ideation, testing and validation of products and prototypes, communication and promotion, and distribution, among others.

The youth consumption culture to which young consumers belong can also guide the company in its choice of the co-creation stage and thus involve them at the beginning, in the middle, or at the end of the collaborative process (see Figure 5.3).

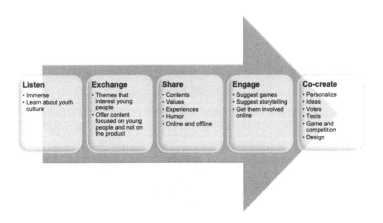

Figure 5.3   Stages of co-creation in youth consumption cultures

Collaborating with young consumers and engaging them in a co-creative process allows companies to adjust and adapt their products and services to the functional and symbolic needs of young people. The collaboration between brands and digital natives can be achieved through different approaches and actions as follows.

3.2.1   Customization and personalization

The sneaker brand Converse allows young customers to personalize their sneakers on the brand's website. For example, young users can customize the Chuck Taylor All Star 1 collection with a simple click and choose between several shoe types: flat sneakers, high tops, and so on. The brand allows users to design the exterior and interior aspects of the product and personalize its colors. Users can also include logos and graffiti and insert a short 12 character message with their names on the outside so that they have a unique personalized product.

3.2.2   Youth engagement through values and hedonism

Communicating the value of a product or service to young consumers requires meaningful content that the brand creates and shares with them. Companies should talk with their younger customers instead of their products. The brand can engage young people by communicating directly with them on social media or through advertising messages by incorporating their youth values.

Social media platforms are considered to be engagement catalysts for these digital natives. Facebook, Instagram, Tumblr, Twitter, and Google+ can be used to interact with young people or offer them fun experiences to live or share with their peers. For advertisers and brands that target young people, engagement is an effective means that creates a closeness with digital natives while reducing the costs of television commercials.

The values that brands share with their targets are, therefore, a significant factor in the engagement of young people. To create engagement, the brand needs to define a purpose or a goal. If the aim of the company is only to sell products, this situation limits creating and strengthening the emotional connection and closeness with young consumers.

However, if the objective of the brand is to show that it wants to make the world a better place by promoting eco-friendly business practices and offerings, in this case, it will have a more sympathetic image, which is in step with the responsible and ethical values of young people. Beyond responsible and ethical values, to engage young people, brands must integrate two main elements in their marketing and communication actions, both offline and online: playfulness and interactivity.

Youth engagement can also build on emerging trends in social media; for example, engagement through play can be implemented by companies and brands using several approaches, such as self-mockery and humor, gamification, and offers that integrate serious games mixing education and hedonism.

MINI-CASE BOX 5.1   "I LOVE POTATOES":
A SERIOUS GAME TO ENGAGE
CHILDESCENTS AND ADONASCENTS
IN SUSTAINABILITY AND RAISE THEIR
AWARENESS OF ENVIRONMENTAL ISSUES

Sustainable development and fun applications are part of the world of consumers from an early age. "I Love Potatoes" is an application for both childescents and adonascents. Its goal is to educate young people and raise
their awareness about ecological issues and the importance of sustainable
consumption.

In the online game, "Chips," the little hero of the adventure, has an important mission: he must save "Potatoland," his wonderful world. In this
world lives a monster who, in exchange for potatoes, offers the inhabitants
everything they want: video games, luxury goods, food, and so on. Chips,
a courageous little character, is thus going on an adventure and will learn to
break free from stereotypes and to consume and live differently.

Like the players of the game, he comes to understand that natural and
environmental resources are not unlimited. This serious game is a playful
way to create an awareness of social change and sustainable development.
Educators and parents are not left out because the ONF (France's National
Forestry Office), which produced the game, also offers educational resources and ideas for activities for young people to do in class or at home. The
goal is to get youths to go further in terms of social innovation, values,
and the overconsumption practices present within today's society in which
young people live and learn to become consumers.

3.2.3   Empathy while co-creating with youth

Empathy is all about communicating emotions that reflect a brand's ability to
put itself in the shoes of the young people with their challenges and paradoxes
and see the world from their eyes. By so doing, companies are able to better
perceive young consumers' needs and expectations so as to orient their communication and marketing strategies accordingly and thus connect with them.

Empathy, therefore, incorporates notions of proximity accompanied by an
open mind, which is receptive to what is happening in the world of young
people. Developing empathy is essential for successful communication with
young people, especially those in the adolescence phase. For example, the
skincare brand La Roche Posay implemented a successful communication
campaign, targeting young people with acne problems, based on empathy that
went viral.

MINI-CASE BOX 5.2   LA ROCHE-POSAY USES SELFIES TO LET YOUNG PEOPLE SHARE THEIR ACNE PROBLEMS WITH OTHERS

La Roche-Posay, a French skincare brand, launched an application for young people with acne. The application, which is called "In Posay Mode," was developed to help young people and adolescents take better care of their skin. According to the brand, one in two acne treatment failures is due to adolescents not taking their acne treatments regularly. To remind them not to forget to take care of themselves, the mobile application offers alerts. In terms of encouraging these young people, the app also allows selfie monitoring: users can take pictures of themselves every day and see that their skin conditions are improving when they follow their treatments. Users will also find a section on what is fact and fiction when it comes to acne so as to inform them and help them better understand the condition.

To sum up, we can say that the democratization of the use of digital technologies and the changing relationship between companies and customers are giving young consumers new powers. These digital natives are no longer passive in their consumption experiences but are becoming more active and eager to interact with brands and other consumers at different levels ranging from ideation to co-innovation.

Brands and advertisers can call on these young consumers regardless of their competencies, knowledge, and creative potential, whether they are experts or merely curious; all opinions count to create a strong relationship with the youth market and thus generate common value.

Co-creating is a strategy that allows young collaborators to actively participate in the generation of ideas and the design of the product/service in line with their needs. For companies, it is also an opportunity to enhance the dialogue with their youth targets and create a strong bond by placing them at the heart of the company's projects and strategies.

3.3   Youth Collaborative Marketing (YCM) to Build Competitive Advantage

Youth Collaborative Marketing is a strategy that can be implemented by companies in different sectors to respond to young people's tangible and intangible needs. These young consumers believe that they too have something to say and that if the brand is a success, it is also thanks to them.

YCM can involve soliciting the ideas, suggestions, or the production of youth to improve a company's products, services, and brand reputation as well as to adapt the brand's offerings to them. This collaborative marketing aiming at young consumers enables brands to gain a sustainable competitive advantage by retaining the youth targets and enhancing their loyalty. Yet multiple challenges and opportunities are related to the implementation of YCM to attract young consumers, as illustrated in Figure 5.4.

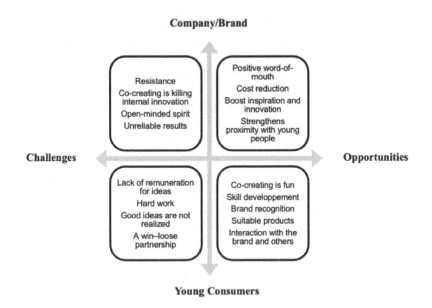

Figure 5.4   Challenges and opportunities of YCM

YCM allows companies to co-create with young consumers and thus develop products and services that are suitable to youth targets and meet the company's objectives at two levels: strategic and operational.

3.3.1   YCM is an effective strategy to improve products and services through youth's testing and voting

For example, the shampoo brand Dop asked young people to vote for their favorite Candy Dop. Likewise, the L'Oréal brand asked young users on social media to choose a candy-flavored fragrance marketed by the company. Young consumers could choose their favorite fragrance on Facebook, Twitter, or Instagram by posting a Tweet or a photo with the hashtag #Dop and the hashtag of their favorite flavor: #candycolores, #crocodiles, or #bananas. A real-time counter displayed the number of votes per fragrance on the brand's website.

Tropicana has designed juice recipes by co-creating with young consumers, taking the interaction with them a bit further to emphasize proximity and exchange. To do this, Tropicana invited young people to choose among their favorite recipes for the following proposed juice products: orange/blackberry, mango/pineapple, and apricot/blackcurrant. The one that got the most votes was launched. Tropicana's objective was to strengthen young people's attachment to the brand by engaging them in the creation process.

As with Tropicana and Dop, each year, Danette, a dessert brand owned by Danone, asks young people to vote on its website for the flavor they would like to find in stores. This involvement allows the brand to get close to its youth targets by considering their opinions and tastes. This way young consumers feel valued and considered by the brand because they are asked for their feedback on its products. Since its first edition to elect the "new flavor of the year," the brand has managed to bring together more than 6 million young voters.

Some brands ask young people for their votes but don't involve them in a co-creation process, which is the case of Amazon and TripAdvisor. With the Internet and social media platforms, young consumers who buy products on e-commerce websites like Amazon or who visit tourist destinations can leave their opinions and feedback. On TripAdvisor, the consumers can even write articles. Studies show that more than two-thirds of young people are influenced by the opinions left by users on websites and forums. That is why companies should encourage young people to provide positive feedback and posts about their experiences with the businesses' products.

3.3.2   YCM is an essential tool in the brand image rejuvenation strategy

To rejuvenate its image and attract new young consumers, Royco, an instant soup produced by the Campbell Soup Company, used collaborative marketing to reach younger and more urban targets. Royco's main challenge was to rejuvenate its customer base and reinvent itself. For young people, Royco products are not seen as "good" or "cool."

To convince the youngest customers, the brand opted for a new positioning, moving from the sale of simple soups to the "snack" of the morning break, which can replace the chocolate bar break or the coffee break. Several collaborative marketing campaigns have been launched by the brand. Young people were then selected to test and evaluate the product but, above all, to talk about it. For Royco, the stake of this collaboration relates to the potential recommendations made by these new "ambassadors" of the product. As a result of the effort, Royco saw a 5 percent increase in its overall sales.

3.3.3   YCM is a tool for brand promotion by young people in their online and offline communities

Very Good Moment, an online community platform, is turning young Internet users into brand ambassadors and advocates who can promote brands in their communities both online and offline. The purpose of this platform is for young Internet users to vote for the "Very Best Moment" – that is, the best photo or video of a moment that has just taken place during the consumption of a product or a brand. How does it work? Users are allowed to post a maximum of five photos or videos. Then the platform selects between one and ten of them to participate in the election of the "Best Host" according to the criteria established in the conditions of use. The video or photo that receives the most votes will be voted "Very Best Moment," and the image must remain at the top of the podium. All members can vote and win prizes, even those who did not participate in the actual "moment." There are five themes for the moments: very friendly: a moment of friendship and complicity; very funny: it is funny or unexpected; very stylish: very classy, or very pretty; very cute: an image that makes you melt; and very sexy. The five themes can be personalized by the brand used during the socialization process.

The partner brand expects young people to have a "very good moment" but also to see its product(s) highlighted in their photos or videos. This is why the brand will vote for the photo or video of its choice during election time. The choice of the brand will automatically add 20 percent more votes on a total already obtained and thus increase the chances of becoming "Best Host." The brand's criteria are the following: the quality of the photo or video; promotion of its products; link with the theme; users of the required age visible in the photo; and interest in the young participants. The winner receives gifts offered by the organizing brand and all those who gave a voice to the photo or video that is ultimately voted "Very Best Moment" wins a gift.

3.3.4   YCM is based on the idea of involving young people in the development of new products

The brand LEGO has created a platform that offers to collect the ideas of young Internet users to develop new products. It is a perfect illustration of the importance of collaborative and co-creative processes for innovation. The brand has launched a site called "Lego Ideas" targeting young consumers. Anyone can submit their idea on the site. Users then have the opportunity to vote for the constructions and figures they prefer, and which they are likely to buy.

When a project receives 10,000 votes, it is chosen by the company. LEGO then takes care of developing the specifications to design and market it. This is how the "Ghostbuster," the "Jurassic Park" car, and the "Yellow Submarine" with the Beatles minifigures were created. In addition, to encourage its community to participate as much as possible and create products that will sell well in the future, the brand has a Twitter account and a Facebook page dedicated to ideas.

To sum up, we can say that the functions of YCM highlight the importance of companies considering their young customers as economic partners able to carry the values of the brand, communicate and promote them among their online and offline communities, and propose creative solutions to improve existing products. Today, co-creation centered on the end-user is booming thanks to the use of social media among young people, who use it to share their ideas and discuss their consumption practices with their peers.

For advertisers and brands targeting young consumers, YCM offers several advantages including the use of the creative potential and ideas of young consumers to innovate, a better understanding of young people and the ability to capture their expectations, and the promotion of brands and new products launched by the company. Thus, by involving young consumers, the company values them and shows them its interest in their ideas by taking into account their opinions and feedback on its products and services.

4.   EMPOWERING DIGITAL NATIVES THROUGH CO-CREATION AND CROWDSOURCING

Young consumer empowerment refers to a form of rebalancing of the "brand–youth" relationship to the benefit of the latter. It is mainly linked to the rise of the use of digital media and can be expressed negatively by brand bashing or expressed positively through youths' desire to participate in the lives of brands. Thus, the empowerment of digital natives can be achieved through crowdsourcing, which is an integral part of co-creation practices across youth cultures. Brands can then leverage co-creation to attract and retain young consumers.

Crowdsourcing is a practice whereby brands appeal to young people mainly through a specialized platform to co-design elements of a marketing policy (e.g., a product concept, choice of a brand, creation of a slogan, etc.). Young people are often rewarded or paid for their co-creative collaborations with the brands. Co-creation, by contrast, represents a form of partnership in which a company and young consumers will each utilize resources to develop the brand in a mutually beneficial direction.

Young people bring their ideas and skills and, in exchange, the company, for example, rewards them financially or with goodies or perks. Online co-creation is becoming attractive for brands, especially in the field of consumer goods. Brands like Coca-Cola, Nike, Danone, and Starbucks involve their young consumers and virtual communities to support them in the development of their communication, products, services, and design among others. The goal is to incentivize youths to contribute new ideas, original content, and disruptive solutions.

The producers of clothing and accessories can also fully benefit from these co-creation tools. Nike, which gives Internet users the ability to personalize their sneakers by going to the brand's "Nike By You" platform, is an example. The more the intervention occurs upstream in the process (ideation or the creation of a concept), the higher the degree of involvement and expertise is from the consumer in general.

This practice is in line with today's youth, who represent the archetype of this consumer, who knows how to take advantage of the new power given by companies. This occurs both because youthhood is a period of life when creativity and innovation find their full expression and because the mastery of digital tools by youths makes them want to engage in the upstream process of the product creation and its marketing.

Moreover, co-creation is one of the priorities in which companies intend to invest quite heavily with youth targets. For example, Bonobo, a clothing brand for young people, recently launched a co-creation campaign on its site in which Internet users are invited to create their "perfect sweet," which is a great outfit. To do this, a dedicated page was created on which users could find a creative brief and a toolkit that allowed participants to view the results of their collaboration in real-time. The participants could then also vote on the creations made by the other competitors. The winner received a sum of money and the opportunity to meet the stylists of the brand to finalize its creation to market the product.

The music radio station NRJ targeting youth has launched an advertising crowdsourcing campaign by offering 30 young illustrators from 17 different nationalities the chance to participate in the creation of its new TV spots. The two spots were rated as the best to be broadcast on both digital and mobile media; yet all the spots benefited from visibility by being brought together in an exhibition in a digital gallery. Thus, the benefits of co-creation and crowdsourcing for both a brand's popularity and youth's empowerment can be explained by two major factors: the satisfaction of digital natives' needs and an increase in a brand's visibility thanks to youth co-creation.

4.1   Co-creation Meets Digital Natives' Needs through the Use of Digital Tools

Digital natives are creative but also seek recognition through their interactions with brands. The high-tech environment in which they live favors the tendency to co-create because it responds to the needs of youths to express themselves and build their personal and social identities through the appropriation of a "cultural object" submitted for the approval of their peers. These young consumers particularly enjoy activities where they are asked by brands to engage in the design of products.

On the other hand, the process of "in real life" co-creation does not make this generation join in because it requires traveling or meeting people in situ. They are, therefore, involved by companies in more upstream co-creation processes than downstream ones, as well as in online operations via platforms, rather than producing something in real life. Brands' co-creation with digital natives gives rise to exchanges and discussions that play a role in social inclusion and thus promote the recognition of a person's peers. This is essential in the stabilization of a youth's identity. However, expressing individuality through a co-creation operation does not mean these digital natives want to differentiate themselves at all costs from others; on the contrary, standardization is even perceived here as being rather reassuring because it makes it possible to become one with your age group.

Thus, it should be noted that there are two main opposing profiles: the opportunists on the one hand, who are focused on themselves, and the involved on the other hand, who are more preoccupied with the task. By taking up the criteria for structuring forms of co-creation, we can thus put into perspective the intrinsic motivations of the "involved" in the search for personal fulfillment. We can then contrast them with those of an extrinsic nature: "opportunists" who will first of all favor the bolstering of their egos or seek tangible gain.

These two profiles like to share their activities on social media but in their friendly sphere: the former for narcissistic purposes and the latter to obtain the advice of their friends to create a collective project. Therefore, co-design responds particularly well to the needs of "involved" profiles, in particular via "co-design" or mass customization. Why? Because it is in line with the desire of these people to express their creativity, talents, and achievements, and gain recognition. It is not primarily the task of creating products that interests them, but, rather, being able to express their talents and be recognized by others.

In a partnership such as this, the value released for the brand, therefore, lies in the co-created object (product or service) that meets users' expectations and in the development of its notoriety among young people through social media. For young participants, it is mainly linked to the experience of co-creation and to sharing it with one's peers. Thanks to the brand, the participants have the opportunity to highlight and promote themselves. It is the staging of oneself and the sociability among peers facilitated by social media that are important to these youths; co-creation is seen only as a pretext in line with this logic.

4.2 Co-creation with Youth Increases the Visibility of the Brand

Even if they participate in the visibility of the brand thanks to the actions that they carry out on these platforms, digital natives do not feel particularly committed to it based on the fact that they have collaborated once with the brand. These young consumers are expecting feedback and clear recognition from the brand so as to create a form of proximity that will help the emergence of a brand community and, beyond that, consider them ambassadors. A significant incentive could lead young people to embark on the adventure of co-creation even if a brand interests them little. However, in this case, there is little hope for complicity once the operation is over. It will be first and foremost for them a windfall of the kind that opportunists are accustomed to.

The different forms of co-creation do not involve all young consumers in the same way. Can taking a picture of oneself with a product, for example, be enough to create a feeling of belonging to a brand? For those less involved, the answer is no. In no way will young people feel the slightest proximity with the brand until it has been able to convey to them this feedback, whether in a tangible form (a reward or gain) or an intangible form (recognition of some sort). Even the least involved youths will be waiting for this signal to feel valued and then want to communicate about (and with) the brand. Thus, young people will be willing to promote a brand that has let them know that they can be proud of themselves.

The brand will have succeeded in initiating this virtuous process by explicitly indicating to these young consumers that it is interested in them and that it appreciates the quality of what they have been able to offer. These consumers will then want to share this with their friends to gain their approval and feel valued. The brand, in turn, will then be able to take advantage of this virality caused by these consumers' need for links and connections.

This need for sharing will be all the greater because the operation will take place on digital social media such as Instagram or Snapchat, where young people spend significant amounts of their recreational time. While opportunist young people will be more likely to use quick and easy-to-use social media, involved ones will make more effort to visit the brand's website and then share their activities. To optimize the link with these empowered digital natives, brands must also consider the profile of the co-creator participants – whether they are involved or opportunists as well as their resulting choices of social media.

KEY TAKEAWAYS

The key takeaways from this chapter underscore the idea that co-creation in different youth consumption cultures reflects the changing role of young consumers who become more and more active and involved in their consumption experiences and their relationships with brands. These young people then develop technical skills and creative potential that are of interest to companies interested in co-creating with youth and thus generating shared values. In the different youth cultures, the young consumer can collaborate with brands on different levels, ranging from the conception of the product to its actual production. Co-creation with young consumers is also made possible thanks to the development of online communication tools and social networks. Young people, who are digital natives, can post their ideas and co-create value with other consumers or with brands.

To fully understand the collaborative process that brands can put in place to build offers with young people, Youth Collaborative Marketing should be implemented by companies as it encourages young consumers to connect and collaborate with brands and share values with them.

6. Digital natives and social media use in youth cultures: what should brands know about blogging?

CHAPTER OVERVIEW

The objective of this chapter is to examine the importance of social media and explore how digital natives are taking ownership of blogs and developing new relationships with brands. To do so, I will first present the specificities of young consumers that influence their use of social media. I will then discuss how this digital native generation acquires social media to develop relationships with brands. The modes of collaboration and the new relationships that are being created on blogs between digital natives and brands will also be discussed at the end of this chapter.

1. SOCIAL MEDIA USE WITHIN YOUTH CULTURES: A VITAL PATH FOR BRANDS

Social media platforms are a prerequisite for brands when it comes to connecting with and engaging young consumers. Each generation is unique in its approach to social media. Digital natives, in particular, are gaining the attention and interest of most brands when it comes to interacting with them on social media. Not only is this because these young consumers have great purchasing power, but also because they are now setting several standards and trends for all age groups, including adults and previous generations.

Digital natives have experienced both the trivialization of the Internet and the birth and the rapid development of social networks and the mobile Internet. Big "social media consumers," these young people toggle from one screen to another and from one platform to another with ease. Therefore, brands are nowadays dealing with a digital native generation that demands immediacy, simplicity, and speed. For these young people, everything should be accessible as quickly as possible and as simply as possible. In addition, these youth have high access to digital devices and platforms. Each of them is equipped, on average, with more than six screens, such as a television, computer, tablet, and smartphone, among others.

Furthermore, studies reveal that these young consumers are driven by the almost obsessive fear of missing something: the "Fear Of Missing Out," or FOMO. They spend almost half of their time outside of school on computers or mobile devices. Brands, therefore, have every interest in making full use of this appetite by offering these consumers the opportunity to stage and broadcast their real-life moments.

Facebook Live and Snapchat are effective tools for this. Thanks to filters on Snapchat, for example, digital natives can replace their hair with fries in a photo when eating at McDonald's. Likewise, a brand like Lacoste allows users on social media to hide crocodiles in the photos they share with its fans. Fans able to find the crocodiles win gifts.

Brands should understand the need to thoroughly rethink their ways of communicating to reach and retain these young consumers. Brands should be able to constantly adapt to and keep up with changes in youth consumption cultures and online communities by addressing them in a determined but very flexible way. To do this, social media platforms allow brands to reach their youth targets directly, not through traditional advertising practices, but by offering youths specific content that will interest them.

As they always have been, today's young consumers are inspired by their peers. But, as far as the digital native generation is concerned, some influencers will have a very special status; they are the stars of social media. As soon as they acquire some form of stardom, their selfies and other posts are bombarded with "likes." Succeeding in associating one of these new prescribers and influencers with a particular brand can, therefore, transform the young user into a brand's "ambassador." The person is then guaranteed to be rewarded with a large number of followers.

Ambassadors such as Hollywood stars have real notoriety. Ambassadors can also be "anonymous" customers who enjoy a certain aura and amount of influence in their private circles. A good ambassador will have a real emotional relationship with the brand and be able to pass on his or her feedback, whether it is the source of proposals for improving quality or correcting a critical misstep before it goes viral. An ambassador should thus symbolize, for digital natives, a set of values, a state of mind, and even a philosophy that enables them to fully believe in this authenticity to which they attach great importance.

To reach this youth target, brands should center the main mechanics of their social media campaigns and then couple them with a presence on more traditional media. Traditional advertising seems to have a bright future despite – or, probably thanks to – a greater mix with digital advertising. Indeed, digital natives are still very fond of traditional media. One way for a brand to reach youth outside of social media is to be present in places where young people's emotional expectations are at their peak, namely when they attend concerts or sporting events.

However, there is a real divide between digital natives and previous generations about how they view their use of digital media. This is because these young people did not experience the beginnings of the Internet and were born in a digital environment that favors instantaneity and the ability to instantly adopt new technologies. They are, therefore, at the same time demanding, volatile, and very impatient. They want to benefit from fast display times, exhaustive product catalogues, fluid navigation, efficient online searches with many filters to narrow down what they are looking for, and a unique shopping experience. Consequently, many elements have become crucial nowadays for the success of a brand's presence on social media and the Internet in general.

The real challenge for companies today, and also the whole online communication dimension, is to develop high-performance applications that consume as little computing power as possible. All the phenomena that have multiplied in recent years, whether 3D, augmented reality, contactless technologies, and so forth, are part of these new tools, which attract digital natives by allowing them to simply and intuitively superimpose virtual elements on real elements.

The dominant usage of smartphones has also enabled the emergence of a new visual language centered on images and photography, which often replace the written word. Digital natives have generated a new language based on images and emojis. Emoticons, which are used to convey emotions, have become essential in a brand's digital communication actions on social media. The rise of Snapchat, Pinterest, and Instagram has, of course, greatly amplified the phenomenon. Digital natives do not distinguish between their online and offline worlds. Brands should ensure that they are present where young people like to spend time and learn how to find the right levers that will succeed in creating bridges capable of interconnecting physical and digital experiences.

MINI-CASE BOX 6.1   THE BUBBLE GUM BRAND MALABAR CREATES A PHYISCAL CONNECTION WITH DIGITAL NATIVES

The bubble gum brand Malabar has recently returned in force by regaining its historic and probably most iconic asset, namely, tattoos. Three new collections were included in the gum packages: "Rings" to wear as jewelry, "Under the Skin" in trompe l'oeil, and "Badass" for the most rebellious consumers. Tattooing is very common among people in their 30s. However, not everyone wants (or dares) to embark on the adventure of getting tattooed permanently. Many people are happy to sport temporary tattoos.

The Malabar brand wanted to take advantage of this phenomenon. The redesign of the tattoos was in line with Malabar's new "Pump Up Your Personality" strategy. After several years of silence, a fresher, more transgressive, and mischievous brand was revealed through the campaign.

What is very surprising about this campaign is that it was designed without using social media in any way. Indeed, there was no mobilization of networks such as Pinterest, Snapchat, YouTube, Instagram, or even Facebook. Even on the brand's Facebook page, the campaign remained quite discreet. Visitors to the site could win packages of Malabar simply by answering questions, such as the following: "In what year did Malabar tattoos first appear?" The brand also ran an old-fashioned campaign by putting posters on bus shelters. But surprisingly, it was Malabar's digital agency that orchestrated the campaign.

2. BLOGGING, A REQUIRED PATH TO CONNECT WITH DIGITAL NATIVES

The relationship digital natives have with social media is particularly complex. Young people's behaviors are multifaceted because of the diversity of online tools, the possibilities offered by platforms, and the social, psychological, and economic influences that come into play. When it comes to social media, the vocabulary is quite broad and non-specific given the multiplicity of the available platforms, such as Twitter, Facebook, Instagram, Pinterest, WeChat, LinkedIn, Tumblr, and personal blogs, among others.

Blogging is a popular practice among young people. A blog is a personal Web page that includes opinions, links, or reviews continually created by its author(s) in the form of posts. An RSS (Really Simple Syndication) feed, or an email alert service, generally allows Internet users interested in a blog to be notified of new posts. Blogs allow young people to share their preferences and feedback on subjects of interest in a personal, free, and critical way. Thus, blogging is particularly interesting because it allows digital natives to generate content and be in contact with people who are their "followers." Blogging is also a way for young people to develop cultural, social, and economic capital by posting textual and visual content that generates attention.

Therefore, companies need to understand how bloggers and brands can interact and create long-term fruitful collaborations. The online diffusion of information by young people on blogs profoundly changes how brands implement their online communication actions aimed at the youth market. A new ecosystem has emerged in which three major actors – bloggers, followers, and brands – interact and create value. Bloggers are full players in this ecosystem in which brands should reinvent the way they contribute and generate value.

2.1　　　Blogging, a Vital Practice in Youth Identity Development

Blogging is viewed by young people as an opportunity for self-expansion and self-development. Gradually detaching themselves from their solely family identities, digital natives will seek to freely assert their personalities. Forming the youth identity involves exploring several possibilities via both online and offline practices and then making choices more independently. In this context, blogs can be used as tools in the service of this identity research. Blogs provide a suitable platform for exploring and expressing the different facets of a blogger's personality, removing barriers such as a person's external appearance, physical abilities, or social status.

Thank to online platforms, young people can participate in different online communities, follow other bloggers, react to information, and share their experiences and preferences. These youths are in a phase of tension and transition during which they will extend and stabilize their identities. They are caught between opposing forces: discovery and engagement; confusion and synthesis. Progressively, they will evolve towards a more stable identity in a phase of self-expansion. Therefore, blogging is a tool at the service of this personal expansion.

Getting involved in blogging activities allows these digital natives to expand their horizons by developing new interactions with brands and followers, acquire new skills, develop their creativity, and assert their personal and social identities. Sharing their passions and enriching their knowledge is the main objective of a youth's blogging. Indeed, creating a blog, since it is both a place for content creation and interaction with the community that reads posts, comments on them, and replies to them, allows young people to discover new passions that they will enjoy sharing with others. The pleasure of discussing a topic around common areas of interest is then a powerful mechanism for being active on their blogs. This motivation is particularly true in the field of fashion, where young bloggers enjoy sharing their passions related to trends, styles, and their favorite brands.

Furthermore, thanks to their blogging activities, young people have become more comfortable when it comes to communicating their identities. The information posted by the blogger creates a digital trail that communicates impressions and shapes one's positioning. The person is aware of his or her image and wants to control and make it attractive using available communication techniques. This can include becoming a "brand person."

The creation of an online profile and the management of associated content and visuals allows young people to communicate and share the positioning of their digital identities. Similar to marketing a product, blogging is about building your image and actively communicating it. One of the challenges for digital natives is to create an image that is close to one's ideal self. In addition, in the quest to forge their identities, young people use blogs to play roles in their communities and define themselves relative to groups. Research has found that peers, or people of the same age, who belong to one's community exert a very strong influence on the references, opinions, and behaviors of these youths.

Moreover, because young people are in a phase of stabilizing their identities, they will want to verify that their desired positioning on their blogs matches the image perceived by their followers. A blog is made to be consulted and is intended to be shared. The blogger will develop expertise to provide attractive content and formatting that is not only visible on the Internet but also recognized as competent and credible. To develop this recognition among one's peers, the blogger will seek to create original editorial content featuring new ideas not present on other blogs.

Sharing one's knowledge with those who consult the blog by informing them, advising them, or stimulating their curiosity also helps to reinforce the feeling that the young person's expertise can be useful to others. Progressively, the gained online notoriety allows these young bloggers to be followed by many online users and have a real influence on their community. Thus, the process of blogging among digital natives ranges from self-expansion motivation to self-improvement and self-esteem as a result of developing their expertise, asserting their identities, and increasing their influence online.

2.2   How Does Blogging by Digital Natives Work?

The blogging process by digital natives goes through several key stages in which brands can play an important role. First, it is a question of young bloggers having the desire to create their blogs and finding sources of inspiration from other Internet users as well as from brands. Then, young people need to understand how to represent themselves with regard to the story being told and its online staging in their blogs. Therefore, three main steps – namely identifying triggers for one's blog creation, defining sources of inspiration, and developing artistic and storytelling narratives – should be considered to understand how blogging works across youth cultures.

2.2.1   Triggers for a blog's creation

Several triggers, more or less rational or emotional, allow digital natives to switch from passive observers to active contributors in their online practices. The first trigger is linked to a particular event in which the young person participates, which deeply marks him or her and that he or she wants to share. Thus, the invitation to an exceptional event or the beginning of new, exciting activity can generate the creation of a blog. The young person will detail his or her experience to make it known and encourage others to try it. From then on, the brand can generate vocations by inviting consumers to exceptional private events.

The second trigger refers to the need to react to, rectify, or bring a different perspective to a phenomenon compared to what is said on social media. In this way, the young contributor sees him/herself as a critic who brings a different perspective or a vision to topics being discussed. For example, a young person who is a fan of a brand that is criticized on social networks may be willing to create a blog to convey more positive information about the brand by sharing his or her own experience. In this case, the brand can encourage loyal consumers to share their opinions and positive moments and experiences they had with the brand to increase its sympathy potential.

A third trigger comes from a feeling of empathy that makes digital natives want to provide other people with useful information or tips. This is the case if a young person has expertise, for example, in the field of fashion or sports and wants to guide other young people who would like to learn about these domains. The brand can then recognize the status of expert and give these bloggers tools to help them speak up and interact with their online communities and followers.

Blogging activity among digital natives can, therefore, be induced by intrinsic motivations linked to the interest and pleasure that a person finds in blogging without expecting any external reward. Alternately, blogging activity can be induced by extrinsic motivations linked to an external circumstance, from the spontaneous sharing of emotions to the presentation of an opinion. In many situations, brands can play an active role in terms of encouraging the emergence of blogs launched by digital natives – blogs by which messages related to the brands' values or products can be effectively communicated.

2.2.2 Searching for inspirational sources for a blog

The source of inspiration for creating blogs can be achieved by observing other bloggers. Even if digital natives are comfortable with social media, they will prefer to first be observers of the blogs that interest them. They will try to identify what they like and what strategies work before launching their blogs. These youth will regularly follow several bloggers as role models and sometimes broaden their horizons by occasionally consulting other blogs. First, the would-be bloggers will seek to analyze how other bloggers, especially those with many followers, develop their personal blogs and websites. Their positioning, the topics covered, and how they feature themselves will be studied. By selecting models to follow, would-be bloggers will be able to identify what best suits them and the identities they want to display and share with their followers.

To develop their inspiration, young people who want to launch blogs can also observe and examine the resources offered by brands. By offering discussion platforms, being creative about their communication, and generating rich content around their brand values, companies can participate in this search for inspiration. For example, more and more fashion brands are including visuals called "street style" on their sites. The trend involves posting spontaneous photos of people wearing a brand's products on the street, rather than posting professional photos of models taken in a studio.

This trend refers to an expectation of young customers, who project themselves more easily in settings that seem closer to their everyday lives. Via initiatives such as "Art of the Trench Burberry," young people are encouraged to be creative while being guided by the brand. Burberry encourages these young users to upload photos of themselves wearing the brand's famous raincoat. The brand can then make a creative montage on its site of all the photos taken by its customers with its products. In this way, brands can serve as models in the way they present "street style" images and encourage the diffusion of photos or videos on young peoples' personal blogs by extending their creative work with the brand.

2.2.3   Developing artistic and storytelling narratives

The presentation of oneself on a blog can be compared to a theater performance where everyone can define the set, the costume, and the light to present oneself in a certain light. The creative dimension is important for young people because it allows them to add their personal touches and increases the interactivity and the attractiveness of their blogs. The young blogger's artistic and graphic talents can enhance the aesthetic and visual aspects to which followers are sensitive. The elements of the web pages, such as the text, photos, and visual editing, among others, allow young bloggers to give free rein to their creativity while trying to maintain a certain coherence and communicate a clear positioning of the blog.

Once launched, the blog allows young people to share their personal stories. Indeed, blogs are places where stories are written and can be understood as a means to achieve the production of the content. The narrative form is used to recount a series of specific events with a beginning, middle, and end. By telling his or her story on his or her blog, in which the reader can at least partially recognize himself or herself, the young blogger will create a stronger connection with his or her community.

These young bloggers choose a writing style, tone, and content. They can also choose a way to share their experiences, for example by systematically mentioning first the place of consumption, the people present, and then the product or service. The elements of content and staging allow young people to create for each blog a unique positioning recognizable by the blog's "followers." Once it is well defined and structured, the blog can be improved based on readers' comments.

Thus, some young bloggers, especially those whose goal is to give a professional dimension to their activity, take the time to evaluate the reactions to the various texts and photos they post to identify what they like and adjust their blogs accordingly.

2.3   How Can Brands Collaborate with Young Bloggers?

Once we understand what digital natives are looking for on blogs, as well as the strategies they are pursuing in terms of exploration, identity creation, and insertion into a community, we need to examine the brand–blogger collaboration modes implemented by both young bloggers and brands to create and engage online communities.

For brands, blogs represent a communication channel that complements traditional media. Partnering with digital native bloggers allows brands to increase their visibility, promote their universe, develop interactions with young consumers, and thus quickly cover a wide target audience. Several modes of collaboration between bloggers and brands are conceivable.

Co-branding is a strategic alliance in which two or more brands are presented simultaneously to consumers. Bringing a blogger and a brand together could, therefore, be seen as a form of a symbolic alliance that enriches the brand's image by transferring the qualities associated with the young blogger to the brand being promoted.

2.3.1   Ambivalent relationships between young bloggers and brands

Young bloggers see brands as a sign of belonging and an affirmation of their identities. Choosing to buy and use a brand is a way for bloggers to showcase themselves by sharing their values. Young people are fans of certain brands that mirror how they see themselves and reject others that do not. The brand is a sign of external recognition that ensures a sense of belonging to a group.

Young people would like to acquire brands to be accepted and recognized by their peers. Because digital natives are particularly sensitive to group pressure and social acceptance, the social benefit will play an important role in their relationships with brands.

Young people recognize the identity and social dimensions of brands and are vigilant about advertising messages. These consumers are informed about products and often feel that they have a good knowledge of the offers and their own needs. They consider it unnecessary for brands to make purchase recommendations and are sometimes suspicious of advertising communications.

Therefore, when it comes to blogging, digital natives seek to assess the risks and benefits of their possible association with a brand for two main reasons:

- The intrinsic blogger–brand relationship. This has to do with risks related to the idea of a blogger being overly influenced when asserting his or her own identity and personal values, such as losing one's freedom. However, the benefit for digital natives is about strengthening one's self-esteem by associating with brands of value and becoming more professional in one's approach;
- The extrinsic blogger–brand relationship. The risks for digital natives refer to projecting an image too strongly associated with a brand or appearing too commercial and the blogger losing his or her authenticity. The advantages for young people lie in terms of being accepted and recognized by one's peers by associating with high-profile brands, such as luxury brands.

2.3.2   Key success factors for brand–blogger collaborations in youth cultures

Young consumers are increasingly seeking co-creative proposals from brands, as highlighted by recent research on customer participation (Pauwells et al., 2016). Co-creation provides young customers with the opportunity to provide their opinions to improve products and thus feel respected by brands (Meuter et al., 2000).

Digital natives appreciate the opportunities to co-create with brands. Brands that co-create with young bloggers ask them for their opinions on product developments or advertising communications, have them test offers before launches, and involve them with the creation of photos or messages, especially if the young blogger has skills in graphic design or journalism.

These activities allow young bloggers to understand a brand and feel involved in the relationship. They will then be able to better communicate and promote the brand's products. Thus, before posting information associated with a brand on their blogs, these young bloggers need first to understand its values and identity. Moreover, collaborating with a brand encourages digital natives to intensify their efforts when writing blog articles or arranging photos so as to match the same level of rigor as the professionals who work directly for the brand.

As Bonnemaizon and Batat (2011) point out, brands can facilitate the co-creation process by helping young people develop their skills via offering them editorial content, advising them on layouts, and giving them tips on how to improve the titles of articles. Thus, the collaboration can be successful, thanks to balanced exchanges that fit in with the expectations of the online community.

Achieving balanced exchanges between brands and young bloggers. The exchange between two parties, namely, the brand and the young blogger, should be balanced to ensure satisfaction on both sides. To create a lasting relationship, the two parties involved should feel that they receive as much as they give. Brands and young bloggers should then define "win-win" collaboration modes that follow different paths:

• When the young blogger is selected by the brand, the aim of the brand is to broaden its target among digital natives by conveying a modern image and reinforcing its visibility and accessibility across youth cultures. The key success factor, in this case, is that the blogger should be perceived as credible, having a large and relevant audience, and should have values aligned with the brand's values;

• When a brand is selected by the young blogger, the objective for the blogger is to assert their positioning, enrich their image, increase their visibility, and encourage the commitment of their followers. The key success factor in this case is to benefit from a valued brand image that is consistent with the positioning and editorial slant of the blog.

On the one hand, brands considering collaborating with digital native bloggers can select among them according to precise criteria to ensure there is a return on the investment. These criteria include the credibility of the blog, the richness of the content and the aesthetics of the layout, the profile of the blog's followers, and the cohesion of the blogger's image with the brand's values. It is also crucial for the brand, before initiating a partnership with a blogger, to take into account the individual's personality, objectives, and the quality of the dialogue with the person's community.

On the other hand, digital natives also have criteria for choosing brands they would like to collaborate with. Thus, a young blogger may decide to partner with a brand that is very consistent with the blogger's identity so as to strengthen it. Or, on the contrary, the blogger may navigate towards brands that are far from his or her positioning. The goal in this case would be for the blogger to broaden his or her audience – but at the risk of making the blog's image ambiguous. Yet the application of these criteria has to be nuanced by the blogger's notoriety and reputation. When starting a blog, a young person may be tempted to gain visibility by accepting any partnership a brand might offer.

Matching the online community's expectations. Digital native bloggers also have to take into account the expectations of their followers in the management of their blogs and their collaboration with brands. These young bloggers should have credible and transparent communications with their audiences. People who follow a blog appreciate feeling close to the blogger and being able to identify with the person, and project themselves into the person's daily world. Brands entering into partnerships should ensure that the proposed collaboration allows the blogger to remain close to his or her audience and avoid constraining the blogger's freedom of expression.

Furthermore, the goal is to get readers to return regularly to a blog, finding new things to discover each time. One of the difficulties encountered by bloggers is, therefore, to generate constant interest. This includes offering a variety of topics and frequent updates to entice visits the blog. In this quest, brands can have a role to play by regularly proposing new offers or experiences relayed by bloggers.

If the balance between renewal and permanence is not easy to find, brands enable young bloggers to better meet the expectations of their communities. Indeed, a brand can offer new content while maintaining a clear position, providing regular information on new products, or communicating operations to be relayed on a blog.

2.3.3   Collaboration between brands and young bloggers

Several modes of collaboration are possible between a blogger and a brand, which can be categorized according to the degree of visibility of the partnership and the degree of personalization of the communication on the part of the blogger. In all cases, it is important to understand the expertise of the brand and that of the blogger. Moreover, the partnership maintains an authentic dimension so that it is appreciated by followers.

A combination of strengths. Digital natives are aware of their skills and influence power. They know that they have a keen awareness and understanding of trends in their communities because they live there every day. With their blogs, they believe they are doing a creative job by producing attractive and useful textual and visual content for their readers. Bloggers also have a similarity and closeness to their communities that gives them strong credibility when they give advice or recommend products. Moreover, most expert bloggers have a thorough knowledge of the topics that interest their communities and the forms of communication that interest their followers. One of the difficulties of promoting brands on the Internet is that it does not allow a person to actually experience a product. For example, unlike a store, it is not possible to touch or try a product on via a blog.

By presenting the product, the blogger can reassure the consumer about how well the product will meet the person's need. Therefore, brands benefit from the collaboration with young bloggers, who can provide more accessible images of the product and advice on how it can be used, so as to remove obstacles to a consumer's purchase.

As for the brands, they have expertise in their products, their values, and their histories. They also have access to consumer data that can give them information on people's attitudes, trends, and how products are used. Brands also know how to communicate their messages in clear and precise ways. The information they transmit to bloggers provides editorial content that enriches the content of a site with relevant information on the brands presented and associated trends.

The collaboration can, therefore, be enriched from the moment the expertise of the brand and the young blogger are respectively recognized. Mutual respect is the key to ensuring a balanced and fruitful partnership. On the one hand, the young blogger will be very proud if a brand indicates that it appreciates the work the blogger has done and will be all the more eager to continue collaborating. On the other hand, the brand will appreciate the digital native blogger taking a professional and creative approach when promoting the brand's values and products.

Modes of collaboration to be considered. Within the framework of the brand–blogger collaboration, the brand should above all fit naturally and non-intrusively into the young blogger's universe and be consistent with its positioning. The relationship can be of a disinterested nature: the blogger freely shares his or her favorites and refers to the brand in an often discreet way. For example, a simple hashtag along with the name of the brand used can appear on the blog. In contrast, the relationship between the two parties can be commercial: the blogger signs a contract with a brand and presents it in an almost advertising way on his or her website.

The selection among different modes of collaboration is made depending on the blogger's maturity, the number of his or her followers, personal goals, and the sensitivity of his or her community. In all cases, it seems crucial for brands to specify the operating rules for the collaboration model and to make the terms of the relationship between the brand and the blogger transparent – whether or not the relationship is contractual.

Authenticity as a core value. Readers of a blog appreciate the authenticity of the content they consult. Therefore, when bloggers mention a brand, they should be careful to maintain the sincerity of their support, which is even more important when they have a commercial collaboration paid for by a brand. It is essential to maintain transparency in the partnership approach and for the bloggers to retain their freedom of speech.

Blogs are sought after for their authenticity, sincerity, and non-verbal discourse. These are essential factors of differentiation relative to brand sites and the professional press. A brand that is perceived as authentic has the following characteristics: maintaining quality standards, respect for heritage, preservation of the essence, and the avoidance of an overly commercial approach (Spiggle et al., 2012).

For a young person, blogging is also about providing intimate information and offering frank and personal opinions not influenced by brands (Moulard et al., 2015). Thus, the authenticity of a blog is a function of its transparency, continuity, and concern for its audience.

To sum up, we can state that before engaging in collaboration, young bloggers have to be convinced of the relevance of a brand and appreciate it. They also should clarify that their choices are motivated more by their passions and concern for their communities than by purely commercial considerations. In this way, bloggers demonstrate that they give priority to the interests of their followers rather than to the profitability of the blogs.

It is also essential for bloggers to ensure continuity in their positioning, and that the way in which they address their communities does not change when the bloggers get closer to a brand. Young bloggers can then choose collaborations that express their values, such as defending a brand that offers fair trade products or defending young fashion designers. Therefore, to ensure effective brand–blog collaborations (co-creation), brands need to gain acceptance and demonstrate that they can add value. Young people want to develop balanced relationships that allow them to meet the expectations of their audiences and have fun.

In the evolution of the brand–blogger relationship, it will be a question of moving towards an increasingly creative and personalized approach to their communication or, rather, towards monetizing their influence. In this context, a brand can have an effective strategy if it does the following:

- Encourages bloggers to immerse themselves in the brand's universe so that they understand the brand's values;
- Favors coherent collaborations in which bloggers and the brand share the same values;
- Allows bloggers to be creative and to remain consistent with how they present the brand;
- Helps bloggers become professional and well-known by allowing them to work with experts and use the communication power of the brand to be visible;
- Respects the work of bloggers, their editorial content, and positioning;
- Clearly defines the "rules of the game" and terms of collaboration with bloggers, especially when the relationships are monetized.

KEY TAKEAWAYS

The key takeaways from this chapter show that in a context in which digital natives are going to use their blogs to meet their identity development needs, brands should offer these people relevant modes of collaboration. As they leave adolescence to reach adulthood, youths are pursuing the dual objectives of developing their own identities and belonging to communities. Blogging provides a platform for personal expression and communication with a community. Young people who blog will be able to play a role and acquire new skills that will allow them to build their identities and develop their expertise. This, in turn, will allow them to be recognized by their peers and thus increase their self-esteem. Moreover, in their relationships with brands, digital natives are both attracted by brands, which allow them to assert themselves, and distrustful of marketing practices that seem manipulative to them.

7. Advertising to digital natives: a hybrid and disruptive way to communicate

CHAPTER OVERVIEW

This chapter tackles questions related to the way in which advertisers should attract young people. It is neither a question of explaining to advertisers how to communicate to this target, nor of drawing a portrait of these young people evolving in the digital world they have always known. Instead, this chapter attempts to analyze the evolution of the technological environment and, consequently, the commercial communication media used by companies to understand how digital natives perceive advertisements and why it is critical for companies to shift to a more hybrid and disruptive form of communication when it comes to the youth market.

1. MEDIA ADVERTISING AMONG DIGITAL NATIVES: WHAT'S NEW?

Unlike other people, digital natives were born in an era in which advertising, the web, social media, and digital devices represent an integral part of their youth consumption cultures. How does this youth generation perceive media advertising? What are young people's media consumption behaviors? What about a new hybrid way of communication combining both digital and traditional media advertising?

The 2000s saw a change in the share of investment in media advertising compared to other forms of communication. The reasons for this were a loss of confidence in traditional media to the benefit of non-media; the emergence of the web (and then digital media); and finally, significant use of hybrid communication, including online ads, product placements, events, sponsorships, and traditional media, among other forms.

Thus, brands should understand digital natives' perceptions of media advertising. Yet, it is difficult to compare this multi-screen generation with previous cohorts since both advertising and the commercial context have drastically changed.

1.1   Media Advertising Perception among a Multi-Screen Generation

Studies state that the perception of media advertising among the generation of digital natives differs from previous generations. This is due not only to the evolution of media content and devices but also to the specific characteristics of this generation, such as their high levels of collectivism, which are reflected by their dependence on social media. Moreover, their mastery of new technologies offers them new ways of consuming media content and advertising.

According to studies, TV seems to be the media experiencing the most changes in its consumption among this youth target. Although youths 13–19 years old watch TV a little less than before, they mostly watch it differently. Thus, they watch more streamed programs than live broadcasts and use their computers when doing so. Also, these young people use tablets and smartphones to watch various videos and media content.

This behavior shows that consuming or watching traditional TV content is no longer part of the habits of today's youths. However, they admit to accessing TV programs or series via other devices, such as computers or tablets. Furthermore, studies show that these young people are permanently connected via their smartphones and are big consumers of social media content on different platforms, such as TikTok, Instagram, and Facebook.

Yet, as shown by several studies, it is important to understand that this generation uses all of these means, often simultaneously, making these people a multi-screen generation. It should be noted that the smartphone remains the main device used by young people. They first use smartphones to listen to music via different applications, then to communicate on different social media platforms, then the web for information seeking, and, finally, to play games.

On average, young people 13–19 years old have three personal devices they can use simultaneously. Many of them can be in front of their TV screens and at the same time using their laptops, smartphones, and tablets. This new way of using media supporting an integrated way of consuming linear and nonlinear content is not without consequences in terms of advertising forms and perceptions among digital natives. Multi-screen media consumption has led to the rise of a new classification of media according to whether or not a company buys space and controls the communication media, namely paid media, owned media, or earned media.

- Paid media refers to advertising on traditional media (TV, the press, radio, etc.), online insertions (banners, videos), search engines, emailing, and comparison search engines;

- Owned media refers to media controlled by a brand, such as brochures, the brand's website, its presence on social media, and its mobile applications;
- Earned media means the audiences generated by conversations and leaders, such as classic word-of-mouth, but also customer opinions on forums, videos on YouTube, blogs, conversations about the brand on social media platforms, and so forth.

Therefore, through their media consumption habits and their mastery of new digital devices and tools, this generation of digital natives is making a strong contribution to earned media. This is not without implication in terms of advertising processing, because on earned media, commercial and non-commercial sources are mixed in a very indistinct way.

1.2   Types of Media Advertising Targeting Digital Natives

Understanding the types of media advertising brands can use to target digital natives is critical when defining and implementing effective marketing and communication actions. Thus, three types of media advertising based on the media uses and consumption among digital natives can be considered by companies, namely integrated, interactive, and interpersonal media advertising.

1.2.1   Integrated media advertising

The concept of integrated communication is not new to advertisers (Pickton and Broderick, 2005). It is based on the recognition that a receiver can be exposed to a wide variety of communication sources and that it is important to ensure that the same message is delivered by these different sources. This concept goes beyond media advertising since it incorporates all forms of media and non-media communication.

Regarding digital natives, the media advertising to which they are exposed should be integrated because it is nested in several media at the same time. These young people move from one media to another or even use several at the same time. For example, when they watch a TV program on the web, they are exposed to a double advertising medium: TV and the Internet. When digital natives share advertising videos on their Facebook pages, there is also a double level of media. Certainly, it can be argued that these consumers are not the only ones exposed to these different media; however, they are the first to master multiple screens simultaneously.

What implications can the integration of media have for the processing of advertising? First of all, the fact that media advertising is integrated into different media makes it less differentiable from its context because these contexts are multiple. For example, if a classic TV ad is highly differentiable from the program that precedes or follows it (it is separated from it by jingles or visuals), what happens when a TV program is viewed on the web (as a replay, via YouTube or any other sharing platform), which also serves as a medium for advertising?

1.2.2 Interactive media advertising

Digital media, and, in particular, the numerous sharing and communication communities used by digital natives, offer interactive possibilities never available in the past. TV and print ads have already attempted interactions via QR codes, websites, and SMS. However, digital advertising offers the possibility of faster and even more immediate interactions. An ad posted on YouTube or a brand's Facebook page can record almost immediate reactions and create a real dialogue with its audiences. Some young people will broadcast the ad to others, share it, and thus the power of the ad content becomes exponential.

1.2.3 Interpersonal media advertising

From the moment a receiver of an announcement shares it with others, thereby generating virtual word-of-mouth, the sender of this announcement can appear as the person sharing it and not as the one who originated the message. Research has shown young consumers prefer personal, non-commercial sources of communication rather than mass and commercial sources. This raises questions about the persuasive power of this type of media advertising. The earned media to which this generation of digital natives is largely contributing is a perfect illustration of today's context.

1.3 How Do Digital Natives Process Advertising?

Does advertising influence digital natives? How do they process it? The questions of discrimination of advertising from its context and the identification of the persuasive intent of advertising have been the subject of numerous studies (De Pelsmacker et al., 2013). This is more the case when it concerns young consumers, who do not necessarily have all the cognitive capacities to process advertising content.

In the case of television advertising, the advertising is very clearly distinguished from its context and announced by separators, while this is not the case on new digital platforms and media. How digital natives process advertising has not been investigated in terms of the mechanisms of attitude formation based on affective, cognitive, or behavioral factors. The existing models, based on hierarchies of advertising effects (Barry and Howard, 1990) and dual models (Petty and Cacioppo, 1986) are nevertheless very useful for classifying the effects of advertising (De Pelsmacker et al., 2013). So, what can we say about the reactions of this digital generation towards media advertising?

First of all, the media and the supports they use are rich in visual and creative content. These characteristics are, therefore, likely to lead to a more "peripheral" processing of advertisements that does not involve an analysis of the arguments about the product or service.

Secondly, this generation, which is accustomed to surfing from one medium to another, will not process information in-depth, leaving room for more emotional persuasion mechanisms. Finally, the blurring of boundaries between commercial and informative content on different media and supports (e.g., YouTube) will not favor identification of the persuasive intent of advertising.

To sum up, we can state that although this digital generation is raised to be critical towards advertisements, this will never prevent digital natives from having a positive reaction to particular advertising content, and even more so if they are not aware that it is an advertisement.

2. USING HYBRID MEDIA COMMUNICATION TO APPEAL TO YOUNG CONSUMERS

Advertising is not the only form of commercial communication present in today's traditional and online media. There is another approach that is mostly used on TV (series, films, and shows), in cinema, and in video clips, namely product placements. This practice is not new and studies on the subject are numerous (Charry and Tessitore, 2016).

Nevertheless, it raises questions of identification. Product placements belong to a paid hybrid communication approach that attempts to influence audiences through non-commercial means (Balasubramanian, 1994). In other words, in a hybrid communication, the persuasive intention is hidden and, therefore, less obvious to identify.

The effects of product placements on the attitudes and behaviors of young consumers are known and need to be considered in a nuanced way. However, the practice can raise questions in terms of protecting young audiences. Digital natives are more likely to be exposed to product placements than the rest of the population. Indeed, youths are big fans of series, video clips, movies, and certain TV programs that may contain them.

A study by Pecheux and Hanot (2016) of young audience members 9–14 years old examined the issue via the program *The Voice Belgium*. The program features many products and services placed on air, and this has given rise to criticism and debate. The results of this qualitative and quantitative investigation revealed the following:

- The majority of young people interviewed did not attribute a persuasive (commercial) intention to a product placement;

- After being exposed to placed brands, young people were more favorable to these brands than before the exposure;
- A screen advertisement containing a placed brand reinforces the effect of the placement in terms of recall and brand recognition;
- Most of the youths surveyed did not recall seeing a product placement warning or logo and did not understand it. Many believed that the logo "PP" was the brand name of the camera.

Therefore, a question should be asked by companies while targeting digital natives through advertising content both online and offline: do young people perceive the advertising broadcast online and on TV in the same way? Studies have analyzed young people's behaviors when interacting with commercials and content both online and through traditional channels such as TV or the press. The studies have shown that most digital natives are not consumers of regularly scheduled TV content due to a lack of time and because of their high consumption of the Internet and their downloading of series and other content. These people consume online content on their computers, laptops, and smartphones whenever they want to.

Moreover, studies state that digital natives think there is less advertising on online platforms. They also believe that on the web, advertisements are less well separated than ads on TV. Another practice that should be considered by brands when targeting digital natives is related to the fact that most young people do not switch to full-screen mode when they watch TV programs on the web, thereby exposing themselves to a whole series of additional ads on the pages visited.

Moreover, most of them are not unduly irritated by the presence of ads on the new platforms. Indeed, this generation seem to be used to the presence of ads on websites or at least say they have become used to it. And their reasoning often goes further since they find legitimacy in advertisements on the new platforms insofar as these platforms are mostly free.

For these digital natives, some ads are more easily identified than others: the fact that it is before a video, the contrast of the ad's colors or shapes, its location on the right side of the screen, the absence of a link between the ad and the content, and the presence of a cross are examples. It is interesting to note that the presence of a brand, a prize, or a promotion in an advertisement allows young people to realize that it is an advertisement. Yet there are advertisements that are not identified as such by digital natives, even when the word "advertisement" appears on it, namely advertisements in the form of articles or editorials.

To sum up, we can say that digital natives seem to tolerate the presence of ads on online platforms although they do not always seem aware of the intensity of the ads. If the overall attitude nowadays is to demonize advertising, or at least to denounce its massive presence, this does not seem to be the opinion of these young people. Also, if the services on the online platforms are free, digital natives see advertising as a normal counterpart, even if they did not choose it.

3. DISRUPTIVE COMMUNICATION TO CONNECT WITH DIGITAL NATIVES

Disruptive communication to better connect with digital natives refers to a hybrid and complex process based on an exploratory and analytical logic guided by critical and experiential design thinking, which brings together four major pillars: critical thinking; experiential approach; empiricism (cognitive and rational approach); and introspective subjectivity (subjective introspection). This section aims first to define the disruption method and then explain how disruption applied to communication and advertising can be used to target and retain young consumers.

3.1   The Disruptive Approach: Back to the Origins

The idea of disruption is not new. It has its first origins in natural sciences, where the concept is used to explain disasters. Its introduction in economics and management sciences dates back to the early 1940s and was used under the term "creative destruction" in the writings of the economist Joseph Schumpeter (1942) with the publication of his book *Capitalism, Socialism, and Democracy*. The idea of disruption was then taken up by Theodore Levitt in his book *Innovation in Marketing*, published in 1962.

In the early 1990s, the term disruptive technology was introduced and defined by Clayton Christensen, an inventor and eminent professor at Harvard Business School. Christensen first used the term in his research articles and then in a book titled *The Innovator's Dilemma*, published in 1997. Several definitions of the disruptive approach exist and vary among authors and disciplines. However, what is important is not the exhaustive definition of disruption, but the perspective from which it is viewed. Following this logic, disruption can be defined according to the following six main perspectives:

- Disruption as an outcome in terms of innovation. This perspective refers to an economic approach through technological innovation and the emergence of the digital economy;
- Disruption as a means to explain social change. This perspective denotes a sociological disruption as a result of the disruption of behavior between generations;

- Disruption as a management model or economic model introducing new alternative business models;
- Disruption as a creative advertising strategy;
- Disruption as a philosophy of life expressed according to a definite ideology;
- Disruption as part of the design thinking process that is both critical and experiential.

The perspective of disruption as part of design thinking has proven its importance in the implementation of communication campaigns aimed at digital natives, who belong to a disruptive, experiential, critical, and creative youth generation.

Unlike design thinking, which refers to analytical and intuitive skills and includes all the work methodologies and tools used for a creative purpose or as part of an innovation project, disruptive design thinking is a complex, dynamic, and evolutionary process. Disruptive design thinking is based on the idea of critical and experiential thinking integrating the analytical and intuitive aspects of design thinking to reconcile various constraints (e.g., economic, technical, operational) and includes different ideas from diverse profiles and resources in a company, such as its engineers, scientists, artists, and young people, among others.

Following a logic based on disruptive design thinking, disruption communication can be applied according to a triptych approach integrating three major factors, namely the disruptor, the culture of the organization, and the environment:

- The disruptor is the bearer of the disruptive idea and can be the creator, the entrepreneur, or the person in charge of the project. In this case, the disruption process is closely linked to the knowledge, career path, training, beliefs, personality, lifestyle, consumption patterns, values, habits, ideology, and philosophy of life of the carrier. All these factors have a direct or indirect influence on the emergence of the idea and the way disruptive advertising is shaped;
- The culture of the organization is another significant factor allowing the creation and implementation of disruptive communication campaigns targeting digital natives. Thus, the organizational culture is defined by the entrepreneurial model, the diversity of internal competencies, and the strong belief in and adherence of the organization's staff to the carrier's disruptive spirit. Indeed, if employees do not believe in the disruption spirit and do not adhere to the values and philosophy, the disruptor will never be able to implement his or her idea. Moreover, to enable a disruptive spirit within the organization, employees should have diverse profiles and com-

petencies that constitute a fusion of brains, and thus of the ideas generating effective disruptive advertisements targeting young people;

- The environment where disruption is launched is critical. It brings together multiple actors: young consumers, institutions, government, companies, and so on. These market actors interact with each other and have different expectations related to what disruption means and what is its added value. Thus, three important elements must be taken into account for the success of the disruptive project: an open environment ready to welcome disruptive ideas and creativity, actors capable of understanding the disruption spirit, and, above all, individuals, organizations, and companies that adopt disruption to meet the needs of their customers, especially the youth segment.

Furthermore, to implement and disseminate a disruptive spirit and functioning, companies need to consider three core competencies:

- Analytical competencies related to the mastery of immersive and exploratory tools to examine consumer behaviors. In contrast to quantitative techniques and surveys, immersive techniques such as self-ethnography, ethnography, or subjective introspection offer an in-depth and exhaustive understanding of consumption cultures and the meanings consumers assign to their practices;
- Critical skills refer to the intellectual ability of the company to develop critical thinking by performing a back-and-forth exercise that alternates subjective and analytical phases;
- Collaborative skills include the ability of the company to co-create with its customers and employees and reap the benefits of the collective intelligence generated by these efforts.

3.2   Disruptive Communication and Advertising

The disruption applied to communication refers to the ability of a company to implement advertising campaigns that mark the minds of its targets, challenge them, and emotionally engage them so as to differentiate the company from its competitors. The creativity that emerges in disruptive thinking is, therefore, the foundation for the emergence of new products and services and, above all, for a new philosophy of life and new ideas that are uncommon and out of step with conventional thinking.

The ideas can originate from several sources that vary according to four major creative paths: empirical, subjective, experiential, and critical (see Figure 7.1). Marketing and brand managers should follow these paths to develop effective and disruptive advertising campaigns and share values with audiences. The four paths are discussed in the following section.

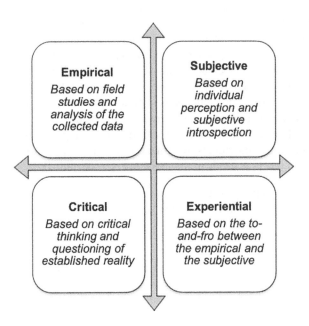

Figure 7.1   Four major creative paths

Empirical disruptive path. This disruptive path includes a rational and analytical approach involving several stages of validation and counter-validation. The process is based on reasoning characterized by the following elements:

- A few solutions are produced by the company to respond to a problem related to strategy, marketing, innovation, and communication;
- The solutions produced are exhaustive and linked to each other;
- The solutions follow a systematic method;
- The solutions have a foundation in the analysis of the environment and its targets;
- To be approved, each solution should be justified and argued.

Thus, the empirical disruptive path allows companies to analyze their context and direct and indirect competition according to three levels of analysis: macro, meso, and micro. While at the macro-environmental level, the company should analyze the impacts related to economic, cultural, social, political, environmental, and technological dimensions. At the meso-environmental level, the company should analyze its direct and indirect competitors and targets, such as its customers. Then, at a more micro-environmental level, it is a question of examining internal organizational actors, namely employees and their interactions with customers. Through this in-depth triptych analysis, marketing and brand managers are then capable of defining accurate and coherent offerings that respond to both the brand's tangible dimensions (e.g., quality and functionality) and intangible dimensions (e.g., relational, emotional, symbolic, and ideological dimensions), which results in an effective and disruptive communication campaign.

Subjective disruptive path. This process refers to a personal and introspective approach that the individual will consciously or unconsciously implement to find ideas, concepts, products, and services that are creative and disruptive. Thus, creative ideas that come from the person's subjectivity and personal interpretation represent several solutions that are produced to respond to a problem. In addition, the solutions produced are in bulk and can be dissociated from each other. In this case, human creativity is at the center of the process, where subjective and unfounded ideas are also considered.

For example, to launch a communication campaign that encourages young people to register to vote, a subjective disruption method can be considered through the logic of personal introspection and individual experiences with young people. Indeed, politicians do not know young people well and wrongly attempt to target them by using youthful language and terms, believing that this is the best way to convince them to vote. However, this approach is not relevant. Young people are not fooled; they are endowed with great intelligence. They know very well that adults are speaking to them to serve their own interests and that the approach is not sincere.

Yet by observing young people around us disrupting political communication campaigns that target youth segments, we can implement effective communication by relying on subjective content that considers the following youth reasoning: voting for a young person is above all about expressing oneself, and digital natives love to express themselves.

In this case, their mode of expression involves using their mouths to speak up. Thus, in the communication campaign, the disruptive idea is to tell them that if they do not register, they will not be able to express themselves, as if they do not have mouths. Consequently, taking the floor away from these young people is much worse than silencing them.

Experiential disruptive path. This path integrates both empirical and subjective approaches described previously. It is a rotating process that evolves and adapts according to the evolution of the experience. The purpose of the process is to generate a disruptive idea, product, innovation, or concept. This path of disruption is based on experiential learning which uses two sources of creativity for the development of creative and disruptive skills, namely a source of intellectual origin and a source related to the central role that experience plays in the disruptive process. The idea of disruption based on experience refers to a dynamic process through two complementary processes: top-down and bottom-up. Together they offer a continuum between the empirical (rational) and subjective (emotional) phases. Thus, the experiential disruption approach is the most complete and the most efficient when it comes to developing unique, creative, and out-of-the-box ideas. Why? Because this approach integrates the cognitive dimension but does not neglect the role an individual's subjectivity plays.

Critical disruptive path. This path refers to the development of critical thinking of reality and the questioning of established social representations. Critical thinking is the main element of generating disruptive ideas and concepts. It is closely linked to the results of a learning process that brings together three components: a multitude of social, transgressive, cognitive, technical skills; theoretical and practical content; and skills and attitudes of the project leader. This process aims to describe a problematic situation for which creative people must demonstrate critical thinking skills.

The problematic situation refers to the existence of one or more possible and obvious options, which explains the interest of using critical thinking to depart from the obvious and bring out disruptive and unexpected ideas that are initially not very obvious. Critical thinking should, therefore, be encouraged at every stage in the creative process; even habitual activities, such as taking notes during meetings, can lead to the development of critical thinking. Indeed, during note-taking, individuals use their critical thinking skills to judge whether the notes they have selected are consistent with the emergence of creative and disruptive ideas.

3.3   Disruptive Advertising: An Effective Strategy to Attract Digital Natives

The underlying idea of disruptive advertising aimed at digital natives follows a postmodern logic that emphasizes the philosophical principles related to the changing structure of society, namely the rise of a fragmented youth identity, the non-existence of absolute truth, and the vanishing of distinctions (Batat, 2019). Thus, disruption grounded on this principle is essential to the success of communication campaigns targeting these postmodern young consumers.

Unlike any other method, disruptive advertising is the approach most in tune with the values, norms, and codes shared by young people who belong to different youth consumption cultures. This section discusses how brand and communication managers can leverage disruption to implement effective advertising and communication campaigns that help them connect with digital natives.

3.3.1 What disruption levers can be used to attract digital natives?

In contrast to traditional communication, in the disruptive perspective, companies should not only meet the functional needs of young people but also attract them by proposing unexpected and unique offerings. In so doing, brand and communication managers can leverage six main ingredients: juxtaposition and fragmentation, empathy, paradox, coolness, kitsch, and recovery.

Juxtaposition and fragmentation. This dimension refers to the combination of two opposite elements within one individual: for example, a person might believe, "I can be this and the opposite of it at the same time." The young person is characterized by a fragmented identity that brings together juxtapositions of several characteristics, which have opposite purposes. Thus, disruptive advertising should be based on the destruction and juxtaposition of youth values following the logic related to the erasing of established hierarchies. This allows for the mixing of genres as a result of questioning the elitist or popular distinction. As a result, offers combining both elitist and popular culture can be proposed.

Also, companies need to consider the consumer's subjective age (the age at which the young person identifies) versus his or her chronological (real) age. The person's gender identification must also be considered. In other words, the male versus female differentiation is no longer relevant as it once was because many profiles have emerged (e.g., metrosexual, androgynous, and transgender profiles).

Digital natives are, therefore, no longer primarily concerned with the values of today's adult society, which is homogeneous, structured, and marked by the absence of diversity. Thus, to communicate effectively with these young consumers, disruptive advertising highlights the salient features and characteristics of this generation. This type of advertising allows people to see fragmentation and juxtaposition through the following multiple lenses:

- The fragmentation of the youth identity. Between previously opposed attitudes, for example, the young person can endorse multiple identities as a consumer. The person can be a musician in the evening, a student during the day, and a high-level athlete on the weekend;
- The fragmentation of society. This phenomenon has led to the rise of multiple tribes of young consumers adopting different consumption practices and brands as a result of media and marketing. The rise of youth vegan tribes is an example;
- The end of traditional sociological models, which means that all lifestyles become legitimate. For these young people, the patriarchal model is waning. Family structures are diverse, and include homosexual, disrupted, and transgender family models.

Empathy. Empathy refers to a way of communicating with digital natives in this form: "I am the only one who understands you because I understand what you are going through." Empathy is a brand's personalized and caring attention to its youth target. Disruptive communication based on empathy to target young people should integrate and translate the brand's emotional capital capable of showing empathy. This will generate positive emotions among young people and create a sense of closeness with the brand.

Paradox. Paradox refers to the idea that "good does bad, and bad does well." A disruptive communication campaign aimed at digital natives can be based on a paradoxical discourse with them, thus contributing to the creation of connivance and confusion among young people. The paradoxical discourse can take several forms based on contradictions related to both rational and irrational behaviors. For example, a youth may think, "I'm eco-friendly, but I don't believe in ecology, so I don't know if I'm *really* eco-friendly." Other examples include "be spontaneous and also control your behaviors" and "be different and also part of the mainstream of society."

Coolness. The concept of "cool" became popular in the 1950s. It was a term used to hide the reality behind a person's detachment. However, the term has been in use for many centuries. It was brought to the New World by West African civilizations forced into the slave trade. In marketing, the term has often been associated with consumer practices and has been defined as unrestrained consumption. Referring to an alternative to resistance and withdrawal is coolness, a way of being, of existing without being there. Coolness used in disruptive advertising aimed at digital natives refers to practices, behaviors, and discourses that highlight the opposite of what is demanded by the rules established by adults and the society.

Kitsch. Kitsch refers to the heterogeneous use, in a communication campaign, of characteristics and elements considered common, old-fashioned, or unpopular. A person wearing white socks with sandals in the middle of summer is an example. However, using kitsch as a tool necessarily requires making a value judgment anchored in a particular cultural setting. For example, what is kitsch in France is not kitsch in Germany.

The kitsch spirit and its translation into an offer or marketing communication are very much in demand among digital natives Why? Because young consumers have evolved and no longer want a straightforward discourse with brand advertising. Brands should show these people that they understand as much by shifting the discourse with them towards kitsch.

Communication should then integrate a style using old-fashioned elements – elements viewed as bad taste by the established culture but valued in their newer use. In disruptive communication aimed at young people, kitsch can be translated according to the idea that the real meaning of a message is the opposite of what's being presented. In other words, you are cool if you're seen as "uncool." Thus, by shifting the discourse, the brands establish connivance and complicity with these digital natives based on the following underlying logic: "*We* know that *you* know that we are deliberately being in bad taste." Such an approach is funny and well received by today's young consumers.

Recovery. Recovery refers to the following logic: "We don't invent anything; we recycle what exists." A disruptive communication aimed at young people is not entirely new or fundamentally original. The idea can be perceived as unique or new by relying on a process of recovering cultural elements that are already well known and integrating them adequately into the communication campaign through a direct takeover of the values in the first degree or an offbeat use.

3.3.2   What disruptive tactics can be used to reach digital natives?

Disruptive communication campaigns targeting digital natives can be implemented by using three main approaches that are relevant and appeal to the youth market through different disruptive combinations: the sacred and profane; realism and hyperrealism; and dirty versus clean.

The sacred and the profane. This approach is based on a juxtaposition that integrates two opposite dimensions: sacred and profane. The sacred allows society to create a separation or opposition between the different elements of the ordinary world. The sacred thus designates what is set apart from the ordinary and commonplace; it is essentially opposed to the profane but also the utilitarian. The profane refers to the ordinary reality, which is defined only in opposition to what is sacred. For instance, a disruption communication campaign aimed at digital natives juxtaposing the sacred and the profane could be implemented by utilizing the Bible or any other religious (sacred) manuscript as a medium to make a product or brand known, loved, and purchased (profane). Indeed, the Bible is the most printed, distributed, and read work on the planet. The Bible can, therefore, enable the dissemination of ideas and their promotion throughout the world. Another support symbolizing the sacred is a flag, which can be used as a communication medium. Yet it should be noted that the sacred and the profane are defined by the cultural context as well as an individual's and community's perception: what is profane for some is not for others, and what is profane versus sacred in one culture is different in another.

Realism and hyperrealism. This technique involves the confluence of two opposite dimensions: the real and the hyperreal. Hyperrealism is the foundation of the hyper consumer society in which young people are evolving. An image is detached from its referents and thereby becomes a strategic component in the marketing and communication discourse. Brand and marketing managers can use the combination of two elements, for example, mixing elements from the world of novels (the hyperreal) to talk about the features and attributes of their products (the real) while targeting digital natives. This approach will endear a brand or a product to young consumers. They will feel immersed in the hyperreal world offered by the narrative and storytelling where the brand or product then becomes a literary novel or a character in a movie.

Dirty and clean. Mixing unexpected elements, such as what is perceived as clean and dirty, in disruptive advertising is another interesting approach to connect with digital natives.

KEY TAKEAWAYS

The key takeaways from this chapter underscore the importance of a hybrid model of communication alongside disruptive content creation companies can implement to reach and connect with digital natives. The consumption of media by young people exposed to different screens simultaneously is very different from that of previous generations. The use of several screens simultaneously raises questions about the possible interactivity of advertisements. Commercial communication towards digital natives is far from being limited to traditional media. Instead, hybrid and disruptive advertising strategies are being used.

8. How are brands designing attractive customer experiences to connect with digital natives?

CHAPTER OVERVIEW

This chapter highlights the importance of adapting youth marketing tools and strategies by integrating the experience of young people in an encounter with the brand or product. This experience marks the transition to a new type of youth marketing, namely the experiential youth marketing that can be implemented by marketers and advertisers to create a strong and sustainable competitive advantage. The chapter start with the limits of traditional marketing techniques aimed at the youth market and then introduces the experiential approach to better connect with digital natives. Digital marketing techniques help companies and brands capture and decode the norms that shape youth consumption cultures and thus offer a customer experience tailored to these young consumers. The last part of the chapter presents examples of brands that successfully designed attractive customer experiences to connect with digital natives and position themselves differently from their competitors.

1.   WHY SHOULD BUSINESSES SHIFT FROM TRADITIONAL TO EXPERIENTIAL MARKETING TO YOUTH?

Today's consumer societies are characterized by the evolution and differentiation of offers and products aimed at young consumers. Marketers and advertisers targeting young people, whether they are childescents, adonascents, adolescents, or adulescents, should question their marketing and communication strategies to differentiate them from those of their competitors. The goal is to build and strengthen loyalty among digital natives throughout their journey to become consumers.

Furthermore, youth behaviors in the consumption field and emerging needs in the different youth cultures have contributed to changing the youth market and, therefore, the levers for creating attractive products and services aimed at young consumers. Thus, creating a strong and durable competitive advantage for companies targeting the youth market must go beyond the idea of satisfying the tangible and functional needs of these people. It must also integrate intangible, symbolic, social, and emotional dimensions of the customer experiences sought by digital natives across different youth cultures.

Considering intangible dimensions in the design of effective customer experiences aimed at young people is vital for companies to attract and, above all, retain digital natives, who are increasingly viewed as product switchers. This approach contributes to reinforcing the attractiveness of a brand or product in a sustainable way because it responds to both the functional and emotional expectations of young consumers.

Following this logic, two main considerations must be taken into account by marketing managers and advertisers targeting digital natives. First, the purchase and consumption of a product or brand should result in a functional, symbolic, social, cultural, and human experience that is coherent with the values and norms shared among different youth consumption cultures. Second, young consumers not only buy and consume products, but also produce meanings rooted in their daily consumption experiences within their particular youth cultures.

1.1   The Limits of Traditional Marketing to Youth

Unlike traditional marketing aimed at youth, from an experiential perspective, products and brands should not only meet the functional needs of young consumers but also provide them with unique, emotional, and meaningful experiences. The experiences should include the following elements:

- Feelings of comfort;
- Positive emotions;
- Feelings of belonging to a family or a common consumer culture;
- Symbols reflecting the world and culture of young consumers;
- Pleasure and well-being;
- Pleasant and memorable sensations.

To shift from traditional to experiential marketing aiming at the youth market, companies should consider a youth-centric approach when defining their marketing and communication strategies. To design effective customer experiences targeting young people, companies should first develop in-depth knowledge of the behaviors across different youth consumption cultures by decoding the meanings and the paradoxes related to youth consumption practices. Furthermore, traditional youth marketing tools such as age segmentation should be re-evaluated to allow companies to implement an experiential marketing strategy adapted to each youth consumption culture.

Traditional marketing is not suited to designing a satisfying consumer experience that creates a sustainable competitive advantage. That is why the advent of experiential marketing is relevant in the context of the youth market as it marks the shift from a logic centered on a product or brand and its functionalities to an era where young consumers' meanings, emotions, and experiences lie at the heart of a company's offerings.

The shift from traditional to experiential youth marketing means questioning the marketing mix and 4Ps (product, price, place, and promotion) often used by marketers and advertisers to target the youth market. Indeed, experiential marketing questions the idea of a functional need to be satisfied, which is the logic behind traditional marketing. The functional need in traditional marketing is linked to the reasoning of the knowledge accumulated by young people and the cognitive aspect of the purchase process.

This reasoning, which is the result of a long process of analyzing information and comparing the advantages and disadvantages of different commercial offers, does not explain the behaviors and reasons that lead young people to swap one brand for another one. Indeed, although a brand may be attractive, it can be suddenly abandoned by digital natives in favor of another trendy brand. The reason for this behavior is not always explained by the quality of the product or the "coolness" of the brand. Young consumers' zapping behaviors may indeed depend on other factors that are mainly subjective, personal, ideological, and emotional.

Experiential marketing thus invites advertisers and marketers to understand the expectations and needs of young consumers from a youth-centric perspective by further exploring their experiences with brands and products consumed in interactions with other social actors within a particular consumer culture. The questioning of traditional marketing aiming at young consumers is then based on two key weaknesses:

- The attractiveness of a brand or product is not limited to the functionalities offered or to its "cool" dimension. A product, whether it is part of everyday life or is consumed exclusively by young consumers, also carries perceived meanings that depend on a person's consumer culture. These meanings strongly differentiate a product or brand by positioning it as a strong symbolic marker in the spirit of different youth consumption cultures (e.g., rappers, rockers, skaters, vegans);
- Digital natives do not always adopt a rational approach in the decision-making process. The decision to buy or reject a product or brand can also be linked to irrational or even paradoxical and contradictory motivations not captured by traditional marketing components and tools.

MINI-CASE BOX 8.1   RED BULL: EXPERIENTIAL MARKETING FOCUSED ON EMOTIONS TO ENGAGE DIGITAL NATIVES

Young people do not just want to be seduced by brands; they also want to be moved and touched by them. An experiential marketing strategy that incorporates strong emotional components is the answer to this trend among today's young consumers. Indeed, what works with young people is anything that allows them to live memorable and emotionally charged experiences. Emotions are thus a vital component of experiential marketing that brands can use to connect with and engage digital natives. Emotionally rich content delivered via videos, images, and text messages, among other media, will have a greater impact on a brand's adoption.

Red Bull is one of the brands that associates content and data with emotions to connect with digital natives. The brand applies moving marketing and communication strategies that combine online data and emotions in advertising. Red Bull has invested in "emotional" data to reinforce its targeted advertisings aimed at young people.

Although Red Bull is a pioneering brand when it comes to creating experiential and emotional content, the company wants to take the next step by mixing emotional and digital data. For example, video is used to mimic the sensations Formula 1 drivers experience. The videos give viewers a glimpse of what the drivers feel during their races. Connected objects also have an important role in the concrete translation of emotions. For Red Bull, connected objects are part of the future of experiential youth marketing. Connected objects are associated with the development of emotional and experiential content with the use of immersive devices and technologies. For example, by placing sensors on an athlete's body, a brand can gather information about the athlete's brain activity and heart rate. Red Bull's objective is to improve the consumer experience by focusing on immersion – that is, by making a young person feel the sensations of a great athlete.

While Red Bull is the leading brand in experiential marketing aiming at digital natives through the use of emotional data, other brands have already expressed interest and even started to process this data. Nokia has looked into the use of hearing and temperature sensors to capture the emotions in photos. Apple filed a patent related to the collection of physiological data to better analyze the emotions of its consumers.

To sum up, we can state that the difference between traditional and experiential marketing aiming at youth lies in the fact that traditional logic does not sufficiently integrate emotional, paradoxical, and subjective dimensions that are part of the young consumers' decision-making process shaped by the norms and codes related to each youth consumer culture. Table 8.1 illustrates the main differences between traditional marketing and experiential marketing aiming at young consumers.

Table 8.1   Traditional versus experiential youth marketing

	Traditional youth marketing	Experiential youth marketing
Objective	Improve the functional attributes and the economic benefits of the product or service	Improve the consumption and purchasing experiences of young people (before, during, and afterwards)
Products and services for youth	Define products and services adapted to youth targets	The competitive advantage lies in the lived experience of the young person and the emotion that flows from it. It is, therefore, a question of proposing an experiential package
Young consumers	Young consumers are rational decision-makers interested in the functional dimension of the product	In addition to functional needs, young people also have irrational, emotional, ideological, cultural, and symbolic needs that constitute an integral part of the youth customer experience and expectations
Market research tools	Use of quantitative and textual methods (questionnaire, focus groups, etc.)	Use of innovative, immersive, exploratory, and experiential marketing research methods

Furthermore, the experiential approach implemented to target young consumers goes beyond the simple logic of product or brand appeal and the satisfaction of functional needs. Young people are more interested in having pleasant and memorable experiences with their peers within their youth cultures. These experiences can be designed by proposing:

- Offers (products and services) anchored in different youth cultures;
- Offers charged with emotion, pleasure, and hedonism that enhance the socialization among digital natives;
- Offers that allow young consumers to share common values with members in their youth consumer cultures and beyond.

1.2   The Rise of Experiential Marketing to Connect with Digital Natives

The experiential paradigm first appeared in the work of researchers Holbrook and Hirschman in 1982. Holbrook and Hirschman's research highlighted the importance of experience as well as the subjective and emotional dimensions related to consumer activities and the decision-making process.

The idea of experiential marketing aiming at young consumers, therefore, takes up the foundations of traditional marketing with its four levels – analytical, strategic, creative, and operational – to incorporate the irrational and subjective aspects of young consumer behaviors. The objective is to develop a new framework for the study of consumer youth cultures.

Experiential marketing aiming at digital natives thus provides a response to youth behaviors and expectations differentiated by the emotional and relational dimensions that animate the daily lives of young people across different youth cultures.

Through this new youth marketing that puts the youth customer experience at the center of a company's strategy, advertisers and marketers can not only able to maximize material and functional satisfaction by responding to the rational needs of consumers. They will also be able to maximize the positive experiences lived by young people within their youth cultures and identify the symbolic factors that allow for the improvement of this experience. This, therefore, helps companies to build loyalty by constructing strong bonds with digital natives.

Multiple challenges can explain the vital need for companies targeting young consumers to shift towards experiential marketing and propose, instead of products, experiences to youth segments. Among these challenges, we can cite the following:

- In today's hyper-consumer societies, a business should evolve in its role from being the provider of goods and services to a producer of experiences;
- Designing customer experiences represents a durable competitive advantage. The goods and services produced and provided by a company are seen as ancillary accessories to create memorable and, above all, unparalleled consumer or shopping experiences;
- One's memorability of the consumption or purchasing experience is a key success factor. It is closely linked to the loyalty of young consumers and the attractiveness of brands, thereby guaranteeing their adoption by youth cultures through positive word-of-mouth;
- The experiential offer aimed at young consumers must be adapted to each individual or group of individuals belonging to a specific youth culture.

Therefore, these challenges lead companies to implement experiential marketing by using different techniques in their offerings aiming at young consumers:

- Theming. This technique helps brands and advertisers to positively stimulate the impressions of young consumers when they encounter the company's offer. The objective is to unify the different tangible and intangible elements provided by the product or brand around a common and coherent history and culture;

- Enhancing positive and unified impressions. This technique helps companies to match young people's impressions with positive cues. Brands need to produce unchangeable impressions young consumers can keep in their minds;
- Elimination of negative elements. The goal is to eliminate negative cues that impact the quality of young people's experience at all levels of the experience (anticipated, before, during, and after the purchase);
- Production of memories and engagement of the five senses. This element produces a mix of memories by offering products and services that young consumers use as a reminder of the experiences they have already had. Using the senses (hearing, seeing, smelling, tasting, and touching) can contribute to creating positive memories.

MINI-CASE BOX 8.2   MICHEL & AUGUSTIN: A FOOD BRAND THAT HAS PLACED YOUTH CULTURES AT THE HEART OF THE CONSUMER EXPERIENCE

From its launch, Michel & Augustin's strategy to connect with digital natives has been based on the integration of the codes and standards of youth cultures by implementing actions both online and offline. The brand positions eating its products as fun, social, and entertaining experiences that young people can share and live. The brand relies on the quality of its products but also on the notions of family, fun, and closeness to its committed communities and the brand's fans. Simplicity and self-mockery are at the heart of a communication strategy that encourages young people to remain themselves, just like the brand, which claims authenticity without the fuss.

To target young urban people, who are fans of new food products and authentic products, the brand focused on the visual identity of its products, which gives it a friendly image with young people. The packaging is designed so that the products stand out on the shelves of supermarkets. For Michel & Augustin, each product should tell a story, thanks to packaging based on happiness, "joie de vivre," and the brand's humorous and offbeat tone.

The idea is to provide young consumers with confidence and strengthen the proximity with them by offering them "friendly" products that speak the same language as they do. This positioning has contributed to increasing the brand's notoriety. Michel & Augustin were awarded the Phénix prize for the best communication campaigns. The originality of the company's communication also comes from the fact that the two creators of the brand do not hesitate to promote their products themselves, thus creating closeness with the young public. The objective of the creators' communication is to encourage a certain interaction and thus involvement in terms of simplicity with young consumers so as to create strong emotional bonds with them. The offbeat and youthful codes of the brand are also reflected on the brand's official website and social media platforms.

2.   CREATING EXPERIENCES INSTEAD OF PRODUCTS: A NEW ERA FOR YOUTH MARKETING?

Customer experience can be divided into four main stages. The first stage refers to the desired experience, which is defined by companies and integrates the culture and brand identity advertisers and marketers want to share with young consumers. The second stage indicates the proposed experience, which is the operational translation of the experience companies want to offer to their youth targets.

Then, the lived-experience stage reflects the result of all the perceptions and emotions a person feels, as well as the knowledge used by young people in a given situation. The last stage refers to the expected experience, which is the anticipation of the experience. Young people can also live the experience of consumption by proxy through the stories of others who have already lived the experience of consumption or purchase.

MINI-CASE BOX 8.3   HOW DOES CHANEL LEVERAGE TECHNOLOGIES AND DATA TO OFFER THE ULTIMATE LUXURY BRAND EXPERIENCE TO DIGITAL NATIVES?

Despite Chanel's minimal e-commerce adoption, the luxury brand is known to be the leader in the world of influence on social media. Chanel has an impressive 40 million followers on Instagram, and 13.1 million on Twitter. We also know that digital natives, born in the digital age, have the highest social media presence of all other generations. Young consumers look for brands that are fond of technology and have expertise in this domain to be modern and relevant. For that, digital native fans chose Chanel to be the most influential luxury brand on social media.

You can see the convenience of the Chanel website from the moment you access it. Users select the region they live in, followed by the language they prefer. The campaigns and content displayed are tailored depending on the consumer's region and language preferences, creating a personalized experience for every region. Chanel only posts what appears to be relevant to the customer.

Second, the design of the website is very minimalistic, a style that is very popular with the digital native generation. The site reflects Chanel's most widespread quote: "Simplicity is the ultimate sophistication." Other than that, the website has clearly visible and easily accessible tabs, classified based on the wide range of products Chanel has to offer, such as haute couture, jewelry, eyewear, fragrances, and so on. Because young consumers are impatient when it comes to digital media, everything must be clear and accessible to keep their interest rising, rather than making it hard for them to access what they are looking for.

Aside from Chanel's user-friendly website, its exceptional digital presence is illustrated by its adoption of successful and interesting brand storytelling, another element that entices digital natives and keeps their interest high. Digital natives tend to value the brand's historical background, which is why luxury brands usually leverage this interest and create "stories" around them, building an emotional connection with young consumers. They do not want to see anything superficial. In fact, they will boycott such brands and "cancel" them on social media.

For that reason, Chanel has told the emotional story of "Inside Chanel," which addresses the background of young Gabrielle Chanel, how she was surrounded by peasants and slowly turned into the world-renowned fashion luxury designer. The story is documented as a micro-series on YouTube. The brand's historical background and how Chanel developed into the position it is currently in worldwide is told. Thus, Chanel has developed quite a reputation among its young consumers thanks to its engaging and active digital presence, positioning itself as a vintage and classy brand but a well-developed and relevant brand among young consumers.

However, Chanel is still behind on the e-commerce side. If Chanel were to be more present in online luxury retail shops such as Farfetch, it would no longer be losing the battle to Gucci and other innovative luxury brands that digital natives love to buy. Chanel would be even more visible and gain a huge competitive advantage over other brands that are winning only at e-commerce. If the collections and collaborations with A-list celebrities that digital natives admire were sold online, Chanel could be exposed to young people even more, and thereby gain more understanding of these digital natives' online behaviors and shopping preferences.

Furthermore, customer experience quality can also be measured at all stages. The evaluation of the quality of the customer experience in youth cultures can be achieved by using multiple measuring models. The most recognized model is the one developed by Parasuraman et al. (1991). These authors developed an instrument that measures the quality of services at the heart of the customer experience by considering five major dimensions: tangibility (e.g., equipment, staff appearance, and physical environment); reliability, which refers to the ability to deliver the promised service reliably and accurately; serviceability, which reflects the willingness to help consumers and provide prompt service; assurance, which denotes the knowledge and courtesy of the staff and their ability to inspire trust; and empathy, which is the personalized attention and caring of staff towards consumers.

Designing an effective and enjoyable customer experience targeting digital natives requires the integration of four main components of the experiential model: a youth's individual characteristics, social and economic interactions, factors related to the lived consumption experience, and the physical environment (see Figure 8.1). These four elements can positively or negatively affect the quality of young people's emotional, cultural, symbolic, and cognitive purchasing or consumption experiences. The elements are presented and discussed below.

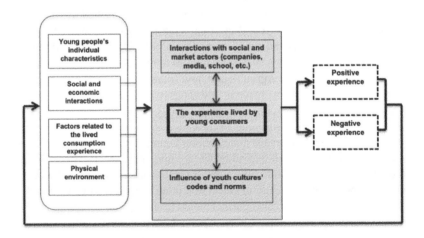

Figure 8.1   The youth experiential marketing framework

2.1   A Youth's Individual Characteristics

Any marketing to youths should include the ability of young consumers to take ownership of commercial offers to redefine the customer experience and its meaning according to the dominant norms in their youth cultures. Individual factors, such as personality, prior experiences, lifestyle, life cycle, and personal motivations, can also have a direct or indirect impact on a digital native's customer experience.

Several studies have shown that individual characteristics affect a youth's reactions to their social environment. In this case, the consumption experience can be modified according to different intrinsic and extrinsic characteristics of a young consumer. Among the factors related to the individual dimensions to be taken into account in the design of an experiential offering aimed at digital natives are demographic and psychographic characteristics.

- Demographic characteristics. Many studies highlighted the importance of personal characteristics, such as age, gender, or education, in terms of the perception and appreciation of the quality of the customer experience lived by a young person. The importance of these variables has already been demonstrated in several areas of youth consumption. Personal variables influence young people's sensitivity to the experiential and social setting and thus their responses to products and services. Thus, a youth's customer experience is unique and depends on the personal characteristics of each young person. These characteristics affect his or her perceptions of the quality of the experience. It is, therefore, critical for marketers and advertisers to assess the demographic and individual variables of a youth's customer experience. These variables are likely to lead to a change in behavior among young consumers;
- Psychographic characteristics. Psychographic variables, such as lifestyles, beliefs, values, and personalities, among others, can lead to significant differences across youth consumption cultures and thus affect young consumers' experiences. Differences in young people's consumption experiences can be significant if we consider a young consumer profile defined by personal characteristics and psychographic variables. Marketing studies show that psychographic characteristics that have an impact on the lived experience can be defined in terms of personality types and the youth cultures to which young people belong, perceptions related to the youths' current or past experiences, the tangible, symbolic, and experiential needs of young consumers, and finally factors such as opinions, lifestyles, values, attitudes, and interests that can be identified before designing experiential offerings aimed at the youth market.

2.2   Social and Economic Interactions

Studies state that demographic and psychographic characteristics can positively or negatively affect the experience of consumption in different youth cultures. These variables are also affected by the typology of human relationships as well as the social and economic interactions that young people have with other social actors. Studies on the impact human relations have on the quality of the experience indicate that two variables – gender and emotional tone – have a strong impact on the satisfaction of young consumers. Moreover, young people who are emotionally involved in the consumer experience are more satisfied than those who are not.

2.3   Factors Related to the Lived Consumption Experience

Young consumers often analyze their behaviors according to the cultures to which they belong as well as the consumption situations they find themselves in. In the consumption experience, the "situation" includes variables such as the presence at the point of sale, feeling advised or accompanied during a purchase situation, and feeling considered by salespeople and other actors present at the point of sale (e.g., other customers). It is, therefore, crucial for marketers and advertisers targeting the youth market to identify the situational factors related to the purchase experience at the point of sale. Thus, situational variables are relevant when it comes to designing suitable and enjoyable consumption and purchase experiences aiming at digital natives.

2.4   Physical Environment

The physical setting is a significant factor that companies should consider when designing satisfying customer experiences aimed at digital natives. Indeed, young people's evaluations of a product and the quality of an experience are largely influenced by the physical environment and its atmospheric variables. Atmospheric variables such as temperature, music, and décor, among others, provide youth with immediate and continued immersion in a positive and enjoyable physical setting. In such a setting, the person can experience a positive and memorable purchasing or consumption situation that can lead to long-term satisfaction and retention.

MINI-CASE BOX 8.4   HOW DOES ABERCROMBIE
& FITCH (A&F) USE THE PHYSICAL
ENVIRONMENT TO ENHANCE YOUNG
PEOPLE'S SHOPPING EXPERIENCE?

Abercrombie & Fitch (A&F) is an American company founded in 1892 by
David Abercrombie and Ezra Fitch. The renewal of the brand in the 1980s
following its acquisition by the Limited Brand resulted in a new marketing
policy targeting young people with a varied range of sports and urban products – products they can buy in experiential and sensory settings.

In each of the brand's stores in the United States and Europe, experiential
marketing is uniformly applied by including sensory and situational elements, ranging from visual to olfactory elements. The visual aspect at A&F
is described by a subdued light bringing serenity and a warm welcome to
the young customers and highlighting the colorful clothes. The tactile aspect is presented through the touch and the fitting of the garments without
the need to resort to salespeople. In the stores, young people can also experience sound as hearing is also solicited by ambient music. Regarding smell
and the olfactory dimension, salespeople have instructions indicating that
they must spray the brand's perfume on the clothes every hour.

These elements enhance the shopping experience by engaging all five
senses of a consumer. The goal is to create enjoyable, positive, and memorable shopping experiences that make young customers stay longer and thus
purchase more items.

3.   HOW ARE BRANDS DESIGNING CUSTOMER EXPERIENCES AIMING AT DIGITAL NATIVES?

This section discusses customer experience strategies implemented by different brands operating within various sectors, including the digital, retail, food,
fashion, and services sectors.

3.1   Designing Youth Customer Experiences in the Digital Sector

The digital sector is by nature an attractive one aimed at digital natives, who
use multiple platforms to satisfy their functional, hedonic, and social needs.
Digital platforms are enhancing the user experience and implementing strategies including the data collected online to engage young users and make
them spend more time on the platforms. How exactly do digital companies
create attractive and engaging digital experiences aimed at the youth market?

To answer the question, I will discuss Spotify, which is disrupting the music industry and gaining more and more users among young people.

Spotify is a digital platform that provides access to music, podcasts, and streaming video covering millions of songs and other content from artists all over the world. Spotify is accessible across a range of devices, including computers, phones, tablets, speakers, TVs, and cars (Spotify, 2019). The music platform primarily targets millennials. According to the brand, 72 percent of its users are between the ages of 18 and 24. This is related to the understanding that Spotify's marketing strategy has in terms of operating data and the streaming habits correlated to younger consumers' preferences for pop culture and their tendency to engage in long hours of listening to music. According to Spotify, the platform has been successful among youth due to its social media elements, such as the ability to add friends, create playlists, share playlists with one's friends, and follow other people's playlists.

Spotify succeeds in orienting its operations on social media platforms. It has done so by making its database accessible, easy to use, and fun. Younger consumers and social platforms are a combination to be considered, especially when making a brand widely accessible and advertised; this is exactly what Spotify is doing. Its platform is all about social interactions. Spotify differentiates itself from competitors by providing a "collective experience that brings people together and opens the door for sharing" (Ascension, 2020).

How does Spotify target digital natives?

Spotify undoubtedly targets young music lovers. Digital natives tend to spend around 143 minutes streaming music every day (SomeSpotify, 2018). The brand closely studied younger consumers' streaming habits, their preferences, and their expectations. Spotify is an interactive music and social platform that encourages the youth market to express their opinions about artists and songs, to share them, and enjoy a very rich database of music, videos, and much more.

The brand introduced itself as a community builder by partnering with Facebook. This allowed users on Spotify to sync their contacts and provided them with a musical platform of interactions with friends. Doing so, in turn, transformed the service into a collective, enjoyable experience. The brand also created SpotifyCares, an account on Twitter that allows fans to keep a line of conversation open for their ideas, complaints, and anything that comes to their minds. Spotify also teamed up with Snapchat to engage young users with short messages, smartly pushing out its exclusive content on one of millennials' most loved applications (Ascension, 2020).

Therefore, we can state that Spotify made it to younger consumers' hearts. The application is loved by this generation for what it provides in terms of unlimited access to music, songs, and artists' news. Young consumers perceive Spotify as a musical platform that engages with them with their friends, allowing them to share, listen, and express their feelings and opinions about the different available data.

How does Spotify redefine the customer experience to attract digital natives?
To improve its competitive attributes, Spotify went a step further in impacting its younger customers by connecting to current cultural trends. For example, as a promotional event celebrating the return of *Game of Thrones* to HBO, Spotify teamed up to create a sub-site that takes a music selection and matches it with one of 15 of the characters on the show so as to generate a customized playlist (Ascension, 2020). This idea engaged many fans around the world.

On another note, Spotify mixed the fascination with celebrities into its platform and worked on attracting younger consumers to engage them by triggering their curiosity to follow their favorite artists' and celebrities' playlists. For example, in 2015, Michelle Obama released a playlist of her favorite female artists to promote her "Let Girls Learn" campaign. Obama's song selection included Beyoncé, Aretha Franklin, and Diana Ross (Ascension, 2020).

When it comes to leveraging technologies to offer the ultimate brand experience and share value with young users, Spotify smartly uses its consumers' data to create fun and exciting campaigns displayed on posters and social media. The company's marketing campaign based its design on data analytics. This was perceived as a bold move that eventually generated positive consequences. The campaign was focused around anonymously releasing their user data in a comedic fashion. Billboards and posters were the platforms and Spotify took to the streets to out their users' weird and wonderful habits, but in a jesting anonymous way (Smart Insights, 2018). The idea was brilliant and widened the scope of Spotify's users.

Furthermore, Spotify continued to challenge new markets and innovated its marketing campaigns to attract a larger number of customers. The company, in association with the advertising agency Leo Burnett, launched a hyper-local OHH (out-of-home) plus digital campaign in India. It was designed in a way to have "a deeply localized and personalized user engagement with millennials. The campaign was targeted geographically based on cities, neighborhoods, and important traffic intersections, with content that depicts relatable life situations and hyper-local cultural nuances" (Sharma, 2019). The whole idea of the campaign was to work on powerful emotional expression through playlists, "no matter how life changes tracks." The campaign was called "There's A Playlist for That."

The main challenge Spotify is facing is to better target young consumers
Spotify needs to carefully address the changing and evolving market. The youth market is tricky and is very challenging due to its continuous changes of demands and expectations. Spotify relies on engaging its young users through

its interesting community platforms and social media. It is indeed an attractive environment to its music fans and artists' fan clubs. The company should keep investing in innovations and work on scaling up its targeted market and consumers' age ranges.

Younger consumers have delicate relationships with their favorite brands; the latter can be threatened by competition, weak adaptability, and a negative reputation. As such, Spotify, and especially after widening its geographical markets, should carefully design and consider the different cultures it intends to attract to avoid any clashes and undesirable marketing consequences.

3.2   Designing Youth Customer Experiences in the Retail Sector

This section introduces the cases of two interesting companies, namely Target and Dollar Tree. Both companies are designing customer experiences to attract and retain the youth segment.

3.2.1   Target's strategy for the digital natives youth market

Target is one of the largest retail companies in the United States. Target offers "high-quality, on-trend merchandise at discounted prices in clean, spacious, guest-friendly stores and its digital channels" (A Bullseye Review, 2020). Among Target's offerings are curated general merchandise and food assortments, including perishables, dry grocery, dairy, and frozen items at discounted prices (Forbes, 2020b).

George Draper Dayton of Minneapolis created the Dayton's department store chain in 1902. In 1962, the Dayton Corporation created Target as a discount alternative chain. Target's mission statement is "To make Target the preferred shopping destination for our guests by delivering outstanding value, continuous innovation, and exceptional guest experiences by consistently fulfilling our 'Expect More. Pay Less. Brand Promise'" (Mission Statement Academy, 2020).

Moreover, the company made sure to align its strategies with what its mission suggests. Indeed, Target is widening its horizon to increase its customers. Target realized the importance of personalization; personalization involves providing customers with a shopping experience that addresses their preferences and expectations (Wertz, 2019).

How does Target attract digital natives?
Target's strategies oriented towards attracting younger consumers involve upgrading the company's groceries and products and their quality to make them organic and natural. Among Target's strategies are offering gluten-free products and millennial-oriented products in the home, beauty, and apparel

areas, and redesigning stores to become more convenient and attractive (Tirico, 2016).

Target's marketing strategy is to introduce its merchandise so it becomes part of people's daily lives. The company has created digital platforms that are easily reached and useful for younger consumers. Target is also opening smaller stores in urban locations to attract younger customers (Wharton University of Pennsylvania, 2016).

Target acknowledges the importance of designing its marketing strategies in a way that addresses younger consumers' expectations. The company invested in creative ways to attract young customers. For instance, Target recently expanded its drive-up service. Using an app, customers can order items and pick them up two hours later. Store associates bring the orders out to customers' cars (Bhasin, 2018a).

Target has increased its competitive edge by investing in delivery operations. The company acquired Shipt, an online company that delivers products to people's homes just hours after the items are purchased (Kuang, 2020). Such an investment has surely attracted younger customers who appreciate speed and quality. Target's strong presence on social media has also helped the company increase its younger customer base and maintain lines of communication and interactions with them.

Young consumers consider Target a convenient shopping experience where they can find their items quickly and for cheaper prices than elsewhere. Target's stores mix quality with affordable and discounted prices. Such a combination is seen as convenient and wanted by younger customers. Target appeals to younger customers who enjoy higher incomes by emphasizing high-quality merchandise and low-cost designer fashions (Kuang, 2020). Target has become the shop of choice for these younger customers because of the convenient and practical shopping experience it provides.

How does Target redefine the customer experience to attract digital natives?
Target makes sure to increase its brand recognition by sponsoring awards shows such as the Grammys, Oscars, Emmys, and Golden Globe Awards.

Target has engaged in socially responsible activities as well (Bhasin, 2018a). For example, annually the company sets aside money, which is invested in donations and given to schools. This socially responsible activity increases Target's appreciation in the public eye, notably among younger consumers.

The company's investment in redefining delivery's convenience played a role as well in attracting young consumers. Such a strategy redefines the shopping experience and makes it more feasible and convenient for these customers who value their time and quality products. Target also acknowledges the importance of training its staff to deliver a friendly, useful, and helpful service during the shopping experience. This provided support is very much appreciated by young consumers who would prefer to be guided and valued when spending their money.

Furthermore, Target adopted ATL (above the line) and BTL (below the line) promotional strategies to increase its customer base and has launched ad campaigns in both electronic and print media via flyers, coupons, newspapers, television commercials, and magazines. On social media, Target displays its ads and promotions on YouTube, Facebook, Instagram, and Twitter (Bhasin, 2018a).

The company also improved the user experience to the point that shopping digital channels provide the same experience as shopping in stores. Instead of blocking the Amazon app or pulling the plug on Wi-Fi to prevent customers from using it in Target stores, Target built a faster network to support digital offerings. It also developed Cartwheel, an online platform that offers customers access to deals and discounts via social media (Maras, 2018). Target's customer relationship management database accentuates its digital service experience. The company collects insights and analyzes them to personalize promotions and ads whenever digital platforms are used. Target goes beyond sending emails with attractive products based on demographic information, such as a customer's age, marital status, and address. The company also identifies brands customers are loyal to (Lipka, 2014).

The main challenges Target is facing to better serve young consumers
Target needs to be attentive to any development the younger market presents, especially given that the competition in retail is high and the company must compete against Amazon and Walmart. It is important to follow the trends and maintain high levels of creativity when designing its marketing strategies. These are necessary measures to maintain its customers' loyalty and interest. Investing in digital innovations and marketing techniques set standards for sustainability and competitiveness.

However, Target might lose some young consumers because its prices sometimes do not reflect "discounted" amounts compared to the competition. It is crucial to remember that what motivates young consumers is the purchasing power discount retailers are providing. If the price issue is neglected, this could harm Target's image as being a shop of choice for youths with less income.

The company has already invested heavily in delivery services. However, it is important to widen its scope of influence and services to reach wider geographical locations and countries to keep up with what the competition is doing. In today's world, speed and quality are much appreciated and desired, especially by young people. The company should constantly reassess its scope of operations to continue to generate progressive retail standards.

3.2.2 Dollar Tree: a convenient retail experience aimed at young consumers

Dollar Tree is "a leading operator of discount variety stores that have served North America for more than 30 years." The company operates 15,000-plus stores across the 48 contiguous US states and five Canadian provinces, supported by a coast-to-coast logistics network and more than 193,000 associates (Dollar Tree, 2020). It also has a Family Dollar segment that includes a chain of general merchandise retail discount stores providing consumers with a selection of competitively priced merchandise in convenient neighborhood stores. The company was founded by J. Douglas Perry and Macon F. Brock, Jr. in 1986, and is headquartered in Chesapeake, Virginia (Forbes, 2020a).

Dollar Tree's increasing profits have made it possible for the company to open stores widely in convenient locations accessible to most customers (especially lower-income families), notably younger ones. The strategic accessibility of Dollar Tree's stores has attracted younger consumers and made it easy to grow the number of customers the company targets. Young consumers are also very much attracted to lower prices. These people are also more tolerant of purchasing products that lack private-label brands but are usually sold for much lower prices (Howland, 2016). Dollar Tree differentiates itself from competitors by abiding by the "dollar" restriction on its prices. If a product does exceed $1, it is usually sold at a price that's lower than the competition's.

Dollar Tree was successful in orienting its marketing and communication strategy towards a competitive one by using social media as a platform for its promotions and item purchases. The company also made its customer service easily reachable. The low-cost retailer clearly understands that social media "is about customer engagement and not solely about making that extra buck" (Parry, 2010). In addition to social media, the company created its own app that allows customers to check out digitally and skip in-store lines. The Dollar General app also features real-time shopping lists and digital coupons (Digital Media Solutions, 2019).

How does Dollar Tree target digital natives?
Dollar Tree acknowledges the importance of its competitive advantage in maintaining its $1 price. It is this strength that is succeeding in attracting younger consumers and gaining their loyalty. This young market is more interested in cheaper prices than brand names. The lower the price, the higher the purchasing power, and the more popular the stores are with this younger audience (Digital Media Solutions, 2019).

As mentioned earlier, the company is also aiming to keep close connections and communication lines with younger consumers who prefer quick and convenient services. The Dollar General app, which features real-time shopping lists and digital coupons, plays a role in engaging younger consumers to interact and target the store for their purchases. It is also important to note that the company has designed its digital platform and social media presence in a way that is perceived to be creative and inspiring. This makes a shopping experience exciting for younger consumers who appreciate trends and newness.

From a youth perspective, young consumers consider Dollar Tree a convenient shopping experience. They find their items quickly and for cheaper prices. The stores are many and widely present in different areas, which makes them accessible and easily reachable for younger customers. The items are diversified and mostly respond to younger consumers' expectations. By being a "one-stop retailer," this makes their shopping experiences easier (CSD Staff, 2018).

Dollar Tree is also present on social media. This presence increases the exposure and promotion of the items sold. Younger consumers appreciate finding their purchases online when deciding to spend their money. Also, maintaining an interactive digital platform provides a chain of communication the company uses to gather feedback, comments, and requests.

How is Dollar Tree redefining the customer experience to attract digital natives?

Dollar Tree made it easy to reach young consumers by adopting a standard that balances quality and price. The convenient prices and locations of its stores add to the competitive aspect when it comes to attracting younger consumers. The latter are seen as less interested in spending on consumables. These youths find that the company's stores fit their principles and expectations (Anderson, 2016).

Dollar Tree's online accessibility and social media presence have also made the company attractive to younger consumers who are "digitally savvy" and "all about convenience" (Castellanos, 2019). The company also created a cart-calculator that "lets in-store customers calculate the exact total of items in their carts, including taxes and discounts, before they go up to the cash register." All these initiatives are oriented towards providing a more convenient shopping experience.

What are the main challenges Dollar Tree is facing to better target young consumers?

Having Dollar Tree Stores located in suburbs and lower-income neighborhoods made them easy targets for crimes such as robbery (MacGillis, 2020). Their sole presence in these areas makes them the "only" visible targets for thieves. As such, Dollar Tree must enhance its security measures and make its stores more safe and secure to avoid robberies and other crimes. Moreover, following the recent events of the COVID-19 pandemic, Dollar Tree's shopping experience still implied a physical presence to purchase items, and the company "shut down its website and announced that it would no longer take online orders" (Debter, 2020). The inability to adapt its purchasing services to the current social context risks its place in being a store of choice.

Any inconsistency in the online sales experience would also harm its profits and could result in a decrease in loyalty, especially among younger customers. That said, Dollar Tree must strategically plan for situations like these to maintain its digital experience standards and refrain from disappointing its younger online users.

3.3   Designing Youth Customer Experiences in the Food Industry

This section discusses two interesting brands that are already part of youth cultures, namely Oreo and Doritos. Each of these food brands is offering customer experiences to connect with digital natives, both online and offline.

3.3.1   Oreo, the coolest brand experience among digital natives

Oreo is a brand of cream-filled cookies (two chocolate wafers with a sweet cream filling in between) that have been around for decades. Oreo was introduced in 1912 by Nabisco and later became popular worldwide (Biscuit People, 2017). The brand's parent company, Mondelez International, was positively impacted financially by the popularity of Oreos. Oreos is a brand that maintains a strong social media presence. The brand constantly comes up with a slogan to match each phase during its evolution and orientation, and it presents its products as healthy and welcomed in every house (Biscuit People, 2017).

Oreo relies on attractive hashtags such as #ProudParents (OREO, 2020) to invite parents and their kids to purchase the delicious cookies. Oreo strives for maximum engagement in its ads and marketing techniques. One of its most famous television commercials is the one in which Oreo cookies are featured with a healthy cup of milk drank by a child. This link to milk made it a first choice and a must-have cookie with every milk drink. Oreo's slogan is: "Milk's favorite cookie." Kids want it; parents get it.

How does Oreo target digital natives?
Targeting younger consumers seems to be a strategy most of the popular brands are adopting since this market is promising and influential. Oreo took the cookie beyond its direct meaning and worked hard to make it more than a cookie. Instead, Oreos means fun and excitement. In all its marketing strategies, the brand focuses on the notion of variety by displaying the cookies in different contexts: musical contexts, social media, stories, and much more (Penfold, 2019). Oreo is thus a family product – it suits what the whole family desires.

A paragraph on MilksFavoriteCookie sums it up: "The positioning of Oreo as a twist-lick-dunk cookie is very luring to kids and teenagers, who are the highest consumers of milk. The brand's adorable ads show children bonding with their parents" (MilksFavoriteCookie, 2014). Oreo's communication strategy is, then, all about originality, creativity, and reactivity. This implies smart ads addressing social responsibility, social support, and appealing products as a link in family relationships (Fernandez, 2018).

When it comes to the perceptions of Oreo, we can state that it is one of the most loved cookie brands by kids. Indeed, the cookie successfully made it to kids' everyday breakfasts, never boring them so that they keep asking for more. Digital natives perceive Oreo as cool, exciting, delicious, and fun. These perceptions are the consequences of the brand's effort to introduce a variety of game-like cookie products, musically inspired innovations, engaging advertisements, and much more.

The youth market is very demanding and changeable. However, because Oreo made it easy to adapt its product, the brand became widely desired and enjoyed. This also means that the younger consumers developed a feeling of loyalty towards the brand. In a survey done in China, results showed that Oreo was increasingly desired by millennials (Jumari, 2017). Oreo succeeded in creating an experience, not only making cookies. On a list of "Kids' Most Loved Brands" in the United States, Oreo cookies scored the highest (PR Newswire, 2015).

How is Oreo redefining the customer experience to attract digital natives?

Oreo persists in delivering creativity and innovation with each product it sells. To attract young consumers, the brand adopted different strategies that made it a top seller cookie and the product of choice in most countries. Oreo is, then, "building personality behind its brand," says David Just, a behavioral economist at Cornell University (Sedacca, 2017). The brand's cookies are differentiated from its competitors by the "crazy" and exciting new flavors the brand offers, instead of sticking to a long-term cookie taste that eventually might get boring.

The brand has also worked on social media campaigns featuring influencers to market its products. For example, during the launch of its Fireworks flavor, influencer Neymar Jr. and actress Ellie Kemper were part of its advertisements. Other engaging strategies include the "Do us a flavor" competition that appeared on social networks. The goal was to engage and give away prizes when consumers suggested their new desired flavors for the next Oreo cookies on the shelves (Sedacca, 2017). The brand is also very active in terms of advocating for social responsibility and diversity. On Gay Pride Day, a cookie was posted on Oreo's official page under a rainbow flag.

Furthermore, the brand moved far and beyond the Oreo as "just" a cookie. Indeed, relying on innovative and creative strategies, Oreo was introduced via online shopping experiences and social media through a variety of technological creations and displays. The Mondelez cookie brand revealed a product that appeals to music fans by creating an Oreo DJ mixer that features three turntables and allows consumers to make music by playing Oreo cookies instead of records (Penfold, 2019).

Other creative ideas were executed by partnering with music stars (Wiz Khalifa) and delivering a music box for consumers to enjoy recording. "You are what you eat," another clever partnership with Snapchat, consisted of scanning packages' codes and unlocking "a Snapchat filter where users were transformed into America's favorite cookie using augmented reality lenses" (Penfold, 2019). Other initiatives and campaigns were introduced such as "Oreo people: show your playful side" to embrace and encourage the weird and the wonderful ones.

What main challenges is Oreo facing to better target young consumers?
The brand, considered a leader in selling cookies' around the world, should carefully maintain its high standards. Indeed, some of its products have received a lot of criticism in terms of taste and ingredients (the new Dough Oreos) (Weiner, 2014). Maintaining quality standards is crucial to the brand's continuity and leading position among its competitors. In addition to maintaining quality, the brand should continue to carefully assess its operating environment (which can differ from one country to another) and deliver products that align with the demands and expectations of each market.

3.3.2 How does Doritos enhance the youth customer experience?

Doritos is a highly favored tortilla chip brand, loved and consumed by people all over the world. Doritos were first introduced in 1964, but not as a product meant to become as popular as the brand currently is. A restaurant in Disneyland called Casa de Fritos invented Doritos when it started reselling old tortillas to people. The tortillas eventually became popular enough that PepsiCo's subsidiary food company, Frito-Lay, introduced them as a tortilla chips brand to the people who favored them.

The brand's first flavor was toasted corn, followed by taco, and then nacho cheese. Nowadays, however, Doritos has a wide range of flavors, from Cool Ranch to Poppin' Jalapeno to Salsa Verde, and more. Doritos even collaborated with different brands to create even more tasty flavors that Doritos lovers would want to try, such as the brand's collaboration with Tapatio Hot Sauce to create spicy red tortilla chips, and its collaboration with Flamin' Hot, which has partnerships with other brands that compete with Doritos, such as Cheetos.

The 56-year-old brand has worked its way up to reach the positioning that it has now. Today, Doritos are the most preferred tortilla chips around the world. The positioning strategy adopted is one of differentiation; Doritos favors treating each of its target markets in the way that it prefers, by adapting its flavors to different cultures.

In a SWOT analysis done for Doritos, it was mentioned that the positioning of Doritos is one of the most important strengths behind the brand, which circulates among the youth group (Bhasin, 2018b). Youths all over the world perceive Doritos as a brand for the bold, with its fiery flavors and crunchy texture. From the feisty colors used, such as red and orange (with a spicy Mexican taste and feel), to the naming of their flavors, such as "Tangy Cheese" and "Heat Burst," all are terms that youth and digital natives specifically can relate to.

Doritos' direct competitors in the chips and snacks industry are mainly its sister companies, Cheetos and Pringles. Both brands are also American made. Cheetos were invented by PepsiCo's subsidiary food company Frito-Lay. Pringles were invented by Kellogg's. Pringles are the "stackable" potato chips placed in a paperboard tube rather than in plastic potato chips bags. Other than the easy and unique packaging Pringles adopts to eliminate excess air in its packages, the brand also has a wider range of flavors for the youth to taste and experiment with. The range is much wider than that of Doritos, which is something that could be of interest to youths, since they despise being limited to a small selection and love being overwhelmed with excitement. A study of how much Doritos and Cheetos were mentioned separately on social media found that Doritos was mentioned 8 percent more often than Cheetos, showing that Doritos is typically more popular among social media users.

Thus, to position itself as a youthful brand among digital natives, Doritos implemented several strategies by creating interesting and fun challenges to target the youth and lock them in as potential customers. The brand excels when it comes to user-generated content. The brand is known to go above and beyond with its ads and challenges, especially during the Super Bowl, the most-awaited and watched football game in the United States. In its annual "Crash the Super Bowl" challenge, sponsored by Doritos, fans are asked to create their best 30-second Doritos ad by showing their love and loyalty towards the brand. A winner is picked with a different prize annually. As much as $1 million has been paid to a winner. The winner's ad is then displayed during the Super Bowl. Youthful fans unleash their innovation and creativity to design and produce their best ads so as to win the challenge and "crash" the Super Bowl. In other words, Doritos aims to make the consumers the stars of its marketing campaigns, breaking the barriers and ice between the company and its consumers.

How does Doritos target digital natives?

Any brand that wants to be relevant and successful in the modern world should always take youths, specifically digital natives, into consideration with their marketing strategies. Doritos constantly tries to make a statement that will grab attention and widen its youthful market. Doritos has made a huge impact in the world of youth-targeting marketing strategies by following two distinct channels (online and offline marketing), becoming the most favored tortilla chips brand in the world, especially among digital natives.

However, in 2018, Doritos ended its annual Crash the Super Bowl challenge after its marketers analyzed the challenge, which started back in 2003. The problem was that, 15 years later, the targeted market for the ad (millennials) were old enough to have kids and, therefore, no longer participated in challenges like this one. Chief Marketing Officer Ram Krishnan told *Business Insider* that the main focus now is on digital natives, and the brand has many plans to extract content from this generation by hosting more user-generated content challenges on a larger scale.

Another youth-targeting marketing campaign, which is more of a hybrid between online and offline channels, is the Doritos "Another Level" campaign. For its offline marketing, Doritos created a logo-less campaign. Billboards all over the United States featured a Doritos ad, only the catch is that the billboards showed a bag of chips without the famous Doritos logo. The ads challenged people to recognize bags of Doritos even without their logos. Doritos was convinced that its young consumers would recognize its "anti-ad" campaign with the logo-less design created by the Doritos team, which would be proof of the brand's strength.

According to Rachel Ferdinando, the senior vice president of core brands of Frito-Lay, the motto "For The Bold" that corresponds to Doritos is now a decade old and outdated. For that reason, the brand will be adopting "Another Level" as its brand motto after looking into digital natives' behaviors and preferences, as well as those of other generations. This motto defines how Doritos challenges people, specifically young consumers, in this case, to take what they love and push it to the next level. Another reason why Ferdinando believes that the new motto could speak better to digital natives is because, after further studying the generation better, they realized that young people care most about authenticity and self-expression. For that Frito-Lay wanted the brand to motivate digital natives to follow what they believe in and be passionate about achieving their hopes and dreams by taking it to "another level."

The "Another Level" campaign turned out to be a huge success and a highly interactive one due to the way it was implemented on social media. Doritos removed all its content and produced a new phase for Doritos where everything was designed without the logo. Fans and followers were asked to show what "Another Level" means to them by crowdsourcing and posting user-generated content. The types of accounts youths favor on social media are those that force them to interact with the account as well as encourage them to take part in challenges and create content for them. This shows why the campaign was a highly successful one for Doritos. The digital ads for this campaign were the largest investment Doritos had ever made, as the brand collaborated with different websites with high exposures to maximize the publicity for this campaign.

To sum up, Doritos goes above and beyond with its marketing campaigns, shifting between online and offline marketing so as to target digital native consumers and grab their attention. The brand is not afraid to try something new, even if it requires removing the brand's logo, which makes up most of a brand's identity. The fact that Frito-Lay did not include the name of the brand in any of its ads and featured only red-and-blue-colored chip bags in its ads on YouTube and TV was a very daring move that was out of the ordinary.

Young people's brand perceptions are different from other generations' in two distinct ways: by preferences and by research. Regarding preferences, almost all generations have different taste buds when it comes to almost anything in their daily lives, which influences their lifestyles and shopping behaviors. Digital natives, for example, care a lot about color coordination, being up on the latest trends, as well as wearing and buying products with visible luxury brand logos. However, older generations, such as the Baby Boomers, care more about convenience and practicality, as well as the quality-to-price ratio. They normally look for things that "get the job done," or, for example, food that satisfies their hunger rather than their appetites.

Second, by research, we mean that the generation looks at a brand's history, its image online, and what it has done to be socially responsible. If a brand produces delicious chips but is not completely socially responsible, it is very easy to boycott the brand as a whole, according to young people. However, other generations, such as the Baby Boomers, barely care about a brand's image and name, or ethics, as long as the product does the job it is meant to do. If a brandless bedding set, for example, covers them and keeps them warm, they could not care less about its design – regardless of whether it is made from faux fur or real fur. Baby Boomers are not as digitally aware of the online resources to check when looking for a brand's actions and stances on socially responsible initiatives.

To dive deeper into our specific case, there are hundreds of different brands for chips and snacks; however, it seems that digital natives have a certain bias or inclination towards Doritos, making it the most favored tortilla chip brand worldwide. For that to happen, it means that Doritos has gone above and beyond to impress youth and succeed, especially to get to the position it is currently in. It also shows that Doritos is a socially responsible and ethical brand that cares about its image, design, and name.

For example, Doritos cares about Gen Z, their interests, their problems, and their communities, especially the LGBTQ+ community. In 2015, Doritos launched Rainbow Doritos, inspired by the LGBTQ+ Pride flag (which is a rainbow). The limited-edition chips were launched in conjunction with the "It Gets Better" project initiated by activist Dan Savage and his partner Terry Miller. The project is home to 630,000 donors and 70,000 storytellers. The Rainbow Doritos were only sold online rather than in supermarkets around the world, and were only available for sale if you donated $10 or more to the cause. The launch of this limited-edition snack not only resulted in donations to support LGBTQ+, but also made a huge statement. The motto behind the flavor, "There's nothing BOLDER than being yourself," encouraged the world and youth generations to be vocal and accepting of themselves and others, no matter how different they might be. Youths nowadays want to normalize the differences between people. Doritos took an explicit and daring step to stand next to them and support their cause. This helped build an emotional connection between digital natives and the brand.

Another incident that occurred with Doritos in 2018 was the development of "lady-friendly chips," which became a highly controversial topic among digital natives who happen to be feminists. Indra Nooyi, the CEO of PepsiCo (Doritos' owner), had observed data showing that women prefer not to "crunch too loudly" or "lick their fingers too generously," which influenced the brand to create pink Doritos that were less crunchy and less powdery.

However, a publicist for the brand suggested that the limited-edition chip was nothing but a rumor, stating that Doritos already had a flavor dedicated to women called "Doritos." In other words, Doritos is genderless and is meant for all people, who are treated equally. The rumor had a negative impact on the brand's perception, most likely due to digital natives. As a result, Doritos made a public statement apologizing for the misconceptions people had of its intentions.

Lastly, a recent incident occurred in the United States when George Floyd, an African-American citizen, was murdered by a policeman in 2020. The murder sparked huge protests across the country and became a rallying cry for the Black Lives Matter political movement. The BLM movement inspired many businesses to show their social responsibility and awareness of the movement. Businesses went above and beyond to show how they value racial equality. On its social media accounts Doritos posted positive statements supporting the movement, and black artists and other people told their stories and showed their murals on the platforms. Doritos' social media planners amplified black voices and opinions when the hype began to cool down, which shows digital natives that Doritos is trying to keep the movement at the forefront until proper justice is served and white supremacy is over.

How is Doritos redefining customer experience to attract digital natives?
Doritos has made quite a few statements in the world of experiential marketing, all thanks to its professional marketing team. This team continues to study
digital natives' behaviors, such as how fast they want an experience to last
before they get "bored." To grab the attention of young consumers, Doritos
has used three different approaches to target them by creating customer experiences that enhance brand loyalty.

First, Doritos created experiential campaigns to test their young customers'
brand loyalty towards Doritos. The first campaign was the famous logo-less
chips campaign in 2019. Doritos was quick to realize that digital natives'
enemies are overt marketers. For that reason, they chose to drop the logo and
show digital natives that they are totally over this obvious type of marketing
and that the brand genuinely cares about pleasing its customers. This in turn
increased the brand loyalty youths have towards Doritos, as these people
succumbed to the logo-less campaign. Doritos won the emotions of this youth
generation through this campaign and built more trust in their community. The
"Another Level" customer experience was a very important, brave, and bold
move for Doritos. Digital natives will expect nothing less from now on. The
campaign showed that the brand is "for the bold."

Doritos also tested its brand loyalty among digital natives when it
launched the Doritos "mystery" flavors in 2014. Doritos launched three new
silver-packaged Doritos with its famous logo colored in red, yellow, or blue,
which revealed a tiny hint about the mystery flavor of the chips. The packaging
also included a "test number" to add more mystery to each flavor. The experience created by the marketing team was somewhat like an online scavenger
hunt to reveal what flavor each of the bags of chips was. Next, Doritos asked
its customers to vote for their favorite flavor. The chip with the highest number
of votes became a new addition to the Doritos family. Also, Doritos gave away
$1,000 in gold to random voters daily, which goes back to the meaning behind
the brand's name *dorado*, which is Latin for gold.

Moreover, to build a youthful, interesting, and eye-grabbing customer experience aimed at digital natives, Doritos used the biggest hub for young people,
which is social media and digital technology. In 2018, Doritos launched its
"For the Bold" campaign in Belgium, where the brand was not very popular
or considered to be as bold as it preaches. To raise awareness about the campaign, the team built a fully digital customer experience on social media that
revolved around daring and bold activities. The team also challenged Belgian
influencers to go on wild experiences as part of Doritos' "What Do You
Dare" campaign. The campaign challenged them to go skydiving blindfolded
or zipline backwards and post videos of these challenges online. To increase
engagement, digital natives were asked to vote for their favorite challenges,
and an influencer had to participate in the highest-voted challenge, giving

followers what they wanted. The campaign created a huge fuss online, and Doritos gained more than 400,000 viewers on YouTube and 1 million reaches on Facebook.

Another action involved Doritos creating challenges that would act as a great foundation to build the most entertaining and interactive customer experience aimed at the youth market. What Doritos did was specifically for the brand's 50th anniversary in 2016, for which it launched its Bold 50 campaign. The effort involved achieving 50 world records, all including a Doritos chip somewhere. Some of the records set were, for example, the highest location to eat a Doritos chip, or the tallest house of cards built using Doritos, or even the furthest distance a Doritos chip could travel and be tossed into a person's mouth. Fans were excited to participate and break these records in honor of Doritos' birthday. The campaign showed just how bold the brand is and how daredevil the fans were.

When it comes to leveraging technology to create unforgettable experiences targeting the youth market, the biggest social media campaign Doritos came up with was the previously mentioned "Crash the Super Bowl" challenge, which required the participants to create an ad tagging Doritos and share it on social media platforms. This digital marketing campaign sparked the interest of tens of thousands of participants around the globe, caused a huge social media buzz internationally, and gave Doritos more and more recognition as a brand.

User-generated content (UGC) has also showed that digital natives fans have huge brand loyalty towards Doritos, and enable even greater reach to the fans' families and friends through social media channels. UGC has also proven how much it can help the brand understand how its fans talk, who its fans are, as well as what they want to see more of from the brand. Some of the important highlights of the outcomes of the event included airing all five finalists' ads during the 2007 challenge; another was the launch of one of the participant's musical careers after composing an original song for a Doritos ad. So, this shows that social media and digital technologies can affect a person's future, which is one of the qualities digital natives look for in a brand – something that promises them a bright future or otherwise motivates them to build one.

Another way of leveraging these technologies is to create a greater social media presence so as to lure young consumers to the brand. To do this, the brand launched its Doritos Mix Cheese Explosion flavor, a new line of chips that included different shapes of chips and cheesy flavors. As part of the campaign for the product, Doritos built a six-story technological and retro arcade in Los Angeles with gaming features and youth-friendly music. This campaign was conducted in collaboration with Twitch, the biggest social video platform for gamers around the globe. Twitch allowed online users to watch the launch. Twitch and Doritos also invited digital native-friendly musicians such as Steve Aoki and Wiz Khalifah to perform on a concert stage in the arcade for three consecutive nights. During the event, Doritos customized a technological experience for its gaming fans by allowing them to control various elements of the musical and gaming experiences via personalized LED wristbands. The wristbands also gave fans the opportunity to unlock bonus content and features with the push of a button.

Doritos collaborated with Twitch again in 2018 to host the "Doritos Bowl," another Doritos-filled experience for the brand's young fans who are passionate about gaming. Doritos chose to feature the most famous gamers on the planet to compete in a tournament of the game "Call Of Duty" (or as digital natives like to call it, CoD). Doritos took the gaming experience to new heights by sponsoring and creating a huge competition for their fans' favorite players globally in the most highly-anticipated game. The event took place in TwitchCon, at the San Jose Convention Center in California, which is home to thousands of passionate gamers, all ready to experience what they called an "epic" event, while consuming their favorite Doritos snacks, watching cosplay models, and even donating to huge fundraisers.

What are the main challenges Doritos is facing to better target young consumers?
The first challenge that Doritos needs to face is joining TikTok, the ultimate hub for digital natives. TikTok is a popular social media platform that is very easy to use and can provide a company with an effortless social media presence and growth. Launched in 2016, TikTok has proven to be one of the most influential social media applications ever because it is a hub for all teenagers and targeted audiences for huge brands. Because it has made its mark in the world of social media and among digital natives, businesses have hurried to leverage TikTok to achieve easy growth by creating increasingly interesting content specifically tailored for young consumers. The content can include recipes, dance challenges, lip-syncing, or any other trends young consumers follow. Doritos needs to take a bold move and create a TikTok account to expand its social media presence and build more brand exposure among digital natives.

In 2020, Doritos collaborated with singer Lil Nas X to create the dance challenge #CoolRanchDance. It started when Lil Nas X starred in Doritos' Super Bowl 2020 ad as the sheriff of the Cool Ranch. There he challenges Sam Elliott to a Wild West dance battle set to Lil Nas X's top song, "Old Town Road." The ad has more than 12.6 million views on YouTube and sparked more than 3,000 TikTokers to recreate the Cool Ranch dance challenge. This in turn provided Doritos with more brand loyalty from its digital native followers, as well as leveraging the "challenge" community on TikTok to generate more positivity among its users – and promote Cool Ranch Doritos chips in a new way. However, collaborating with TikTok stars from outside the platform is very different than collaborating from the inside: if Doritos had an account on

TikTok and then created this dance challenge with Lil Nas X, there would have been much more engagement and exposure. This is especially true if Doritos had reposted its favorite dances on its verified account. This would have prompted more young people to participate in the dance challenge and created a better connection with them and built loyalty to the brand.

Another challenge Doritos could face relates to corporate social responsibility. Some accusations have been made to the effect that PepsiCo needs to take more corporate social responsibility. The company received some bad press after it came to light that Doritos were made using unsustainable palm oil harvested on land reclaimed by burning down rainforests. However, PepsiCo states that this is untrue, and that the accusations, which were made by the activist group Sum of Us, are patently false and mischaracterized PepsiCo. PepsiCo continued to defend its stance of corporate social responsibility by ensuring that its palm oil is sustainable and is produced with no deforestation occurring.

3.4   Designing Youth Customer Experiences in Fashion

Nike is a leading sportswear brand. The company worked on different aspects and has taken various strategic approaches to reach wider markets and more consumers. Nike has done so by adapting to market evolution and trends and shifting its tactics to a more personalized and customized promotion of products (Safdar, 2019). Nike delved into digital data collecting methods through its apps, ensuring a customized optimization of product preferences for consumers. Nike's advertising slogans became very popular and influential. "Just Do It" is an example. The company takes its slogans seriously in the way it engages itself with the community.

In an interview, Nike founder Phil Knight explains that the company acknowledges the attention it attracts and, therefore, uses it to implement socially responsible projects, such as sports clinics for youth. "We're underwriting a series called Ghostwriting that the Children's Television Workshop is developing to teach kids how to read and write," says Knight. "We're doing it because we think it's the right thing to do, but we also want the visibility" (Willigan, 1992).

How does Nike target digital natives?
The company's intelligent strategies engage younger generations by allowing them to feel like part of a challenging movement. This is fueled by Nike's YouTube channels, hashtags, TikTok, and many other easily accessible social media tools – tools that allow young people to create their own fun and purposeful content (Maguire, 2020).

Nike succeeded in impacting younger customers through its supportive social-purpose strategies that encourage young girls and boys to fire-up and feel ready to do it! As Nike spokesperson Vizhier Corpus smartly stated: "If you are a parent interested in raising a girl, who is physically and emotionally strong, then look to sports as a means to that end" (Vilá and Bharadwaj, 2017).

In addition, Nike's retail distribution strategy raised marketing standards in the field and became a successful reference for its competitors (Danziger, 2017). Nike's Triple Double Strategy aims to double its "cadence and impact of innovation, its speed to market and double its direct connections with consumers" (Danziger, 2018). This strategy increased Nike's revenues, which grew rapidly between 2018 and 2019. The emotional ties it creates with its consumers is another influential approach to attract loyal and long-term customers. Phil Knights says: "To create a lasting emotional tie with consumers, we use the athletes repeatedly throughout their careers and present them as whole people. So, consumers feel that they know them" (Willigan, 1992).

Nike managed to establish values that express ethical support to youth communities. A section on Nike's website is all about helping kids lead healthy and active lives. The company's "storytelling" technique in its marketing campaigns inspires both young people and adults, motivating them to achieve what they think they cannot achieve (Ghausi, 2018). Nike's ads rarely feature its products; instead, the ads inspire the audience by building "emotional branding" (Islam, 2020). Moreover, the company is all about spreading videos that show young persons (and not athletes) challenging themselves to "just do it"; it labels these advertisements under "Find your Greatness," for example, an encouraging statement to do what you think you cannot do.

The socially conscious activities add to the aspects of loyalty this brand is creating. One of these activities is "innovating to get kids moving." On its news website, Nike challenges the idea that kids are "made to play." Instead, Nike claims that kids are also "made to train." The statement is then elaborated on by digital resources the company provides that help kids and their families stay active indoors.

Nike is aiming to "help children cultivate a healthy relationship with movement so that living healthy becomes a sustainable part of their lives" (Nike News, 2020a). A more in-depth analysis of the content of this news page reveals that "sustainability" is achieved by motivating kids to be in motion and active, which "creates emotion for athletes of all ages and abilities," says Nike Master Trainer Brian Nunez.

Likewise, Nike is targeting youth by being transparent and real in its ads and campaigns, some of which are controversial. Millennials are very much impressed by this directness, which could affect older generations differently (or even negatively) (Masunaga, 2018). "Nike by You" introduces a whole new level of brand personalization by making products more unique and customized to the personal preferences of buyers. For example, NikePlus members can have one-on-one sessions with a designer to customize select shoes – adding dip-dye, embroidery, and more – and walk away with uniquely designed footwear.

Nike's commitment to sports and fitness made it a strong, if not the ultimate, choice for shy younger consumers who want to get involved. The platform it introduces is simple, fun, and exciting. The younger generation is attracted to the brand's creativity. In fact, in a statistical survey posted on *Business Insider*'s website, 72 percent of teens said Nike was their favorite activewear label. The study revealed these young consumers have positive perceptions of Nike's training programs and athletes' corners. This young generation disagrees with their parents, who prefer to diet instead of engage in physical activity. Young consumers believe exercising is essential for being healthy and fit, which is exactly how Nike is delivering its message (Lutz, 2015). As such, the company has taken a more realistic approach, which has impacted the younger generation emotionally and personally, who appreciate transparency.

That brings us to an additional perspective – one that describes young consumers as motivated and encouraged to stay active and in motion. The fact that Nike presents its campaigns as the main motivator to become more active and stay healthy builds appreciation and optimism among younger consumers, who develop loyalty and preferences for such reliable and supportive brands.

On another note, younger consumers are inspired by the athletes and celebrities that Nike utilizes in its marketing strategy. These consumers appreciate a certain path that summarizes strength, challenges, and achievements and builds trust towards the brand. Younger consumers prefer Nike over other brands because it works to establish strong bonds of trust, honesty, and practicality with its customers.

How is Nike redefining the customer experience to attract digital natives?
Nike's success in becoming one of the toughest competitors in the sportswear market is greatly related to its intelligent and innovative marketing and advertising strategies. Indeed, Nike is listed on the Forbes list of the Worlds' Most Powerful Companies (Madden, 2012). The way the company redefined the fashion experience was by making its products more desirable. Spike Lee is an example of how powerful Nike's selection of an advertising strategy is. The Jordan Brand Lee took on as a project was realized in an engaging yet desirable way, which made it more of a lifestyle product, far beyond sports (Madden, 2012).

Nike's Triple Double Strategy is all about innovation, "service and delivery to market, and an intensified connection to consumers" (Ingvaldsen, 2019). Such diversification and customization directly impact younger consumers who feel they have a say in the products they are buying. The company scored top in fashion and style, and loyalty, and continues to be the leader in all key categories relating to consumers.

The company continues to take the sport fashion experience to a different level by selecting young athletes to wear its products through sponsorships with local leagues, clubs, and federations (Lutz, 2015). Nike's partnership with professional athletes also inspires young consumers to select it as their brand of choice.

Moreover, Nike persists in making sports fashion a valuable experience by highlighting consumers' creativity and engagement. NikeCraft, for example, is a digital workshop experience designed to "inform, inspire, and foster a creative community" (Nike News, 2020b). Interestingly enough, the company keeps its consumers, especially the young ones, challenged through its digital platform to "Just Do It." The platform helps them surpass their limits and gets them on the move to exercise and play sports. Different challenges on the platform are led and posted by athlete celebrities, such as the football player Cristiano Ronaldo. The Ronaldo initiative was launched by Nike and called "The Living Room Cup." It is a digital workout series that offers a new space to compete against Nike pro athletes via weekly fitness challenges.

When it comes to leveraging digital media and technology to design the ultimate sports fashion experience aimed at digital natives, Nike takes very seriously its commitment towards innovation and creativity. The company's platforms are now a benchmark of influence and engagement in marketing and promotions. Younger consumers are easily attracted to these digital platforms, whether they are on social media, Nike's website, or apps created by Nike.

For example, Nike's Phenomenal Shot was created after a partnership with Google during the FIFA 2014 World Cup. In conjunction with Google, consumers could enjoy their favorite players in 3D in real-time and personalize them with filters, captions, and stickers (Islam, 2020).

Nike's self-lacing shoes were another successful and influential technological achievement the company offered to young consumers, relieving them from worrying about their laces or tripping on them when they are loose. The HyperAdapt is a shoe that includes sensors and automatically molds shoes to the shape of people's feet when they step into them. This exciting product was ultimately successful and desired, and promised a future for other exciting products yet to be created. "Winner Stays" was one of Nike's most successful ads. It featured teenage boys transforming into football superstars, making them fierce players during a game. The ad received more than 107.8 million views.

Nike's platforms are all about data collecting, aiming at gathering more personalized information about their consumers to promote their favorite, most preferred, products. Most importantly, the company has aced its role on social media, orienting its content towards a conversation, and not just product postings and promotions. This commitment is indicative of the use of a lot of engagement with consumers to build their excitement, specifically the excitement of young consumers.

The main challenges Nike is facing to better target young consumers
Due to increasing competition, Nike is under a lot of pressure to maintain its leading position in the younger consumers' market. The company should correct what critics cite as negative factors (the use of child labor by its suppliers, unfair working conditions, and so on) (Rizwan et al., 2016). That argument is supported by the fact that the younger generations are much more informed, through online platforms, about all sorts of news and trends in the market. To avoid falling into a controversial debate and losing customers because of negative media attention, Nike should invest in responding to its internal weaknesses and bettering its position vis-à-vis the critiques.

Additionally, Nike should not back down on its commitment to innovation and creativity. Any shortage (or disappointment) in product delivery will be severely criticized and judged by its fans, especially after raising the bar high. Since those targeted are young consumers, Nike should carefully reassess its pricing strategies: the more expensive it is, the fewer young consumers the company will have. Young people would rather get high-quality products (e.g., Adidas, UnderArmour, and Reebook brands) and spend less money on Nike products. Price revisiting is essential in this sense, especially when the competition for this young, promising market is becoming more aggressive.

Because Nike already acknowledges the importance of creating trends and responding to market changes, the company should maintain this level of commitment in regards to the young consumers' market spending evolution. Maintaining social engagement is another important aspect of ensuring Nike's stability as a leader of influential sportswear brands.

3.5   Designing Youth Customer Experiences in the Services Sector

This section discusses two companies that are also competitors: Starbucks and Dunkin' Donuts. Both are targeting digital natives by designing suitable and enjoyable customer experiences aimed at the youth market.

3.5.1   Is Starbucks offering the ultimate coffee experience to youth?
Starbucks is a world-renowned coffeehouse chain that has more than 30,000 stores around the world. It was founded in Seattle in 1971 by Jerry Baldwin, Gordon Bowker, and Zev Siegl. Today it is the most popular coffeehouse and coffee bean roaster in the world; every person is likely to try Starbucks at least once in his or her lifetime. The company is known for mixing different flavors of syrups and creamers with different types of coffee beans from all over the

world, such as Nariño from Colombia, the French Roast, Caffe Verona, as well as Ethiopian and Kenyan roasts.

People, especially digital natives, are known to be "hooked" on Starbucks, with their coffee dates almost always meaning a Starbucks date. For that reason, Starbucks positions itself as a relatively iconic and "young" brand. It has a special marketing strategy targeting youngsters who order their iced caramel lattes before pulling all-nighters to study for their exams. Starbucks also strives to become people's "third place" after their homes and their workplaces. This means that going to Starbucks has become part of their routine and not just an outing.

Likewise, the Starbucks "secret menu" (which is no longer a secret) is an unpublished menu with more than 200 different flavors created by Starbucks fans. Mostly, digital natives are the ones who keep up with the new trends created by the Starbucks secret menu lovers, taking aesthetic pictures of the famous pink drink, or unicorn drink, and posting them on social media to show their aesthetically pleasing drinks to their friends. Doing so increases the word-of-mouth about the secret menu. The Starbucks secret menu was created by Starbucks baristas who love inventing new flavors and experimenting with different syrups and creamers until they can achieve the perfect taste for people. However, when customers order a drink from the secret menu, they need to give the barista specific measurements and ingredients, because not all baristas are aware of every single Starbucks flavor.

Regarding the competition in the coffee shop marketplace, Starbucks' biggest competitors are Tim Hortons (also known as the Canadian Starbucks) and Dunkin' Donuts. In a study done by Sukhpal Saini in Canada, 8 out of 20 people are more likely to get Starbucks, whereas 6 out of these 20 people are more likely to get coffee from Tim Hortons. Some people surveyed said Timmies (Tim Hortons) is cheaper but that Starbucks is a place for sitting down and occasions. Starbucks is known to be more upscale and luxurious than Timmies, whereas Timmies gives more of a friendly and traditional vibe to its drinkers. Starbucks is also slightly more expensive than Timmies but offers more value (12 oz. for a small cup of Starbucks versus 10 oz. for a small cup at Timmies). Both Starbucks' and Dunkin's marketing strategies and coffee options are relatively similar. However, despite Starbucks being 20 years younger than Dunkin', it has substantially higher annual revenues.

How is Starbucks targeting digital natives?
Starbucks' new targeted customers – digital natives – cannot be in the same marketing mix as its other coffee consumers because the coffee chain is not a one-size-fits-all type of model. Instead, Starbucks works on enhancing the current coffee experience by attracting digital natives with its four favorite strategies, the 4 Ds: dependency, digital, dedication, and dialogue.

Dependency. Starbucks is currently realizing that its wider audience, if not a more specific one, consists of teenagers who are digital natives and Starbucks' upcoming coffee addicts. Unlike cigarettes and alcohol, no law prohibits children from coffee consumption, which is why you can always find teens entering schools with Starbucks branded white cups filled with their favorite coffees and creamers. Starbucks is not sure whether or not it will add any items that appeal directly to kids' and teens' preferences, aside from the company's current milk and hot chocolate options. However, Starbucks can already see that teens are ordering 16 oz. Caramel Frappuccinos, which are three times more caffeinated than a 12 oz. can of Pepsi. Starbucks also observes how this youth generation depends on coffee to concentrate on studying for their exams and even just waking up in the morning.

Digital. Starbucks has also moved its marketing strategies to digital natives' favorite channel, which is digital media. Social media is probably the only thing more addictive than coffee for this youth generation. For that reason, Starbucks rode the digital natives' bus to learn all types of slang and dialect that youths normally use to implement them on its social media platforms. This new communication style is the new trendy language, especially for digital natives because they can fully absorb and dissect it. That is the sole reason why Starbucks now has 18.2 million followers on Instagram alone, proving its successful stance. Digital natives tag the Starbucks account and connect with their fellow Starbucks addicts, forming an online community that shares photos while drinking their favorite coffees. Similarly, Starbucks' Tweet-a-Coffee campaign in 2013 on Twitter helped the brand gain recognition on social media. The campaign asked people to tag their friends' accounts and "@tweetacoffee," which would give them access to a $5 coupon, thereby improving Starbucks' direct response with users.

Dedication. Starbucks proved how loyal digital natives are when 70 percent of the consumers promised to come back to the brand that they love. For that reason, Starbucks is dedicated to serving these young customers in the most generous way possible: by granting them access to free music and apps after they subscribe to the company's "My Starbucks Rewards" program via Starbucks' app. Now, instead of reaching for their wallets, they reach for their phones to pay for their drinks or claim their rewards. This program in turn creates brand loyalty because the youth feel like Starbucks genuinely cares about them enough to grant them all these freebies.

Dialogue. Starbucks' seating area harkens back to the days where people would meet face-to-face instead of meeting on their webcams. Because 87 percent of youths would much rather meet in the digital world than in the real world, according to a Cisco study, Starbucks acts as the midpoint between the two. The company does so by persuading digital natives to come to meet up with their friends and families at Starbucks' urban-like upscale coffeehouse, creating an environment and culture where digital natives feel comfortable going out and interacting with people face-to-face.

When it comes to the perception of Starbucks across different youth consumption cultures, a study was conducted by surveying 300 young people to see how loyal they were to the company. For what reason do they owe such immense loyalty towards Starbucks? Most of the criteria related to the sweet coffee smells that attract these customers, as well as the great variety of Starbucks' high-quality coffee. Customers were also keen on following Starbucks' corporate social responsibility projects as well as website innovations. For these reasons, we can see that Starbucks' younger consumers perceive the brand to be one with a reputable image due to its popularity among people in general, as well as a brand that follows up on its corporate social responsibility initiatives. This is an interest digital natives have with regard to any brand.

These young consumers prefer Starbucks to McDonald's now. Gone are the days when these youths got excited over a Big Mac; instead, they are now more excited about Iced Caramel Macchiatos. According to Goldman Sachs, this youth generation is more likely to visit a coffee shop (Starbucks) than a burger joint (McDonald's). Starbucks has higher brand equity and a more favorable image among younger customers than McDonald's in general. This partly results from the design of its coffee shops, which attract youths more than cheap-looking food courts. Coffee shops make young people feel like they are successful grownups going out on coffee dates before or after work.

From what Starbucks spokesperson Brandon Borrman has seen, Starbucks has now become more of a family destination, with younger customers who are less than 18 years old being their regular customers and most often ordering heavily caffeinated drinks. Borrman suggests that Seattle-born Starbucks should take responsibility for these young consumers because even if they perceive the brand to offer a safe space where they can drink coffee and "act older," it does not mean that Starbucks should encourage that indirect influence. Instead, Starbucks should offer more "kid-friendly" menu options – more than just hot chocolate and milk – or at least provide sizes smaller than a 12 oz. drink.

How does Starbucks redefine the coffee experience to connect with digital natives?

When we refer to customer experience, we are talking about something much broader than a mere product or a small service that involves targeting the consumer's emotions and five senses when entering a shop. For that reason, Starbucks intends to enhance its highly loved customer experience by improving its coffee making and reintroducing its favored coffee bean smell, which customers notice when they enter a Starbucks store. In so doing, Starbucks focuses on three aspects, experience, product, and social responsibility, to redefine its customer experience to attract more consumers – especially youngsters.

Experience. Starbucks went above and beyond by redesigning its store layouts and aesthetics to provide a more welcoming hangout place for its young consumers who normally meet out for coffee. What it did exactly was design a relatable atmosphere, depending on the region in which a store is located. For example, in New York, Starbucks designed its stores to give consumers a more Broadway-like, theatrical feel with loft designs and spotlights. In the South, however, Starbucks designed its stores to be reminiscent of farms or beaches, which are more likely to be seen there. This can give youths a sense of belonging because whatever surrounds them at Starbucks reminds them of home. Also, Starbucks designed its new drive-thru experience to give youths the "home-away-from-home" feel.

Product. Whatever is Instagrammable is digital natives' favorite new drink, which is why Starbucks goes above and beyond when creating new flavors or packaging ideas. The company established Starbucks Reserve, which is a "lab-like" roastery, to experiment with different flavors before rolling them out to customers. Nitro Cold Brew and Cascara Latte are Starbucks' iconic coffee experiments that made it onto the menu and became popular among young consumers, especially after cold brew became the new hipster trend in 2016. Other than drinks, Starbucks also invested in its food business by introducing new items on its food menus, such as on-the-go salads, sandwiches, and egg bites. These menu items became digital natives' favorites, especially after studying at Starbucks for three-plus hours and getting hungry; they no longer have to leave Starbucks for lunch or dinner. They can now stay and order food there.

Social responsibility. Due to how international and world-renowned Starbucks is, its sustainability and social responsibility measures must continue to be highly recognized to remain in the industry, especially in an era when climate change is the biggest concern for the future of the world. By 2020, Starbucks aimed to commit to purchase 100 percent ethically produced coffee beans, according to its Coffee and Farmer Equity Program. This action of corporate social responsibility could attract thousands of sustainability-driven digital natives, who are now more concerned, active, and vocal than any other generation to date about CSR. Also, Starbucks aims to decrease food waste. In 2016, it partnered with Feeding America by donating leftover foods before closing time every day. Starbucks hopes to deliver 50 million meals as a result of this initiative and avert 60 million pounds of food waste from entering landfills.

Furthermore, to design effective and enjoyable coffee experiences, Starbucks leverages technology to connect with digital natives. CEO Kevin Johnson was once asked whether Starbucks is considered a "tech-company." Johnson agreed it was because Starbucks is no longer just your local coffeehouse that you grab your coffee from and leave. Instead, it is now a destination built on experiential modern retail, which is why Starbucks has now extended its customer relationships by entering the world of digital.

Because Starbucks considers itself to be "the third place" people go to after home and work, the company must create an innovative digital experience for younger consumers to validate this image. To increase Starbucks' mobile app usage, the company had to develop a new project to retain users of the app. One of Starbucks' projects was the loyalty program on the app, which lets consumers collect points from their orders and redeem a free drink or meal with their points. These efforts worked. Starbucks found that the number of daily active uses of the app increased by 14 percent in less than one year.

Moreover, with regard to the experiential aspect of Starbucks, according to Netguru, Starbucks' digital transformation started when coffee was linked to data. Because Starbucks generates almost 90 million transactions weekly all around the world, it has a massive amount of data to analyze so as to understand and to shape consumers' preferences and tailor a good customer experience. Subsequently, Starbucks' Digital Flywheel initiative was born. The initiative mainly focuses on four distinct pillars to shape the company's online marketing, namely rewards, personalization, payment, and orders. The brand also aims to shorten waiting lines as well as make the Starbucks experience more convenient.

From these pillars, Starbucks can learn to understand and leverage these data-pulling technologies to create personalized experiences for its digital native customers, who very much prefer such experiences. The key is to understand what coffees each customer is ordering, how their taste varies by weather and time, and adjust Starbucks' offers to them accordingly. These personalized offerings can help lock in the digital native customers and increase sales by being more cost-efficient.

Likewise, social media, which is the digital native's middle name, plays a huge role when implemented well. Due to Starbucks' unique branding and aesthetically pleasing content, young consumers are head over heels in love with the brand. On Instagram, digital natives can learn new Starbucks recipes to recreate at home, have their creative Starbucks photography reposted, as well as read new articles about coffee and new trends.

UGC is also one of the main pillars of digital marketing; it is where Starbucks leverages the art of free marketing from its loyal customers. Consider the pumpkin spice latte, which has been a huge hit for Starbucks and the biggest autumn drink trend to date: people have created memes and even made accounts with that name, which Starbucks has reposted to boost its marketing among digital natives and push sales up further.

What are the main challenges Starbucks is facing to retain young consumers?
Starbucks, in particular, could face numerous problems when trying to target digital natives, especially since it is shifting from an adult experience and incorporating it into teenage life. Coffee and caffeine, in general, are scientifically better for people over 18 years old. Consequently, convincing digital natives and their parents that coffee-drinking is not as harmful as people think it could be a problem for Starbucks. However, because today's youth consider coffee to be socially acceptable to drink, even for those under 18, they have solved more than half the challenges Starbucks may have encountered along the way. Parents no longer think coffee is "forbidden fruit" for their children.

While Starbucks is working on its digital transformation, its mobile application and online loyalty program are no longer enough for young consumers; every other brand is already doing the same. Consequently, Starbucks faces a technological problem in the digital age, because it is somewhat behind on the digital aspect of the brand. It needs to improve its existing features, whether they are on its mobile application or its website or are related to the company's e-commerce. The company has to innovate and think of ways to create new features digital natives can enjoy. This generation is known as a "fast" generation: they want everything to change, and they get bored easily, which is why Starbucks has to work fast before its young consumers switch to a more innovative and technologically aware coffee brand. Starbucks should also consider improving its coffee-making machines to prepare more coffee in a shorter amount of time and, therefore, offer a super-fast service for its impatient young consumers.

Other than technology, Starbucks could be facing a challenge financially. Increasing its prices by leveraging customer loyalty can only go on for so long. When targeting a new, younger market of people who may not have jobs yet and only small allowances, it's hard to imagine them being addicted to something that may be out of their reach financially. Starbucks is known among digital natives as the "expensive" coffee place, meaning that it is only for occasions and not a routine-like destination after home and work, as Starbucks aims to be.

3.5.2 How does Dunkin' Donuts attract digital natives?

Dunkin' Donuts defines itself as the world's leading baked goods and coffee chain. The company serves more than 3 million customers every day. Its website states: "True to our name, we offer 50-plus varieties of donuts, but you can also enjoy dozens of premium beverages, bagels, breakfast sandwiches, and other baked goods." The company has more than 11,300 restaurants worldwide. It has 8,500 restaurants in 41 states across the United States, and over 3,200 international restaurants across 36 countries.

The company's competitive edge is its ability to look for the best buys at lower prices. Its locations across the globe makes it an easy choice for young customers. The accessibility of its stores makes it a quick choice for delicious bites and tasty hot drinks. The company's marketing strategy is all about exploring new menu items and innovating products, as well as effectively reflecting this on digital platforms, reachable to all. Dunkin' Donuts has continued to innovate in the mobile and digital technology space while loyalty programs and one-to-one marketing have become critical components for growth and differentiation among coffee and QSR (quick-service restaurant) brands (Olenski, 2017). The company's focus on mobile apps gives it an edge with its younger customers.

How does Dunkin' Donuts target digital natives?
Dunkin' Donuts has been able to make a significant shift in terms of making its products attractive and desired. Indeed, the company maintains a marketing strategy of understanding its younger customers' expectations and provides them with excellent and quick customer service by cutting order times and waiting lines (Bohannon, 2017). The company's logo is fascinating with its fun colors and has a memorable effect on young people. Moreover, the way Dunkin' presents its donuts in colorful boxes and with attractive toppings is perceived as appealing and desirable by young people. Another important aspect of the company's strategy is making its prices affordable to younger consumers and providing them with promotions, discount coupons, and many other innovative and money-saving tools.

Furthermore, younger consumers are infatuated with Dunkin' Donuts products. They are considered delicious and tasty, easy to buy, and affordable. More importantly, the company has worked on building trust with its customers. Young consumers value trust, which is a core component to building a stable relationship with the company. These customers are in constant interaction with Dunkin' Donuts. It is a youth's favorite brand for its quick delicious bites and money-saving expenditures. Dunkin' Donuts also plays an important role in interacting with younger customers. The people who work in its stores are friendly, helpful, and enjoy serving them.

How does Dunkin' Donuts redefine the customer experience to attract digital natives?
Dunkin' Donuts created a mobile application that effectively serves its younger customers and keeps them engaged and active with the brand. Dunkin' Donuts, loyalty program, DD Perks®, is designed to provide the company's customers with rich, personalized experiences via the delivery of content and offers relevant to their individual preferences (Salesforce, 2016).

The company uses television ads that are exciting and fun and positively impact both older and younger customers. Dunkin' redefines the customer experience by planning events via its social media presence, maintaining interactive websites, through advertising, signage, the in-store environment, the company's community presence, and, of course, the product itself (Deal, 2010).

Dunkin' Donuts also makes sure to set the bar high when mixing its strategies with technologies. The company has diversified the way in which it promotes its products to attract a wider base of fans and younger customers. Dunkin's tagline is "America runs on Dunkin'" and the company's cheeky TV spots poke fun at "highfalutin" sounding coffee with esoteric names available at more upscale shops (Deal, 2010). Dunkin' has also created catchy slogans aired on TV and radio. The company also sponsors activities such as Liverpool Football Club and the New York Mets. In addition, Dunkin' keeps in touch with its loyal fans via Twitter and Facebook and various other promotional activities (Bhasin, 2020).

The main challenges Dunkin' Donuts is facing to better target young consumers
One challenge the company faces is being able to adapt to constant environmental pressures and changes. Anything that could impact its prices has a direct impact on its younger customers, who appreciate high quality and cheaper prices. Also, Dunkin' Donuts must strive to maintain its leading position in its industry and work hard to keep moving forward.

KEY TAKEAWAYS

The key takeaways from this chapter show that the emerging behaviors and needs among young people have contributed to a changing competitive environment and, therefore, to the levers of a brand's appeal. Thus, a company's competitive advantage goes beyond the functionalities offered by brands. It now plays out in the experience digital natives have with a brand and the emotions that flow from it. The integration of the emotional, relational, ideological, symbolic, hedonic, and subjective dimensions of an online and offline offering aimed at young people are vital for companies to meet the expectations of young consumers and build their long-term loyalty. Therefore, an experiential youth marketing strategy that incorporates four components, namely a youth's individual characteristics, social and economic interactions, factors related to the lived experience, and the physical environment, are needed to design suitable and engaging customer experiences charged with positive emotions offered both online and offline.

9. How to study youth consumption cultures: towards immersive market research tools

CHAPTER OVERVIEW

This chapter tackles questions related to the obsolescence of quantitative tools used in market research to examine digital natives' behaviors and attitudes towards brands and products. In this chapter, I introduce exploratory and immersive tools companies should utilize to develop an in-depth understanding of the youth market and its paradoxes. Immersive and exploratory market research methods bring together a set of tools relevant to the study of young people's offline and online consumer experiences and cultures. These immersive and interactive tools allow companies to explore the meanings young consumers assign to their consumption practices and decode the symbolic, emotional, and subjective dimensions that emerge during an encounter with a product or service. The chapter will focus on exploratory qualitative methods and new tools to understand and analyze youth behaviors and attitudes within different youth consumption cultures.

1. THE LIMITS OF QUANTITATIVE SURVEYS AND THE RISE OF EXPLORATORY MARKET RESEARCH TO STUDY YOUNG CONSUMERS

The market research sector has changed a lot over the last 15 years. It is a market that for a very long time has remained fairly focused on two main types of research – qualitative and quantitative – offered by two categories of market players: large groups and small companies or artisans, mainly present in the field of qualitative research. The issues related to research have always been diverse. They include consumer insights, sector expertise, and media performance, among others.

Today, however, the skills and techniques required have gradually expanded with the digital age and the importance of social media, new interactive tools, and big data. New horizons have opened up for predictive and prescriptive analysis, such as modeling, contribution, and attribution. This is allowing the emergence of new and more digital-profile players capable of processing and analyzing an exponential volume of data and competing directly with the historical players in terms of their deliverables and deadlines.

With this immediacy brought by digital technology, traditional players in the market research companies should now develop more advanced expertise to differentiate themselves, even though technology allows correlations to be detected that escape the unaided human mind, making it a tough competitor.

Nowadays, the challenge for the sector is to integrate and reconcile all types of data (e.g., discursive, spontaneous, and observed data) to offer a holistic framework for data analysis. Indeed, the issue for brands is the volume of proprietary or third-party data and their relevance for the development of a marketing strategy or an advertising campaign, especially when it comes to the youth market.

Focusing everything on correlation analysis is to deny what underpins the relevance of the market research business, namely the initial understanding of "why" people do things. This could be a good definition of an insight, where it is a question of understanding the tension that manifests itself at a given moment when it comes to a young consumer's behavior. If companies targeting youth understand it, they will be better equipped to imagine the levers that will solve this problem and reinforce "how" digital natives will behave, adopt, or reject brands.

Moreover, the social instinct of young people is more easily revealed through communities, mainly thanks to social media. In these communities, whereas in the past young people used to position themselves either against or for the leader, they now alternate between voluntary submission to a more expert peer and claiming their competence. In other words, young consumers can be both someone's king and someone else's valet. Communities are thus more easily analyzed and quantifiable.

Furthermore, there are many more invariants in youth consumption cultures than is commonly thought. Today's young consumers experience the same situations as their parents did at the same age. The only change lies in their permanent access to information and entertainment via digital technology, which sometimes detains young consumers or gives them a mastery of things without the necessary maturity. For example, these young people are exposed at a very early to the issues of sexuality on the Internet without discernment and solicit their elders less about the topic, even though the associated anxieties are still there. Online communities have, therefore, become a challenge in the field of research and provide a lot of resources for investigations of young people.

The methods that can be used to study young people's consumer behaviors can also be image-based, as young people may not have the educational or emotional resources to clearly express their expectations or opinions.

Lexicological or semantic analysis is also a good way to separate the wheat from the chaff by disassociating mimicry from the systematic rejection of real insight about the target. Also, to study young consumers in their different youth consumption cultures, innovative ways to capture their attention and empathize with them to facilitate their expression have to be considered by companies.

Design thinking, for example, is an innovation management methodology that fits well with this generation. Here young people, under a certain pressure to generate ideas, become more creative as they prototype and test them live to come up with something concrete. Furthermore, co-creation dedicated to understanding the experience of young people can be an effective tool, but companies should always ask the question of which profile to co-create and for what purpose. Ethnographic research, which allows young people to describe a consumer activity and follows them in this activity, is an interesting approach to co-creation, especially when young people have difficulty expressing themselves.

Alongside traditional methodologies (e.g., interviews, focus groups, or questionnaires), retroactive approaches can also be used to identify subsequent changes in behavior or listen to social networks to capture the reality of young people. Using Tumblr to ask young consumers to illustrate their lives or talk about their consumption practices is an example.

These techniques highlight the creativity of young people and bring out relevant data in terms of innovation or marketing strategy. Finally, to study young people properly, it is also necessary to immerse oneself in their culture by following their favorite media, music, and hobbies, for example. Thus, it is essential to develop interdisciplinary knowledge to understand young people and their behaviors before conducting market research.

For advertisers and marketers targeting the youth market, including chil-descents, adonascents, adolescents, and adulescents, qualitative and exploratory tools are then best suited to develop an in-depth understanding of the paradoxes and the meanings young consumers assign to their consumption practices – meanings shaped by the codes and norms prevailing in each youth consumption culture.

Therefore, companies should shift to a more exploratory and immersive approach in terms of market research because it allows a company to gain an in-depth analysis of both tangible (functional) and intangible (symbolic, emotional, social, ideological) needs that make the behaviors of these digital natives different compared to previous generations. The next section introduces and discusses the relevance for companies targeting the youth market of shifting towards exploratory market research tools.

1.1   Exploratory Market Research: A Closer Look at Youth Consumption Cultures

Unlike quantitative studies that aim to measure variables related to the purchasing process, exploratory methods are qualitative in nature. They provide immersive insights that help companies gain a deeper understanding of the driving forces and the features of youth consumption cultures, young consumers' behaviors, and their perceptions of brands within different youth cultures. Table 9.1 provides a synthesis of the elements that differentiate the qualitative and quantitative approaches used in market research.

Table 9.1   Qualitative versus quantitative techniques

Criteria	Qualitative	Quantitative
Logic	Exploratory with a bottom-up approach. The interviewer produces new hypotheses from the data collected	Confirmatory with a top-down approach. The interviewer tests his or her hypotheses by collecting data
Objectives	Explore, discover, and build	Describe, explain, and anticipate
Approach	The study of behaviors in their natural environment	The study of the consumer behavior under the control of certain variables
Final report	A narrative report illustrated with verbatim quotes	A statistical report with correlations, comparisons, and statistically significant results

In the field of youth marketing, qualitative methods can be used to understand young consumers' behaviors through the collection and the analysis of two categories of data: discursive (e.g., verbatim and discourse) and visual (e.g., images, icons, and video). Moreover, numerous methodological approaches can be applied depending on the objectives and the phenomenon being studied.

To deeply understand the behaviors of digital natives, three approaches are likely to be implemented by companies: descriptive, explanatory, and exploratory research (see Figure 9.1). Nevertheless, when studying young consumers who belong to different consumption cultures, the exploratory approach is preferred due to its relevance. It allows a deep understanding of new phenomena that can emerge in the four interrelated youth segmencultures: childescence, adonascence, adolescence, and adulescence.

Exploratory market research allows businesses aiming at digital natives to better anticipate the motivations and attitudes these young consumers have towards their brands, products, or advertisements. Before explaining how the use of new exploratory market research tools is relevant when it comes to analyzing youth consumption cultures, let us first have a look at the advantages of qualitative methods in the field of youth marketing.

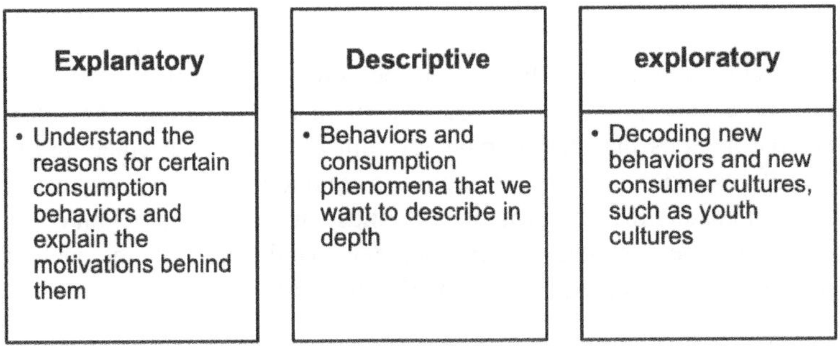

Explanatory	Descriptive	exploratory
• Understand the reasons for certain consumption behaviors and explain the motivations behind them	• Behaviors and consumption phenomena that we want to describe in depth	• Decoding new behaviors and new consumer cultures, such as youth cultures

Figure 9.1   *Three study approaches: explanatory, descriptive, and exploratory*

Given the limitations of quantitative studies that use questionnaires to under-stand the motivations, needs, and attitudes of young consumers, qualitative methods are the most appropriate, if not vital, approach for collecting relevant and deep insights on young consumer behaviors and perceptions. This is done by being as close as possible to the social reality of digital natives.

By allowing young consumers to express their cultures, their functional and symbolic needs, their perspectives, and their experiences, qualitative methods aim to understand the reality of the youth universe and cultures from the per-spective of young people – and not from what the company thinks it knows about the youth market. In other words, qualitative tools allow companies to see the world through the eyes of a young person. Distinct from surveys, the qualitative approach brings out issues that a questionnaire tends to quantify. The approach is often used to:

- Identify the real reasons for how young consumers behave and the choices they make;
- Examine groups of consumers that are difficult to access with a question-naire (e.g., the homeless);
- Define a consumer's representations, needs, and perceptions;
- Identify the codes and norms that shape consumption cultures;
- Examine the existing phenomena: "what exists," "why it exists," and "how it exists or in what form," rather than quantifying it;
- Identify new creative and unexpected ideas and convert them into innovation;
- Provide an in-depth description of a particular case of consumer practices, situations, or individuals;

- Analyze the meanings young people in different consumer cultures assign to their consumption, brands, and products;
- Identify the dynamics and social interactions in youth consumption cultures that often escape the attention of marketers because they are tacit and underlying.

In the exploratory qualitative logic, the researcher does not need to recruit large numbers of young participants as is the case in quantitative studies. The number of participants can vary from one to a few dozen people. The issue of representativeness and the reliability of the results is nonetheless important, however, and requires careful consideration in the composition of the study group.

The more representative the group is of the total youth population in terms of its diversity, the more relevant the data obtained will be. Although the limitations of qualitative methods are mainly due to their subjective and interpretative nature, they are nevertheless crucial for studying the behaviors of young consumers who belong to different youth consumption cultures.

1.2 How Brands Can Innovate by Shifting to Exploratory Market Research Studies

Exploratory market research using qualitative tools has the benefit of allowing data to be cross-checked by placing the behaviors and experiences of young consumers in their context, that of youth consumption cultures. This method also helps businesses analyze and understand the codes and norms that shape the perceptions, behaviors, and attitudes young consumers have towards their products, brands, and advertising.

Furthermore, exploratory market research is a source of inspiration for brands looking for new ideas to target the heterogeneous youth market with values and content that speak to them. In youth marketing, the importance of implementing exploratory studies is related to the evolution of consumer trends in our contemporary societies and new emerging behaviors. This is especially the case when it comes to young, connected, and informed digital consumers who express their values through their consumption modes and brands selected. Among the benefits exploratory studies provide in terms of understanding youth consumption cultures, we can cite the following:

- Exploratory research allows companies to better understand the stakes of the transformations generated by the technological context and the importance of emotions and youthful consumer cultures while examining the behaviors of digital natives;

- Exploratory studies are the only studies that allow marketing and research managers to use a fairly wide range of methods: motivational studies, interviews (individual, dual, and group), projective techniques, and documentary analysis, among others;
- The use of different methodological tools helps research managers in their marketing analyses, which facilitates decision-making by bringing together as many elements as possible to gain an in-depth understanding of youth consumption cultures and behaviors from the youth perspective rooted in a particular consumer culture;
- This methodological approach helps decision-makers understand the subtle and tacit behaviors and symbolic dimensions that make up youth consumption cultures and play a significant role in the adoption or the rejection of certain products and brands.

MINI-CASE BOX 9.1   AN OVERVIEW OF AN EXPLORATORY STUDY EXAMINING DIGITAL NATIVES' CONSUMPTION COMPETENCIES

Study context and objectives. The objective of this exploratory study (Batat, 2014) was to determine what "consumption competence" means from a youth perspective by questioning whether young consumers see themselves as competent or vulnerable consumers. Eighteen portraits of young participants 11–15 years old were obtained. For professionals, educators, and parents, digital natives as consumers represent a mystery that requires an in-depth study. This was a study shaped by different consumption cultures and subcultures. The study attempted to answer three main questions: how do digital natives perceive themselves in society? How do they define consumption competencies? Are they competent or vulnerable actors?

The exploratory study. Answering these questions required setting up of a deep and long-term immersive exploration within the youth sphere. This strategy helped the researcher to understand, through immersion in the world of digital natives, how competencies in the consumption field are defined by youths and how they perceive themselves as consumers. A long-term (6 month) exploratory study based on participant and non-participant observations and interviews allowed the investigator to gain acceptance from participants, who were not very collaborative since they did not appreciate the authoritarian presence of adults. Then, the method of portraits was used to define each youth profile, including the consumption activities and behaviors and analysis of all the documents produced by participants (e.g., photographs of consumer objects from their world, drawings of rooms, and collages), in order to speak in a visual way about their consumption practices.

What were the main results of the study? The results show that the consumption competencies of digital natives are contextualized. They emerge and are shaped in several youth consumption cultures that are considered a subdivision of the global culture. The youth consumer culture is defined by elements such as the digital and interactive context in which young consumers evolve, and also digital natives' need to belong to a group and to socialize. Transgression and self-transcendence, do-it-yourself, self-esteem and identity construction, the self-concept, and symbolism are all aspects sought by young consumers through their social and consumption experiences. The analysis revealed 11 dimensions of consumer competence.

What are the marketing implications of the study? The study showed that consumer competence has multiple meanings among digital natives. Moreover, this consumer competence exists only if it is recognized by members of the group who share the same youth culture and values. We cannot say that a young consumer is competent in the absolute. On the contrary, we will say that he or she is competent in a particular field to carry out a particular activity. Moreover, digital natives develop creative competencies they use by acquiring and diverting the global consumption culture to build their own identity and consumer cultures. This study provides a better understanding of the skills of young people that can be applied in the field of youth marketing. Companies will be able to rely on some of the competencies defined by young people to establish commercial relationships with them through the implementation of devices to uncover the skills of young consumers for the co-creation of offers – thus involving them in the process of sharing, design, and production.

What is the value of this study? When digital natives have digital skills, the production of online content can generate value. Thus, companies can set up actions to accompany the young person in the process of building skills in areas such as music, media content, and online practices, among others. By involving digital natives and recognizing their consumption competencies, companies targeting the youth market can build loyalty and a long-term relationship with them. This creates a strong competitive advantage.

Studying young consumers and their youth consumption cultures by using exploratory qualitative techniques constitutes a real source of innovation and differentiation for businesses. It allows them to get to know these digital natives and their cultures by adopting a "bottom-up" way of thinking – one in which the starting point is young consumers and their perceptions of their consumption practices within a particular youth cultural context.

2.   IMMERSIVE MARKET RESEARCH TOOLS TO DECODE YOUTH CONSUMER BEHAVIORS

Beyond the traditional qualitative techniques, such as interviews, focus groups, and motivational studies, often used by market researchers to understand the youth market, there are additional and alternative tools for analyzing the intangible aspects of youth consumption practices (e.g., ideological, symbolic, and experiential aspects). These tools allow companies to capture the so-called "hidden obvious" and thus analyze in a contextualized manner the "why" of certain paradoxical behaviors characteristic of youth consumption cultures.

These unconventional, immersive, and interactive tools include the following techniques: youthnography, immersive observation, auto-ethnography, photography, narratives, and netnography. Although these tools are still underused by companies, they are better suited to the study of tangible and intangible aspects of young consumers' behaviors and attitudes towards brands and products in different youth consumption cultures. The tools are presented and discussed below.

2.1   Youthnography, an Ethnography of Youth Consumption Cultures

Youthnography is an exploratory, interactive, and immersive methodological approach that is part of the alternative methods used to provide an in-depth analysis of youth consumption cultures. Youthnography allows companies targeting the youth market to understand the social interactions between young consumers and market players, as well as the internal interactions within each youth consumption culture.

Youthnography aims at analyzing the symbolic and emotional dimensions related to the consumption practices of young people that emerge in their experiences within a different youth segmenculture, namely the childescence, adonascence, adolescence, or adulescence consumption cultures. The main objective of this method is to go beyond the cognitive and rational vision by adopting a symbolic and sociocultural perspective of the behaviors of youths.

For example, youthnography aims to study how young consumers construct and develop attitudes towards brands and products in their youth cultures, and how the codes and norms in these cultures contribute to the formation of attitudes and consumption habits among digital natives. Furthermore, youthnography uses visual and verbal data from audio and video recordings of the behaviors of youths in real-life consumption situations. Interviewers should, therefore, immerse themselves in a particular youth consumption culture when they seek to understand and connect with young people and thus get accepted as members of the group.

When youthnography is utilized, young consumers remain in their natural environments. It is up to the interviewers to make an effort to integrate and make themselves invisible and part of the group. Thus, collecting data in this framework allows an ethnographer to observe behaviors and make young people react in real-time.

For marketing and brand managers, the contribution of youthnography in terms of knowledge about young people and their consumer cultures is critical. Youthnography helps market researchers to identify, categorize, and analyze consumer cultures, subcultures, counter-cultures, and micro-cultures of youth consumption practices and behaviors. In these different cultures, we will be able to identify behavioral typologies and segmencultures according to the norms shared by the young people who belong to a similar consumption culture.

Youthnography, therefore, requires companies to work as closely as possible with young consumers. In so doing, the ethnographer should develop a ritual and a strategy to enter youth cultures and get access to the consumption sphere of digital natives. Moreover, the implementation of youthnography can be diversified according to the problem being studied. Investigators can choose between two major techniques:

- Multi-site youthnography. This consists of following several fields, several groups of young people, and several consumption practices in various youth cultures at the same time. This technique is facilitated by the frequent back-and-forth between data analysis and the "field." Consequently, it is necessary to build loyalty among young people to ensure their participation in the study;
- Quick-and-dirty youthnography. This is an accelerated method in line with the rapid changes and developments in contemporary society. The practice of ethnography within youth cultures has become more fragmented, faster, and more mobile. This technique is important when it comes to studying the youth market to launch technological innovations.

2.2 Immersive Observation in Youth Consumption Cultures

Immersive techniques require a great capacity for socialization and observation while interacting with young people in different consumption cultures being studied. Immersive observation is a technique that is used to collect verbal and nonverbal data on the consumption behaviors observed in different groups of young consumers. This method was developed by anthropologists seeking to understand unknown cultures and social phenomena. The main benefit of using immersive observation in the study of youth cultures is to discover, through observation and interaction, the elements that make up and organize consumption practices among digital natives in their place of life.

Participatory observation implies an active immersion in the world of young people. Thanks to this immersion, tacit information that is not easily accessible with other methods is made available and allows for a better understanding of certain internal workings, which remain difficult to capture by actors outside of the youth consumption culture. Immersion in the world of young consumers allows the researcher to collect deep and rich insights from several sources:

- Direct observations in the field by sharing young people's lives and consumption activities with their families and friends while at school, on vacation, at home, at the supermarket, and so on;
- In-depth comprehensive interviews via occasional conversations as well as formal and informal exchanges related to the consumption practices of young people;
- The analysis of personal documents such as diaries, blogs, and social media content in which young people reveal in their own language, their point of view on their consumption practices, and the world around them.

Figure 9.2 presents the steps the observer should follow to collect data on digital natives' practices embedded within different youth consumption cultures.

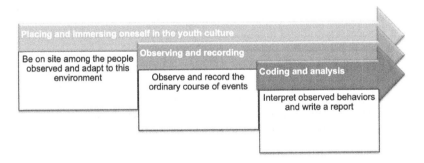

Figure 9.2   Steps to observing youth cultures

2.3   Auto-Ethnography to Unveil the Codes Shaping Youth Consumption Cultures

Auto-ethnography is a qualitative methodology focused on the young person as an observer of his or her consumer practices and culture. This self-observation, which is fueled by self-centered personal reflections, aims to develop an introspective narrative that brings together the aspects of consumption perceived by the young person as significant and meaningful.

To examine youth consumption cultures and analyze their functional and symbolic dimensions, personal subjective introspection is derived from the experiences of the self-observed young consumer. This allows companies to understand the meanings and significance the young consumer assigns to his or her consumption practices embedded in the youth consumer culture to which the person belongs.

The advantage of auto-ethnography is that it allows 24-hour access to the field in real-life daily situations described in a diary a young person fills out each day in autobiographical form. For example, the cosmetic brand L'Oréal used introspective tools to learn more about young females' makeup routines. Thus, observing and understanding women's beauty routines and strategies is a crucial source of inspiration for the brand.

Observation methods should be constantly renewed for the development of new insights and new products. In so doing, L'Oréal implemented immersive and introspective techniques based on the observation of women's morning and evening routines as they apply and remove makeup. The study results were also frequently enriched and documented through observation techniques at women's homes or in salons.

2.4   Using Photography to Study Youth Consumption Cultures

Photography can reflect the involvement of young people in the investigation of their consumer culture by offering them the opportunity to express themselves and thus reveal their practices and behaviors through representative photos of the objects that constitute their consumption. This method allows companies to capture visual insights of subjective photographs representing the world of consumption of young people.

Photographs are vital because they allow companies to unveil how young consumers understand their consumption experiences – experiences that they would not be able to verbally express through a to-and-fro between the field and the photographs. This helps interviewers refine their results.

The use of photography, drawings, and collages in the study of youth consumption cultures helps marketers understand the symbolic dimension of youth consumption practices. To refine the analysis of visual data, youth photography can be combined with other qualitative techniques, such as participant observation, interviews, and ethnography, among others.

2.5   Narratives of Youth Consumption Cultures

Collecting stories and narratives of young consumers' daily lives and consumption practices is an exploratory method that originates in the social sciences and can be used in marketing to understand youth practices that are socially constructed within a predefined consumption culture. The life story describes the young consumer's narrative discourse about his or her consumption universe when interacting with other young people who belong to the same youth culture. To generate youth narratives, several steps should be followed in the process:

- Identify the problem to be studied;
- Select an individual to be learned from;
- Collect the individual's personal and social stories;
- Deepen the history of the individual both over time and space;
- Collect stories from other individuals;
- Synthesize all the stories told by individuals;
- Rewrite and tell the individual or collective story.

In the collection of youth stories and narratives, all the practices, meanings, and consumption situations retained by the young consumer are commented on in a subjective and detailed manner. These discursive and subjective insights are key for companies targeting the youth market because they are produced and described by young people according to their importance in their daily lives. Thus, the hierarchy of events is not necessarily chronological. It may also reflect a classification according to the importance that these practices represent for the young person.

2.6   A Netnography of Youth Consumption Cultures

Netnography, which is a combination of the words *net* and *ethnography*, is a research method for virtual environments and communities. Its founder, Robert Kozinets, published his first research on the subject in 1997, followed by a book on netnography first published in 2010 (Kozinets, 1997, 2006, 2015). The goal of netnography is not only to understand but also to share the common passion that drives members of the online and offline community. This method takes the classic steps of ethnography and adapts them to the study of online behaviors and communities.

Netnography applied to youth consumption cultures is an online immersion technique on different social media platforms and blogs; the main objective is to analyze the discourse and exchanges between young people on the Internet. This method is based on the collection of qualitative and quantitative data on the Internet generated by online brand communities.

Like ethnography, netnography focuses on the study of online communities by using several methodological tools such as online interviews or online participatory observation.

This technique is, therefore, an adaptation of qualitative and quantitative methods often used to study young consumers in a real context to make them correspond to the online context with few adjustments. Overall, netnography can be conducted through participating or non-participating observations by following five main steps:

- Defining the objective of the study;
- Selecting an online community to integrate;
- Engaging in observation and immersion;
- Collecting and analyzing data;
- Making recommendations and offering solutions.

The advantage of using netnography for qualitative studies is that it allows young people to express themselves freely about their consumption practices without the fear of judgment. This allows interviewers to collect more personal information because there is no physical interview. To conduct a netnographic study among digital natives, the investigator or researcher should follow four main stages described by Kozinets (2015):

- Entry stage. The first step in the netnography process is to make an "entry" whereby the interviewer prepares the field before selecting the community to be studied and beginning the analysis. It is important to define a clear objective and question. Then, a web-based identification of communities consistent with the defined objective is delineated. This step is used to select the groups most relevant to the objective. It is, therefore, essential to cross-check as much information as possible about the chosen community and its participants.
- Data collection stage. Several types of netnographic data need to be integrated during the collection process. There are data available within the virtual community in the form of texts written by group members. In addition, other data concerning external elements of communication with the subjects, such as their voices, silences, and so on, are available within the virtual community in the form of texts written by group members. Other data are also considered, such as the data produced by the interviewer/ researcher. Notes, reflections, and remarks are written by the person during the observation process. If the researcher/investigator adopts a participa-

tory attitude, contact can be made with members to conduct individual interviews or start a new discussion.

• Data analysis and interpretation stage. This stage involves analyzing the messages using classification to identify off-topic messages. Next, an analysis using the constant comparative method is performed by the investigator. During this process the data are coded with variables that reflect the behavior of participants. This requires the researcher to take an "emic" approach to achieve a deep level of understanding of the culture. Next, an "etic" approach is needed to conceptualize the findings.

• Validation and ethics stage. Netnography is a method that facilitates the validation of data by participating members. Members of the virtual community can be contacted and presented with the results of the netnographic research to gather their comments and demonstrate transparency. Feedback is key because it allows members to nuance the results, which improves their understanding.

To sum up, we can state that on the methodological and empirical level of the study of young consumers and their practices rooted in the different youth consumption cultures, exploratory market research studies bring together more appropriate techniques and make it possible to respond exhaustively to the objectives of the study. These methodologies are relevant to market studies conducted among young people because they allow for an in-depth study of youths' cultures and subcultures, their interpretative strategies, and the sociocultural dimensions of consumption in ordinary and experiential consumption fields, such as tourism, art and culture, leisure and sports, and entertainment, among others.

KEY TAKEAWAYS

The key takeaways from this chapter underscore why it is important for companies to shift to a more exploratory market research logic. Unlike quantitative studies that aim to measure variables related to the purchasing process, immersive and exploratory market research methods provide rich and deep insights to better understand the codes and norms that shape the consumption practices of young people in their youth cultures. In addition, exploratory tools allow companies to decode the meaning digital natives assign to brands or products within different youth cultures. Thus, the immersive exploratory methodology allows marketers and advertisers targeting young consumers to better anticipate their motivations and attitudes towards brands, products, and advertisements. Immersive and exploratory tools that can be used to analyze youth behavior include youthnography, participant and non-participant observation, auto-ethnography, photography, youth narratives, and netnography or online ethnography.

10. Are digital natives eco-friendly consumers?

CHAPTER OVERVIEW

This chapter examines the attitudes and behaviors digital natives have towards the environment. The chapter also examines their capacity to be changemakers and promoters of sustainable consumption modes so as to influence the behaviors of older generations. The following questions are considered: do digital natives care about sustainable development? What are their attitudes and behaviors regarding the environment? And who are the main socialization agents influencing youth behaviors when it comes to ecological issues and the impact of their consumption on the environment?

1. DO DIGITAL NATIVES CARE ABOUT SUSTAINABILITY AND ECO-RESPONSIBILITY?

Digital natives are familiar with the sustainability discourse prominent in the media, schools, and politics. Various studies have found that one's generation is a more important determinant of a person's ecological attitudes and behaviors than the person's chronological age (Menz and Welsch, 2012). An eco-responsible individual strives to respect nature and the environment. How then do digital natives behave when it comes to the environment? Do they care about sustainability and the ecological and social impacts of their consumption activities? To answer these questions, I examine young people's attitudes towards sustainability and how they perceive sustainable and eco-friendly behaviors.

1.1 Digital Natives' Perceptions of Sustainability

According to Francis and Davis (2015), young consumers are sensitive to environmental issues and are already involved in eco-friendly activities. The activities include making second-hand purchases, recycling, recovering water, avoiding packaging, using clean energy, enjoying activities in the natural environment, and limiting waste.

When it comes to ecological knowledge, studies show that young people comprehend the various environmental risks related to water pollution, deforestation, the disappearance of certain species, and carbon dioxide emissions. Young people are also capable of changing their daily consumption activities to fit with sustainable values, such as using alternative modes of transportation, recycling, buying eco-friendly products, and turning off lights that are not being used. They also have an interest in and support non-governmental actions and associations such as Greenpeace and the World Wide Fund for Nature.

Environmental understanding is based on values and encompasses beliefs and an affective dimension that make young people sensitive towards the environment (Leppänen et al., 2012). This sensitivity has three axes: sensitivity to major environmental facts, personal involvement with the environment, and collective environmental involvement through associations and non-profit organizations. Studies show that digital natives express sensitivity towards the environment through their compassion and concern, for example, by believing in preserving the planet for future generations. These people also demonstrate personal involvement (e.g., setting an example for others). However, regarding collective involvement, few of them want to belong and become active members within a particular non-profit organization.

Furthermore, these studies reveal a generational difference in attitudes towards the environment between parents and their children. Thus, older generations have stronger environmental attitudes than younger generations do. This difference can be explained by the fact that youthhood is characterized by a search for identity and the search for autonomy, which can often result in young people rejecting the values of adults. However, taking up an environmental cause is no longer a way to oppose older generations because the latter are also sensitive to environmental issues. Thus, younger generations may be less interested in sustainability as a result. It is then important to question whether these young consumers are less sensitive to the environment compared to previous generations and what factors impact their environmental engagement.

Indeed, not all digital natives have the same attitude towards the environment. Different variables can influence their sensitivity. One variable is a person's level of education, as revealed by Meeusen (2014). Meeusen states that digital natives with higher levels of education are more receptive to environmental causes than those with lower levels of education.

Regarding the impact of gender on environmental sensitivity, although there is no real consensus, more studies have found that there is greater environmental sensitivity among girls than boys. An analysis of these studies shows that boys have more individualistic values, whereas girls are more defined by collective and thus more responsible values.

1.2   How Do Digital Natives Define Responsible Behaviors?

Pro-environmental behavior is defined as consciously seeking to minimize the negative impact of one's action on the environment and thus contributing to the preservation of the world. This can be done by minimizing energy resources and consumption, using non-toxic substances, and reducing waste (Kollmuss and Agyeman, 2002). For young people, several behaviors can be considered as having a positive impact on the environment. The behaviors include, for example, saving electricity, reducing one's water consumption, recycling, not throwing away bulky items, buying eco-friendly products, and considering alternative modes of transportation. For Autio et al. (2009), there are three types of environmental profiles of youth:

- "Environmental heroes" are characterized by eco-responsible attitudes and behaviors, and their choices are guided by an environmental prism. The cost of eco-responsible products is a potential obstacle for this type of teenager in the future;
- "Anti-heroes" are aware of environmental concerns but wish to live their lives comfortably and easily, unlike eco-responsible consumers who deny themselves materialistic pleasures. Anti-heroes also tend to be fatalistic: they believe the planet will be destroyed no matter what we do;
- "Anarchists" take a critical view of the capacity of corporations to be responsible, highlighting their immoral character (such as destroying native habitats). In this sense, the capitalist interests of business are, for this profile of responsible young consumers, incompatible with environmental or social causes. Anarchists are part of a critique of today's consumer society and thus resist consumption.

Yet this study reveals that there is a clear gap between the eco-responsible attitudes and eco-responsible behaviors of today's youth. Indeed, pro-environmental attitudes do not always lead to pro-environmental behaviors.

Francis and Davis (2014) state there are different reasons for people not being eco-responsible in terms of their actions. In line with the studies mentioned, research by Uitto et al. (2015) highlights a problem of linearity between the cognitive dimension of the pro-environmental attitude (the intention to act favorably towards the environmental cause) and actual pro-environmental behavior. These authors emphasize that the shift from intention to behavior is highly context dependent. Moreover, intending to act or acting in a pro-environmental way is reinforced by psychosocial constructs. Having values related to the environment and the perception of one's self-efficacy (a person's confidence in his or her ability to implement changes) contribute to the transformation of the intention to act in a pro-environmental way into actual pro-environmental behavior.

Young people are aware of ecological issues and believe that it is important to protect the environment. However, when it comes to the youths' fundamental life goals, environmental protection ranks low. Moreover, this generation thinks that they are making, in their own way, an average contribution to environmental sustainability. In fact, studies show that digital natives have a pessimistic vision of the future of the planet and seem daunted by the associated commitment to preserve it. This assumption echoes the study by Uitto et al. (2015), which found that this generation does not think it can change society.

2.   HOW DO YOUNG PEOPLE LEARN TO BECOME SUSTAINABLE CONSUMERS?

Digital natives can learn to become responsible consumers who are aware of the impacts of their consumption activities on the environment by socializing themselves and interacting with different socialization agents. Those agents include their families, the media, their schools, and their peers, among others. Thanks to socialization, these young consumers acquire skills, knowledge, and attitudes useful for their engagement and behaviors when it comes to socially responsible consumption activities.

Although the socialization process related to developing an eco-friendly consciousness occurs during a person's childhood, its effect is not limited to that period. Indeed, many responsible consumption patterns during one's adulthood are influenced by a person's experiences in childhood and adolescence. Growing up in an environment with which they will interact, children cannot be indifferent – voluntarily or not – to the environmental discourse dominant in today's Western societies. In light of this observation, it is necessary to study "environmentally friendly socialization" when it comes to questioning the potential of digital natives to become an eco-responsible generation.

The results of research on how young people and children acquire eco-friendly behaviors and thus become more responsible consumers can provide us with a better understanding of the formation of digital natives' current beliefs, attitudes, and behaviors when it comes to environmental sustainability. In other words, digital natives are not born sensitive to the environmental cause; they become sensitive to it over time.

The issue is, therefore, to understand how this digital native generation acquires sensitivity, skills, and knowledge about the environment and how socialization agents – namely, one's family, peers, school, and traditional and online media – influence the process.

2.1 How Does Family Influence Digital Natives' Eco-Friendly Behaviors?

The role parents play in the socialization process of their children is significant during childhood. That role then diminishes during adolescence with the appearance of other socialization agents, such as a child's peers. To what degree, then, do parents play a role in the propensity of young people to feel concerned about the environment?

There is a slightly higher propensity among young people to talk about the environment with their mothers than with their fathers. This finding by Luchs and Mooradian (2012) reveals that environmental values are different among young males and females. Young females are generally more expressive in terms of their communication and have more empathy relative to young males. In addition, mothers appear to be more concerned than their digital native daughters about being involved with charitable or social causes (e.g., Ogle et al., 2014).

To sum up, the environmental cause is, indeed, transmitted from parents to their children, and the transmission appears to be gender related. Girls are more likely to be the target of this transmission than boys are, and the transmission is thought to occur through observation and teaching.

In addition, the more sensitive parents are to the environment, the more they talk with their children about sustainability and eco-friendly behaviors, and the more their children are aware of environmental causes. Thus, studies show that a child's ecological awareness is influenced by the frequency of communication about the environment with his or her parents as well as by the parents' ecological awareness. However, it is well-established that parental influence, when it exists, does not explain a significant part of a person's ecological awareness. This suggests that other socialization factors are important for these digital natives to develop sensitivity towards the environment.

2.2 Do Peers Influence Digital Natives' Eco-Friendly Behaviors?

Peers are considered a key socialization agent during adolescence. They influence a person's beliefs, attitudes, and behaviors, which allows young consumers to integrate, through a certain number of codes, into the groups they join. Although peer socialization has been studied in different contexts, scant research has been conducted on the weight of this agent when it comes to digital natives adopting or rejecting eco-friendly behaviors.

The eco-friendly socialization of digital natives that is under the influence of peers appears to revolve around three dimensions, namely discussions about the environment among peers, the influence peers have on a person adopting responsible behaviors, and the existence of environmental norms within the peer groups. Yet discussing environmental issues among peers is only an occasional activity. Often it results from external teaching or information.

Some initiatives have been conducted by organizations and associations to promote sustainability among young people by focusing on peer groups. For example, the "Young People for the Environment" prize, instituted by companies and non-profit organizations, aims to connect with peer groups in order to help young people become proactive when it comes to changing the attitudes and behaviors of their relatives. The organizers of the prize aim to better understand how the communication system and its substance (which messages) and form (which projects via which media) can be implemented to do so.

MINI-CASE BOX 10.1   VEJA, AN ETHICAL AND POPULAR SNEAKERS BRAND IN YOUTH CULTURES

The sincerest brands are often those that are most appreciated by digital natives. Veja, which has always claimed to follow an ethical and ecological model, has never hidden the fact that it is simply impossible to manufacture sneakers that are 100 percent environmentally friendly. However, the company, which was founded in 2005, is sparing no effort to reduce its impact on nature. Its organic cotton is produced by farmers' associations in South America and is grown with respect for people and the environment. Wild rubber only accounts for 35 percent of the soles of Veja's sneakers. The leather for the shoes is not produced using fair-trade practices because cattle breeding requires extensive fields and a significant financial investment. To reduce its carbon footprint, Veja transports its products by boat to Brazil, where they are assembled, and then ships them by barge to Paris's suburbs.

2.3   How Do Schools Influence Sustainability Perceptions among Digital Natives?

Elementary school, high school, and college are places where youth's knowledge, know-how, and interpersonal skills are constructed. Overall, in schools, the environment is examined in a rather transversal way: through economics, biology, and geography courses. In addition to the knowledge acquired, schools are increasingly setting up sustainability programs that encourage students to behave in environmentally conscious ways by adopting behaviors such as recycling and reducing the waste related to the students' consumption activities.

The aim of incorporating such a curriculum is that if young people learn to behave sustainably at school, they will do so routinely at home or due to their conviction. As a result, young people will potentially become active environmental proponents. Studies show that a significant proportion of students who have followed a program or instruction related to the environment say that it has a significant influence on them. Their mothers are even more likely to find that school plays an important role in providing information about the environment.

In the past, there has been a lack of consensus on the extent to which schools should act as socializing agent in terms of promoting eco-friendly practices. However, more recent studies focusing specifically on the environment seem to show that schools are an important socializing agent in terms of knowledge and the awareness of eco-responsibility. According to Meeusen (2014), the environment may not be a topic of paramount importance for young consumers. When young people are asked what topics are important in their lives, topics such as employment and crime score higher than the environment (Meeusen, 2014).

Yet even if digital natives are informed, to what extent will other sensitivities be stronger and, indeed, more likely to be translated into behaviors than the environmental cause? The answer is related to the optimism digital natives have about the future of the environment.

If research highlights a significant connection between learning about sustainability in schools and digital natives' sensitivity to the environment, to what extent does this sensitivity translate into actual behavior? To our knowledge, such an evaluation of the effectiveness of educational programs has not been implemented. In addition, whereas environmental sensitivity is an important and necessary concept, it is not sufficient to develop sustainable and eco-friendly behaviors among young people.

Pro-environmental programs implemented in schools seem to contribute to increasing students' environmental engagement from a cognitive point of view but contribute much less to increasing young people's pro-environmental behaviors (Uitto et al., 2015).

To sum up, these studies also highlight the fact that encouraging young people to become proactive rather than reactive has a greater impact. More generally, school and the family are major agents of the environmental socialization of digital natives.

MINI-CASE BOX 10.2   TEACHING ENVIRONMENTAL SUSTAINABILITY AT SCHOOLS: A FRENCH CASE

The governmental measures adopted by the French education system to promote sustainability include the following:

- Integrate sustainable development into all school programs and in all disciplines, from kindergarten to high school, while renewing current programs; interdisciplinary practical teaching of "ecological transition and sustainable development" is being implemented;
- Define the key pathways for environmental education and sustainable development throughout France, to reward the best educational projects in the field of sustainability;
- Define clear objectives and monitoring indicators in terms of education for sustainable development; the generalization of schools or projects integrating sustainable development or eco-school labels in elementary and high schools;
- Promote the "sustainable development generation" competition to highlight student initiatives related to sustainable development, in partnership with different stakeholders such as NGOs.

2.4 How Do Traditional and Online Media Influence the Eco-Responsibility of Youths?

Recent studies highlight the importance of the media as a source of socialization. The digital native generation has experienced a lot of media coverage related to the environment. It is a current topic relayed through different TV programs, movies, and documentaries. Traditional media, such as newspapers, TV, and radio, are significant sources of information for young people regarding the environmental cause (Larsson et al., 2010).

Even if the environment is a theme found in the media, little information exists on the capacity of the media to be an agent of environmental socialization. Existing studies highlight the important role this agent plays in environmental socialization, mainly through TV and magazines. Young people say they watch programs that make them more sensitive to the environmental cause and relish related discussions with their parents and friends.

Studies of the media as an agent of environmental socialization among digital natives do not mention the Internet. This observation may be questionable given the propensity of young people to be connected to the Internet. In this sense, it is surprising not to consider the Internet as a medium of environmental socialization. Consequently, online media and social media platforms do not seem, for the moment, to be key agents for the transmission of knowledge, attitudes, and behaviors towards the environment.

3. CAN DIGITAL NATIVES INFLUENCE ADULTS' SUSTAINABLE BEHAVIORS?

Eco-friendly behaviors in youth consumption cultures are influenced by both intragenerational interactions with a person's peers and intergenerational exchanges represented by their family. The intergenerational influence refers to a reverse, top-down socialization process in which children can influence the behaviors of their parents in terms of environmental sustainability.

3.1 Reverse Sustainable Socialization among Digital Natives

A few studies have examined how parents and grandparents acquire new information from their children or grandchildren. Indeed, the family should be considered a place of interactions, a moving system or "family flow." In other words, the family should be a place of circulation (of ideas, values, learning, etc.) and interactions in which all family members are involved (Kerrane and Hogg, 2013).

Reverse socialization is the process whereby parents acquire new values, skills, attitudes, and roles through their children. Having assimilated knowledge about the environment, through socialization, children will influence their parents and thus constitute a promotional vector of sustainability knowledge. However, studies show that reverse socialization is strongly influenced by parenting styles and the ability of children to "give" and their parents to "receive." Parenting styles include intra-familial principles, norms, and rules.

Carlson and Grossbart (1988) developed two categories, namely "warm" and "cold" parenting styles. Warm parenting refers to permissive parents who seek to restrict their prescriptive scope as much as possible without, however, exposing their children to any danger. Warm parenting is based on the idea of equity between the child and the adult. If parents allow their children to express themselves, they are exercising authority based on the well-being of their children. Therefore, communication is an important element in this type of family. In contrast, cold parenting includes two main aspects: authoritarian parents who see their children as subordinate to the various normative prescriptions inherent in the family unit, and neglectful parents who are distant from their children. For these parents, the child is self-involved; parents such as these resist the advice and control of their children.

Studies have found that warm parenting styles are more likely to lead to reverse socialization (Grossbart et al., 2002). Parents see their children as agents of socialization within the family and believe they are capable of contributing, developing, and sharing knowledge, especially when it comes to eco-friendly consumption behaviors.

3.2 Are Digital Natives Legitimate Actors for Environmental Change?

As mentioned, a few studies have looked at how digital natives can have a strong influence on their parents' adoption of pro-environmental consumption behaviors (Easterling et al., 1995). Yet the question to explore is whether these young consumers *want* to play a role as socialization agents to change their parents' behaviors. If this is the case, are these young people considered legitimate actors for environmental change?

Ecological reverse socialization refers to the influence young people exert on their parents to change their knowledge, skills, and attitudes regarding environmental issues. Easterling et al. (1995) highlighted a set of variables likely to come into play within the framework of the phenomenon of ecological reverse socialization.

First and foremost, a youth's capacity to feel concerned appears to be necessary for ecological reverse socialization to occur. This capacity remains a function not only of a certain cognitive status (young people appear more likely than younger children to reflect on higher level topics) but also the degree of a person's exposure to environmental subjects and the intensity of the individual's ecological socialization.

If a youth's ability to be sensitive to environmental issues exists, then, depending on the communication model that exists within the family, the phenomenon of ecological reverse socialization can take place. The propensity of the parents to be sensitive to responsible behaviors, as well as the family's resources (available time, income, and residential location) also affect the process. That said, the family unit usually does not consider a child's ecological expertise to be superior to that of the child's parents.

Ecological reverse socialization can nonetheless be a virtuous circle; young people or children who have been socialized about ecology, in turn, socialize their parents. Moreover, Watne and Brennan (2011) state that young people not only influence their parents in terms of ecology but also that their parents count on them to advise them about environmentally friendly product choices.

It has been shown that "warm" mothers are more likely to accept being influenced by their children in terms of ecology than are "cold" mothers. Furthermore, it also appears that the degree of expertise that the mother thinks her child has with regard to ecology will moderate this relationship. Nonetheless, ecological reverse socialization can take place within the framework of a parental style qualified as cold if the mother believes that her child has a higher level of expertise than she does. In contrast, expertise does not come into consideration if a mother has a "hot" parenting style.

Culture has an effect as well. A study conducted in Vietnam (Aleti et al., 2015) points out that eco-friendly products are seen as new in Vietnam and that young people 18–25 years old should have a better knowledge of and interest in them. However, this is not the case. Indeed, the level of knowledge of these products is the same for parents as it is for their children. In fact, parents show a higher interest in these products than their children do.

Another variable that should be considered in terms of ecological reverse socialization is related to the frequency of communication that exists between parents and their children. The frequency of communication also moderates ecological reverse socialization when there is a warm parenting style.

Thus, in families with a warm parenting style, the young person will engage in bilateral strategies such as negotiating, using specific arguments, and his or her expertise. The strategy implemented in families with a cold parenting style is different; the young person will try to influence his or her parents by demanding, insisting, and thus being part of a unilateral strategy. Indeed, it is conceivable to think that young consumers, having heard about the environment since childhood, are more likely to be environmentally sensitive than people who belong to previous generations. However, geopolitical and economic upheavals are massively reported by the media and can, therefore, hamper environmental efforts. In other words, given the oftentimes bleak news disseminated by the media and public opinion, it may be hard for young people to muster up an interest in environmental causes.

This context may shed light on some recent findings showing that the parents of digital natives are more environmentally sensitive than digital natives themselves. Furthermore, if parents are more environmentally aware than their children are, it is probably because they are concerned about their children's future. In contrast, their children are more likely to be concerned about the short term (and not the long term).

Overall, digital natives have favorable attitudes towards the environment. However, the attitudes do not necessarily translate into them adopting sustainable and ethical behaviors. The lack of translation seems to be rooted in a pessimistic and fatalistic view of the future – one in which young consumers do not believe they can act to make a real difference. This is manifested by their engaging in routine ecological behaviors that seem to be less the result of an environmental conviction than an economic one.

It has also been shown that having parents concerned about the environment only weakly explains the eco-responsibility of their children. Likewise, the environmental socialization by one's peers seems very occasional. As for the media, TV shows are an element of socialization, whereas the web is not perceived as a medium for environmental socialization in youth consumption cultures. The flagship socialization agent is school. However, the pro-environmental programs implemented in schools contribute more to increasing students' environmental knowledge and commitment from a cognitive perspective but contribute much less to increasing students' pro-environmental behaviors.

Despite this somewhat pessimistic picture regarding the commitment of digital natives to sustainability and eco-friendly behaviors, a question remains: is ecology a theme of reverse socialization across generations, and, if so, under what conditions? The answer is "yes" because young consumers can be a potential catalyst for behavioral and attitudinal changes in their parents' ecological behaviors. As mentioned, ecological reverse socialization depends on parental styles, the ecological expertise within a family, and the frequency of communication among family members. The antecedent element, however, lies in the propensity of digital natives to feel concerned about the environmental cause.

More globally, it seems appropriate not only to continue the socialization of the youth generation in terms of environmental sustainability, but above all, in the light of the research called for, to act at the source – that is to say, to act on the reasons that result in this generation insufficiently engaging in actions linked to sustainability. Thus, it is the pessimism and fatalism of youth that must be combated so that digital natives believe it is possible to change the situation and that everyone's action has consequences.

To sum up the relationship between digital natives and environmental sustainability, it is vital to emphasize the four core ideas that brands, institutions, and educators should integrate when implementing eco-friendly actions aimed at this generation:

- Youth's attitudes towards environmental sustainability. Digital natives have a favorable attitude and sensitivity towards the environment, even if their parents seem less inclined. However, the weight of this attitude becomes less important when the measurement is no longer carried out in an absolute but relative manner – in other words when other problems such as violence and unemployment are assessed jointly. Girls and young people with higher levels of education are more receptive to the environmental cause. Thus, attitudes towards the environment seem to be acquired rather than innate.
- The sustainable behaviors of youths. There is a clear difference between a favorable predisposition towards the environment and the development of pro-environmental behaviors among digital natives. The difference can be explained by the cognitive and financial costs of pro-environmental actions. Another explanatory element lies in the doubts young people have about their ability to change things. Consequently, it is necessary to modify the perception of the self-efficacy of digital natives.
- Youths' ecological socialization. Parents transmit environmental sensitivity to their children, even if this does not seem to represent a significant

percentage of the environmental sensitivity of youths. The influence of a youth's peers seems, in this case, to be in operation. However, it must be noted that although peer socialization has been the subject of marketing studies in various fields, the environment has not been sufficiently examined. Consequently, this does not allow us to estimate the weight of peer socialization on the environmental sensitivity of digital natives. The media appear to be real sources of information likely to influence the environmental sensitivity of young people. Finally, school is an important socialization agent in terms of a person's knowledge and awareness of eco-responsibility.

• Youths' ecological reverse socialization. Digital natives can, under certain conditions, be agents of the socialization of their parents when it comes to environmental matters. The various factors to consider in this regard are parental styles, the ecological expertise of young people, their propensity to feel concerned about the environmental cause, and their communication about it with their parents. This reverse socialization appears to be a key element of sensitivity to the environmental cause. However, to translate that sensitivity into more pro-environmental behavior, it is necessary to act on the negative perceptions a young person may have about his or her self-efficacy.

KEY TAKEAWAYS

The key takeaways from this chapter show that digital natives are sensitive to environmental issues and can also influence the behaviors of older generations. This chapter highlights, among other things, that the digital generation has its own practices and perceptions intrinsically linked to environmental protection. This "sustainable native" generation has grown up during the economic and financial crisis. Yet many digital natives place environmental preservation at the top of the list of their concerns, and that is embodied by their ability to move the terms of debate where they consider previous ones have failed.

Conclusion to *Youth Marketing to Digital Natives*

The objective of this book was to rethink traditional marketing thinking applied to digital natives and to offer a new youth marketing framework – one that provides a better understanding of the foundations, tools, and strategies of the current approach to youth segmentation and marketing to digital natives. Furthermore, this book introduces a sociocultural approach and a youth-centric perspective to be applied to the youth market through the introduction of three marketing concepts: youth consumption cultures and subcultures, segmenculture, and experiential youth marketing. As several chapters have clearly shown, segmentation, branding, collaborative marketing and youth competency, youth experience, and digital and immersive exploratory market research methods, such as youthnography, are significant strategic elements – elements advertisers and marketers in charge of designing and promoting offers and brands aimed at young consumers, especially digital natives, should consider in their marketing and communication strategies both online and offline.

In the evolution of youth marketing, experiential, digital, and collaborative approaches that take into account different youth consumer cultures are particularly relevant. Indeed, marketing to digital natives that is grounded in the different youth cultures to which they belong provides marketers and advertisers with more coherence. This type of marketing does so by opting for a structured approach to understanding the new levers that serve to create a sustainable competitive advantage and to build loyalty among young consumers – thus adapting to the tangible and symbolic needs in the different segmencultures: childescence, adonascence, adolescence, and adulescence.

These fields of youth culture, customer experience, and exploratory market research tools are areas of expertise that are still evolving. Many books and analyses are still being produced on the subject. In the coming years, we will undoubtedly witness an increasingly precise and strategic advancement of our knowledge on this subject.

References

Alba, J., & Hutchinson, J. (2000). Knowledge calibration: What consumers know and what they think they know. Journal of Consumer Research, 27, 123–156.

Aleti, T., Brennan, L., & Parker, L. (2015). Consumer socialisation agency within three-generational Vietnamese families. Young Consumers: Insight and Ideas for Responsible Marketers, 16, 172–188.

Ariès, P. (1973). L'enfant et la Vie Familiale sous l'Ancien Régime. Paris: Seuil.

Autio, M., Heiskanen, E., & Heinonen, V. (2009). Narratives of 'green' consumers: The antihero, the environmental hero and the anarchist. Journal of Consumer Behaviour, 8, 40–53.

Baker, S.M. (2009). Vulnerability and resilience in natural disasters: A marketing and public policy perspective. Journal of Public Policy & Marketing, 28, 114–123.

Baker, S.M., Gentry, J., & Rittenburg, T.L. (2005). Building understanding of the domain of consumer vulnerability. Journal of Macromarketing, 25, 128–139.

Balasubramanian, S. (1994). Beyond advertising and publicity: Hybrid messages and public policy issues. Journal of Advertising, 23, 29–46.

Bandura, A. (1977). Social Learning Theory. Englewood Cliffs, NJ: Prentice-Hall.

Barry, T.E., & Howard, D.J. (1990). A review and critique of the hierarchy of effects in advertising. International Journal of Advertising, 9, 121–135.

Batat, W. (2008). Exploring adolescent development skills through Internet usage: A study of French 11–15 year olds. International Journal of Consumer Studies, 32, 374–381.

Batat, W. (2010). Le Comportement de Consommation des Jeunes Âgés de 11–15 Ans: Les Modalités de Construction des Compétences de Consommation dans la Société Digitale. Paris: Éditions Connaissances et Savoirs, Collection: Sciences Sociales.

Batat, W. (2014). How do adolescents define their own competencies in the consumption field? A portrait approach. Recherche et Applications en Marketing (English Edition), 29, 25–54.

Batat, W. (2017a). Les Nouvelles Youth Cultures. Paris: Éditions EMS, Collection 0–25 ans.

Batat, W. (2017b). Comprendre et Séduire la Génération Z. Comportements de Consommation et Relations des Postmillennials avec les Marques. Paris: Ellipses.

Batat, W. (2019). Experiential Marketing: Consumer Behavior, Customer Experience and the 7Es. New York: Routledge.

Batat, W. (2020). How can art museums develop new business opportunities? Exploring young visitors' experience. Young Consumers: Insight and Ideas for Responsible Marketers, 21, 109–131.

Batat, W., & Tanner, J.F. (2021). Unveiling (in)vulnerability in an adolescent's consumption subculture: A framework to understand adolescents' experienced (in) vulnerability and ethical implications. Journal of Business Ethics, 169, 713–730.

Belk, R., & Costa, J.A. (1998). The mountain man myth: A contemporary consuming fantasy. Journal of Consumer Research, 25, 218–240.

Blasius, J., & Friedrichs, J. (2003). Les compétences pratiques font-elles partie du capital culturel? *Revue Française de Sociologie*, 3 (44), 549–576.

Bonnemaizon, A., & Batat, W. (2011). How competent are consumers? The case of the energy sector in France. International Journal of Consumer Studies, 35, 348–358.

Bourdieu, P. (1979/1984). *Distinction: A Social Critique of the Judgment of Taste*, tr. R. Nice. Cambridge, MA: Harvard University Press.

Bourdieu, P. (1986). The forms of capital. In J.G. Richardson (ed.), *Handbook of Theory and Research for the Sociology of Education*. New York: Greenwood Press, 241–258.

Bowlby, J. (1946). *Forty-Four Juvenile Thieves*. London: Tindall and Cox.

Brim, O.G. (1966). Socialization through the life cycle. In O.G. Brim & S. Wheeler, *Socialization after Childhood: Two Essays*. New York: Wiley, 1–49.

Buckingham, D. (2004). *Constructing the Media Competent Child: Media Literacy and Regulatory Policy in the UK*. http://www.medienpaed.com/05-1/buckingham05 -1.pdf.

Buckingham, D., Bragg, S., & Kehily, M. (2015). Rethinking youth cultures in the age of global media: A perspective from British youth studies. Journal of Childhood and Adolescence Research, 10, 265–277.

Burt, C. (1925). *The Young Delinquent*. London: University of London Press.

Cardona, O.D. (2004). The need for rethinking the concepts of vulnerability and risk from a holistic perspective: A necessary review and criticism for effective risk management. In G. Bankoff, G. Frerks, and D. Hilhorst (eds.), *Mapping Vulnerability: Disasters, Development and People*. London: Earthscan Publishers, 37–51.

Carlson, L., & Grossbart, S. (1988). Parental style and consumer socialization of children. Journal of Consumer Research, 15, 77–94.

CDC (2015). *Births: Final Data for 2013*. https://www.cdc.gov/nchs/data/nvsr/nvsr64/ nvsr64_01.pdf.

Charry, C., & Tessitore, T. (2016). Product placement, its supporters and detractors: A quest for balance. In P. de Pelsmacker (ed.), *Advertising in New Media and Formats: Current Research and Implications for Marketers*. Bingley: Emerald Group Publishing, 265–290.

Christensen, C.M. (1997). *The Innovator's Dilemma: When New Technologies Cause Great Firms to Fail*. Boston: Harvard Business School Press.

Cohen, A. (1956). *Delinquent Boys: The Subculture of the Gang*. London: Collier-Macmillan.

Cohen, P. (1972). *Subcultural Conflict and Working-Class Community*. Working Papers in Cultural Studies CCCS, University of Birmingham.

Cook, D. (2005). The dichotomous child in and of commercial culture. Childhood, 12, 155–159.

Cook, D. (2008). The missing child in consumption theory. Journal of Consumer Culture, 8, 219–243.

De Pelsmacker, P., Geuens, M., & Van den Bergh, J. (2013). *Marketing Communications: A European Perspective*. London: Pearson Education.

Debesse, M. (1972). *Les Etapes de L'éducation*. Paris: PUF.

Donnison, S. (2007). Unpacking the millennials: A cautionary tale for teacher education. Australian Journal of Teacher Education, 32, 1–13.

Easterling, D., Miller, S., & Weinberger, N. (1995). Environmental consumerism: A process of children's socialization and families' resocialization. Psychology & Marketing, 12, 531–550.

Ekström, K. (2005). Roundtable: Rethinking family consumption tracking new research perspectives. ACR North American Advances, 32 (2), 493–497.

Elliott, R., & Cova, B. (2008). Interpretive consumer research as cultural critique. Consumption, Markets & Culture, 11, 71–72.

Erikson, E.J. (1968/1972). *Identity: Youth and Crisis*. New York: Norton.

Feldman-Barrett, C. (2018). Back to the future: Mapping a historic turn in youth studies. Journal of Youth Studies, 21, 733–746.

Feldman-Barrett, C. (2019). Making space for youth culture history: Berlin's Archiv der Jugendkulturen. Space and Culture, 22, 405–418.

Ferguson, S. (2008). Generation Y as community: Consuming cool globally. Consumer Culture Theory Conference, Boston.

Fields, B., Wilder, S., Bunch, J., & Newbold, R. (2008). *Millennial Leaders: Success Stories from Today's Most Brilliant Generation Y Leaders*. Plymouth: Ingram Publishing Services.

Francis, J.E., & Davis, T. (2014). Exploring children's socialization to three dimensions of sustainability. Young Consumers: Insight and Ideas for Responsible Marketers, 15, 125–137.

Francis, J.E., & Davis, T. (2015). Adolescents' sustainability concerns and reasons for not consuming sustainably. International Journal of Consumer Studies, 39, 43–50.

Gordon, M. (1947). The concept of subculture and its application. *Social Forces*, 26, 40–42.

Grossbart, S., Hughes, S.M., Pryor, S., & Yost, A. (2002). Socialization aspects of parents, children, and the internet. Advances in Consumer Research, 29, 66–70.

Hall, E.T. (1956). *The Silent Language*. New York: Doubleday.

Hall, E.T. (1976). *Beyond Culture*. New York: Anchor Books.

Hall, S., & Jefferson, T. (1976). *Resistance Through Rituals: Youth Subcultures in Post-War Britain*. London: Routledge.

Hazel, D. (2001). Centers turn to curfews as a last resort to cope with teens, shopping centers today. https://www.icsc.org.

Heilbronner, O. (2008). From a culture for youth to a culture of youth: Recent trends in the historiography of Western youth cultures. Contemporary European History, 17, 575–591.

Hofstede, G. (2001). *Culture's Consequences: Comparing Values, Behaviors, Institutions, and Organizations Across Nations*, 2nd edition. Thousand Oaks, CA: Sage Publications.

Hoggart, R. (1957/1970). *La Culture du Pauvre*. Paris: Éditions de Minuit.

Holbrook, M., & Hirschman, E. (1982). The experiential aspects of consumption: Consumer fantasies, feelings, and fun. Journal of Consumer Research, 9, 132–140.

Holt, D., & Thompson, C. (2004). Man-of-action heroes: The pursuit of heroic masculinity in everyday consumption. Journal of Consumer Research, 31, 425–440.

House, R.J., Hanges, P.J., Javidan, M., Dorfman, P., & Gupta, V. (eds) (2004). *Culture, Leadership, and Organizations: The GLOBE Study of 62 Societies*. London: Sage Publications.

Irwin, J. (1970). Notes on the status of the concept subculture. In K. Gelder (ed.), *The Subcultures Reader*. London: Routledge, 66–70.

Kandel, D., Griesler, P.C., & Hu, M. (2015). Intergenerational patterns of smoking and nicotine dependence among US adolescents. American Journal of Public Health, 105 (11), 63–72.

Kerrane, B., & Hogg, M.K. (2013). Shared or non-shared? Children's different consumer socialisation experiences within the family environment. European Journal of Marketing, 47, 506–524.

Kjeldgaard, D., & Askegaard, S. (2006). The glocalization of youth culture: The global youth segment as structures of common difference. Journal of Consumer Research, 33, 231–247.

Kline, S. (2006). A becoming subject: Consumer socialization in the mediated marketplace. In F. Trentmann (ed.), *The Making of the Consumer*. New York: Berg, 199–221.

Kolb, D.A. (1984). *Experiential Learning: Experience as the Source of Learning and Development*. Englewood Cliffs, NJ: Prentice-Hall.

Kollmuss, A., & Agyeman, J. (2002). Mind the gap: Why do people act environmentally and what are the barriers to pro-environmental behavior? Environmental Education Research, 8, 239–260.

Kozinets, R. (1997). "I want to believe": A netnography of the X-Philes subculture of consumption. ACR North American Advances, 24, 470–475.

Kozinets, R. (2006). Click to connect: Netnography and tribal advertising. Journal of Advertising Research, 46, 279–288.

Kozinets, R. (2015). *Netnography Redefined*, 2nd edition. London: Sage Publications.

Larsson, B., Andersson, M., & Osbeck, C. (2010). Bringing environmentalism home: Children's influence on family consumption in the Nordic countries and beyond. *Childhood*, 17 (1), 129–147.

Leppänen, J.M., Haahla, A.E., Lensu, A., & Kuitunen, M. (2012). Parent-child similarity in environmental attitudes: A pairwise comparison. The Journal of Environmental Education, 43, 162–176.

Levitt, T. (1962). *Innovation in Marketing*. New York: McGraw-Hill.

Luchs, M.G., & Mooradian, T.A. (2012). Sex, personality, and sustainable consumer behaviour: Elucidating the gender effect. Journal of Consumer Policy, 35, 127–144.

Mannheim, K. (1952). *Essays on the Sociology of Knowledge*. London: Routledge & Kegan Paul.

Martin, C., & Turley, L. (2004). Malls and consumption motivation: An exploratory examination of older Generation Y consumers. International Journal of Retail & Distribution Management, 32, 464–475.

Mason, M., Tanner, J.F., Piacentini, M., Freeman, D., Anastasia, T.T., Batat, W., Boland, W., Canbulut, M., Drenten, J., Hamby, A., Rangan, P., & Yang, Z. (2013). Advancing a participatory approach for youth risk behavior: Foundations, distinctions, and research directions. Journal of Business Research, 66, 1235–1241.

McCandless, B.R. (1969). Childhood socialization. In D.A. Goslin (ed.), *Handbook of Socialization Theory and Research*. Richmond, KY: Rand McNally, 791–819.

Mead, M. (1935/1963). *Sex and Temperament in Three Primitive Societies*. New York: Morrow.

Meeusen, C. (2014). The intergenerational transmission of environmental concern: The influence of parents and communication patterns within the family. The Journal of Environmental Education, 45, 77–90.

Menz, T., & Welsch, H. (2012). Life-cycle and cohort effects in the valuation of air quality: Evidence from subjective well-being data. Land Economics, 88, 300–325.

Meuter, M.L., Ostrom, A.L., Roundtree, R., & Bitner, M.J. (2000). Self-service technologies: Understanding customer satisfaction with technology-based service encounters. Journal of Marketing, 64, 50–64.

Miller, K. (2007). Examining the role brand fit plays in Generation Y's propensity to purchase. Australian and New Zealand Marketing Academy (ANZMAC) Conference, New Zealand.

Minkiewicz, J., & Bridson, K. (2007). The relevance of role models to older aged Generation Y consumers. Australian and New Zealand Marketing Academy (ANZMAC) Conference, New Zealand.

Moulard, J., Garrity, C., & Rice, D. (2015). What makes a human brand authentic? Identifying the antecedents of celebrity authenticity. Psychology & Marketing, 32, 173–186.

Murdock, G.P. (1965). *Social Structure*. Pittsburgh, PA: University of Pittsburgh Press.

Namer, G. (2006). *Karl Mannheim, Sociologue de la Connaissance: La Synthèse Humaniste Ou le Chaos de L'absolu*. Paris: L'Harmattan.

Nielsen, S.F., & Thing, L. (2019). Trying to fit in: Upper secondary school students' negotiation processes between sports culture and youth culture. International Review for the Sociology of Sport, 54, 445–458.

Nuttall, P. (2007). For those about to rock: A new understanding of adolescent music consumption. *Advances in Consumer Research*, 35, 624–629.

Ogle, J., Hyllegard, K.H., Yan, R., & Littrell, M.A. (2014). Mother and teen daughter socialization toward ethical apparel consumption. Family and Consumer Sciences Research Journal, 43, 61–77.

Parasuraman, A., Berry, L., & Zeithaml, V.A. (1991). Refinement and reassessment of the SERVQUAL scale. Journal of Retailing, 67 (4), 420–449.

Parsons, T. (1942). Age and sex in the social structure of the United States. *American Sociological Review*, 7, 604–616.

Pauwells, V., de Kerviler G., & Janssen, C. (2016). Investigating the relationship between co-creation and corporate social responsibility: The role of co-creation type. AMS 19th World Marketing Congress, Paris.

Pecheux, C., & Hanot, M. (2016). Product placement in family TV shows: A need for more legal constraints? Academy of Marketing Science Conference, Paris.

Pechmann, C., Levine, L., Loughlin, S.E., & Leslie, F. (2005). Impulsive and self-conscious: Adolescents' vulnerability to advertising and promotion. Journal of Public Policy & Marketing, 24, 202–221.

Pendergast, D. (2009). Generational theory and home economics: Future proofing the profession. Family and Consumer Sciences Research Journal, 37, 504–522.

Petty, R., & Cacioppo, J. (1986). The elaboration likelihood model of persuasion. *Advances in Experimental Social Psychology*, 19, 123–205.

Piaget, J. (1975). *L'équilibration des Structures Cognitives. Problème Central du Développement. Études d'épistémologie Génétique*. Paris: PUF.

Pickton, D., & Broderick, A. (2005). *Integrated Marketing Communications*. New York: Prentice-Hall.

Reynol, J., & Mastrodicasa, J. (2007). *Connecting to the Net Generation: What Higher Education Professionals Need to Know about Today's College Students*. Washington, DC: NASPA.

Ringer, A.C., & Garma, R. (2006). Does the motivation to help differ between Generation X and Y? Australian and New Zealand Marketing Academy (ANZMAC) Conference, New Zealand.

Ritzer, G. (1993/1996). *The McDonaldization of Society*. Thousand Oaks, CA: Pine Forge Press.

Roedder-John, D. (1999). Consumer socialization of children: A retrospective look at twenty-five years of research. Journal of Consumer Research, 26, 183–213.

Rohrer, I. (2014). Anthropology and youth. In I. Rohrer (ed.), *Cohesion and Dissolution*. Wiesbaden: Springer, 37–46.

Roudet, B. (2009). *Les Jeunes en France*. Quebec: Presses de l'université Laval.

Schumpeter, J. (1942). *Capitalism, Socialism, and Democracy*. New York: Harper.

Schwartz, G. (1978). Book review of *Resistance Through Rituals: Youth Subcultures in Post-War Britain*, by Stuart Hall and Tony Jefferson. American Journal of Sociology, 84, 789–791.

Secord, P.F., & Backman, C.W. (1964). *Social Psychology*. New York: McGraw-Hill.

Shultz, C.J., & Holbrook, M. (2009). The paradoxical relationships between marketing and vulnerability. Journal of Public Policy & Marketing, 28, 124–127.

Solomon, M.R., Bamossy, G., Askegaard, S., & Hogg, M.K. (2010). *Consumer Behavior: A European Perspective*, 4th edition. London: Prentice-Hall.

Spiggle, S., Nguyen, H.T., & Caravella, M. (2012). More than fit: Brand extension authenticity. Journal of Marketing Research, 49, 967–983.

Statista (2020). Estimated median age of Americans at their first wedding in the United States from 1998 to 2019, by sex. https://www.statista.com/statistics/371933/median -age-of-us-americans-at-their-first-wedding/.

Tamesberger, D., & Bacher, J. (2014). NEET youth in Austria: A typology including socio-demography, labour market behaviour and permanence. Journal of Youth Studies, 17, 1239–1259.

Taylor, S.L., & Cosenza, R.M. (2002). Profiling later aged female teens: Mall shopping behavior and clothing choice. Journal of Consumer Marketing, 19, 393–408.

Thorndike, E. (1932). *The Fundamentals of Learning*. New York: Teachers College Press.

Tufte, B. (2004). Children, media and consumption. Young Consumers: Insight and Ideas for Responsible Marketers, 5, 69–76.

Uitto, A., Pauw, J.B., & Saloranta, S. (2015). Participatory school experiences as facil-itators for adolescents' ecological behavior. Journal of Environmental Psychology, 43, 55–65.

United States Census Bureau (2006). Total population for the world: 1950–2050. http://www.census.gov/ipc/prod/wp02/wp-02001.pdf.

Van De Velde, C. (2008). *Devenir Adulte: Sociologie Comparée de la Jeunesse en Europe*. Paris: PUF.

Von Hippel, E. (2005). *Democratizing Innovation*. Cambridge, MA: MIT Press.

Voss, K., Spangenberg, E.R., & Grohmann, B. (2003). Measuring the hedonic and utilitarian dimensions of consumer attitude. Journal of Marketing Research, 40, 310–320.

Ward, S., Wackman, D.B., & Wartella, E. (1977). *How Children Learn to Buy*. Thousand Oaks, CA: Sage Publications.

Watne, T., & Brennan, L. (2011). Behavioral change starts in the family: The role of family communication and implications for social marketing. Journal of Nonprofit & Public Sector Marketing, 23, 367–386.

Wiedmann, K., Hennigs, N., & Siebels, A. (2009). Value-based segmentation of luxury consumption behavior. Psychology & Marketing, 26, 625–651.

Wortham, S. (2011). Youth cultures and education. Review of Research in Education, 35, vii–xi.

Yalch, R.F., & Spangenberg, E.R. (1993). Using store music for retail zoning: A field experiment. ACR North American Advances, 20, 632–636.

Yildirim, C., & Correia, A. (2015). Exploring the dimensions of nomophobia: Development and validation of a self-reported questionnaire. Computer Human Behavior, 49, 130–137.

FURTHER SOURCES

A Bullseye Review (2020). Corporate overview. https://investors.target.com/corporate -overview.

Acosta, G. (2016). Doritos lures millennials with technology, gaming and music. https:// drugstorenews.com/center-store/doritos-lures-millennials-technology-gaming-and -music.

Akgün, S., & Yalım, F. (2015). The reasons of young consumers' choice on chain café stores: A research on Starbucks. https://www.econjournals.com/index.php/irmm/ article/view/1296/pdf.

Alkhaldi, M. (2015). The value creating strategy of Starbucks. https://digital.hbs.edu/ platform-rctom/submission/the-value-creating-strategy-of-starbucks/.

Anderson, G. (2016). Why are affluent millennials shopping in dollar stores? *Forbes.* https://www.forbes.com/sites/retailwire/2016/06/21/why-are-affluent-millennials -shopping-in-dollar-stores/#2886ceaa1653.

Antonelli, W. (2020). A beginner's guide to Instagram, the wildly popular photo-sharing app with over a billion users. https://www.businessinsider.com/what-is-instagram -how-to-use-guide.

Ascension (2020). Spotify reaching the millennial market. *Ascension Strategy.* http:// ascensionstrategy.com/spotify-reaching-the-millennial-market/.

Bhasin, H. (2018a). Marketing strategy of Target Corporation. *Marketing91.* https:// www.marketing91.com/marketing-strategy-of-target-corporation/.

Bhasin, H. (2018b). SWOT analysis of Doritos. *Marketing91.* https://www.marketing91 .com/swot-analysis-doritos/#:~:text=Positioning%3A%20Doritos%20has%20been %20positioned,that%20it%20is%20being%20sold.

Bhasin, H. (2020). Marketing mix of Dunkin Donuts. *Marketing91.* https://www .marketing91.com/marketing-mix-of-dunkin-donuts/.

Bhasin, K. (2012). The psychological secrets behind nacho cheese Doritos. https:// www.businessinsider.com/nacho-cheese-doritos-brand-2012-12.

Biscuit People (2017). The short history of Oreo Cookies. https://www.biscuitpeople .com/magazine/post/the-short-history-of-oreo-cookies.

Bohannon, C. (2017). Dunkin' Donuts balances mobile, traditional marketing to protect brand personality. *Retail Dive.* https://www.retaildive.com/ex/ mobilecommercedaily/unbalanced-mobile-strategies-lead-a-pathway-toward-low -roi-a-dunkin-exec-says.

Business to Business (2013). The great Goya family. https://stories.wf.com/great-goya -family/.

Castellanos, S. (2019). Dollar General boosts digital strategy. *The Wall Street Journal.* https://www.wsj.com/articles/dollar-general-boosts-digital-strategy-11570646318.

Chrzanowska, N. (2020). 4 examples of digital transformation: Starbucks, Adobe, KW and more. https://www.netguru.com/blog/digital-transformation-examples.

CSD Staff (2018). Dollar stores gain popularity with customers. *CStore Decisions.* https://cstoredecisions.com/2018/12/31/dollar-stores-gain-popularity-with -customers/.

Danziger, P.N. (2017). Nike's challenges in the U.S. market. *Forbes.* https://www .forbes.com/sites/pamdanziger/2017/10/27/nikes-challenges-in-the-u-s-market/ #55f8702127df.

Danziger, P.N. (2018). Nike's new consumer experience distribution strategy hits the ground running. *Forbes.* https://www.forbes.com/sites/pamdanziger/2018/12/01/nikes-new-consumer-experience-distribution-strategy-hits-the-ground-running/#ebd957f1d066.

Deal (2010). How Dunkin' Donuts keeps its customers happy. https://superhypeblog .com/marketing/how-dunkin-donuts-keeps-its-customers-happy.

Debter, L. (2020). Dollar Tree killed off online ordering when coronavirus struck— now it's paying for it. *Forbes.* https://www.forbes.com/sites/laurendebter/2020/03/31/dollar-tree-online-orders-coronavirus/#64e0851d1843.

Delventhal, S. (2020). Starbucks vs. Dunkin': What's the difference? https://www .investopedia.com/articles/markets/120215/starbucks-vs-dunkin-donuts-comparing -business-models.asp#:~:text=Dunkin'%3A%20An%20Overview&text= Starbucks%20has%20a%20larger%20footprint,beyond%20the%20U.S.%20more %20extensively.

Denys, E. (2018). Doritos – for the bold. https://www.semetis.com/en/resources/ presentations-and-cases/doritos-for-the-bold.

Digital Media Solutions (2019). Dollar stores are exceeding expectations. *Insights. Digital Media Solutions.* https://insights.digitalmediasolutions.com/articles/dollar -stores-continuing-to-thrive.

Dispatch (2020). Instagram vs TikTok: The battle between social media plat- forms. https://wp.nyu.edu/dispatch/2020/02/20/instagram-vs-tiktok-the-battle -between-social-media-platforms/#:~:text=In%20other%20words%2C%20while %20Instagram,terms%20of%20gender%20and%20age.

Ditch the Label (2021). Official website. https://www.ditchthelabel.org/.

Dollar Tree (2020). About us. https://www.dollartreeinfo.com/about-us.

Doritos (n.d.). Official Instagram account. https://www.instagram.com/doritos/.

Doritos (2019). Anti-Ad :60. https://www.youtube.com/watch?v=tbwoKm5U0tM& feature=youtu.be.

Dove (n.d.). Dove Self-Esteem Project. https://www.dove.com/uk/dove-self-esteem -project.html.

Dove (n.d.). Our mission. https://www.dove.com/uk/dove-self-esteem-project/our -mission.html.

Dove (n.d.). Uniquely Me: A tool to help build self-esteem in young people. https:// www.dove.com/uk/dove-self-esteem-project/help-for-parents/uniquely-me-a-tool -to-help-build-positive-body-confidence.html.

Dunkin Donuts (n.d.). Official website. https://www.dunkindonuts.com/en/about/about -us.

Edie Newsroom (2015). PepsiCo defends Doritos' palm oil policy. https://www .edie.net/news/5/Doritos-palm-oil-policy-defended-by-PepsiCo-after-SumOfUs -campaign/.

Edwards, G. (2015). The legend of Doritos. https://www.maxim.com/entertainment/ legend-doritos.

e.l.f. Cosmetics (n.d.). About e.l.f. beauty. https://investor.elfcosmetics.com/about-elf -beauty-old.

Ellwanger, S. (2019). Doritos sheds logo in new campaign targeting Gen Z. https://www .mediapost.com/publications/article/339693/doritos-sheds-logo-in-new-campaign -targeting-gen-z.html.

Fernandez, J. (2018). How did the brand Oreo manage to become one of the leaders of the cookies market? *Medium.* https://medium.com/marketing-marques-innovation

-bordeaux/how-did-the-brand-oreo-manage-to-become-on-of-the-leaders-of-the
-cookies-market-c5d08212ba0a.

Forbes (2020a). https://www.forbes.com/companies/dollar-tree/#7940fdfb17fe.

Forbes (2020b). https://www.forbes.com/companies/target/#598e56785274.

Foster, L.B. (2018). 5 ways Starbucks is innovating the customer experience. https://
www.qsrmagazine.com/consumer-trends/5-ways-starbucks-innovating-customer
-experience.

Frank, J. (2017). Doritos were originally Disneyland trash. https://www.businessinsider
.com/doritos-flavors-disneyland-trash-frito-lay-frontierland-brand-chips-tortillas
-2017-1#:~:text=In%20the%20early%20days%20of,by%20Frito-Lay%20in
%201966.

Frito-Lay North America (2018). Doritos and Twitch join forces to host the boldest
gaming event ever: Doritos Bowl at TwitchCon 2018. https://www.prnewswire.com/
news-releases/doritos-and-twitch-join-forces-to-host-the-boldest-gaming-event
-ever-doritos-bowl-at-twitchcon-2018-300712927.html.

Ghausi, N. (2018). Win more business by copying Nike's storytelling playbook.
Entrepreneur. https://www.entrepreneur.com/article/318320.

Goya Foods (n.d.). GOYA encourages families to stay safe and prepared amidst natural
disasters and COVID-19 pandemic. https://www.goya.com/en/our-company/press
-room/prepare-for-hurricane.

Goya Foods (2020). Goya distributes 400,000 pounds of food to families in New York
and New Jersey. https://www.prnewswire.com/news-releases/goya-distributes-400
-000-pounds-of-food-to-families-in-new-york-and-new-jersey-301103458.html.

Hammett, E. (2019). Vegan beauty: How conscious consumers are driving innovation
in ethical cosmetics. https://www.marketingweek.com/how-conscious-consumers
-are-driving-vegan-beauty/.

Heilpern, W. (2016). Doritos tells us why it has had enough of its 'Crash the Super
Bowl' contest. https://www.businessinsider.com/doritos-explains-last-ever-crash
-the-super-bowl-2016-1.

Howland, D. (2016). Dollar stores attracting more wealthy millennials. *Retail
Dive.* https://www.retaildive.com/news/dollar-stores-attracting-more-wealthy
-millennials/421128/.

Ingvaldsen, T. (2019). New data showcases Nike outranking competition in consumer
perception. *Hypebeast.* https://hypebeast.com/2019/5/nike-outranks-competition
-consumer-perception.

Islam, Z. (2020). Nike's marketing strategy: You should be (just) doing it too. *Referral
Candy.* https://www.referralcandy.com/blog/nike-marketing-strategy/.

Joachimsthaler, E., & Aaker, D.A. (1997). Building brands without mass media.
Harvard Business Review, 75 (1).

Jumari, S. (2017). Oreo and HP steal hearts of Chinese millenials. *Print Innovation
Asia.* https://www.printinnovationasia.com/single-post/2017/04/07/Oreo-and-HP
-steal-hearts-of-Chinese-millenials.

Kuang, C. (2020). Target competitors. *Investopedia.* https://www.investopedia.com/
ask/answers/051915/who-are-targets-tgt-main-competitors.asp.

Lim, S. (2019). Coca-Cola encourages Thai millennials to have more meals with friends
and family. https://www.thedrum.com/news/2019/12/20/coca-cola-encourages-thai
-millennials-have-more-meals-with-friends-and-family.

Linn, A. (2007). Starbucks rethinks stance on young customers. https://www.nbcnews
.com/id/wbna20608492.

Lipka, M. (2014). What Target knows about you. *Reuters*. https://www.reuters
.com/article/us-target-breach-datamining/what-target-knows-about-you
-idUSBREA0M1JM20140123.

Lutz, A. (2015). Nike just got a great sign it will dominate in the future. *Business
Insider*. https://www.businessinsider.com/nike-is-the-top-teen-retailer-2015-4.

MacGillis, A. (2020). How Dollar stores became magnets for crime and killing.
ProPublica. https://www.propublica.org/article/how-dollar-stores-became-magnets
-for-crime-and-killing.

Madden, L. (2012). Spike Lee is still the best Nike Jordan brand pitchman. *Forbes*.
https://www.forbes.com/sites/lancemadden/2012/12/05/spike-lee-is-still-the-best
-nike-jordan-brand-pitchman/#586c81646e52.

Maguire, L. (2020). Marketing to Gen Z during Covid-19. *Vogue Business*. https://
www.voguebusiness.com/consumers/marketing-to-gen-z-during-covid-19

Maras, E. (2018). How Target is embracing the human touch to beat the competition.
Retail Customer Experience. https://www.retailcustomerexperience.com/articles/
how-target-is-embracing-the-human-touch-to-beat-the-competition/.

Masunaga, S. (2018). Nike targets youth with provocative ad campaign. *The Detroit
News*. https://www.detroitnews.com/story/business/2018/09/05/nike-kaepernick
-campaign/37724717/.

McLaughlin, A. (2019). Nike ID rebrands as Nike By You. *Creative Review*. https://
www.creativereview.co.uk/nike-id-rebrands-as-nike-by-you/.

MilksFavoriteCookie (2014). Segmentation, targeting, positioning. *The World of
OREO*. https://milksfavouritecookie.wordpress.com/2014/09/21/segmentation
-targeting-positioning/.

Miller, B. (2016). Doritos launches 'Bold 50' campaign to celebrate 50th anniversary.
https://www.chewboom.com/2016/03/07/doritos-launches-bold-50-campaign-to
-celebrate-50th-anniversary/.

Mission Statement Academy (2020). Target mission and vision statement analysis.
https://mission-statement.com/target/.

Nichols, R. (2016). The importance of including social media as seen in Crash the Super
Bowl Doritos campaign. https://sites.psu.edu/comm473/2016/02/25/the-importance
-of-including-social-media-as-seen-in-crash-the-super-bowl-doritos-campaign/.

Nike News (2020a). https://news.nike.com/news/nike-training-club-premium-workouts
-for-kids.

Nike News (2020b). https://news.nike.com/news/nike-living-room-cup.

Ogilvy Agency (2011). The Friendship Machine. https://www.adsoftheworld.com/
media/ambient/cocacola_the_friendship_machine.

Olenski, S. (2017). Time to make the donuts: How the Dunkin' Donuts brand stays relevant. *Forbes*. https://www.forbes.com/sites/steveolenski/2017/03/06/time-to-make
-the-donuts-how-the-dunkin-donuts-brand-stays-relevant/#e0ff5765556a.

OREO (2020). Twitter. https://twitter.com/Oreo/status/1276908149757394945?ref_src
=twsrc%5Egoogle%7Ctwcamp%5Eserp%7Ctwgr%5Etweet.

Parry, T. (2010). Dollar Tree's social strategy is worth a buck. *Chief Marketer*. https://
www.chiefmarketer.com/blog/dollar-trees-social-strategy-is-worth-a-buck/.

Penfold, K. (2019). Oreo takes it beyond the biscuit to target Gen Z consumers.
Because Blog. https://www.becausexm.com/blog/oreo-takes-it-beyond-the-biscuit
-to-target-gen-z-consumers.

PR Newswire (2017). OREO is the #1 brand among kids 6–12. *CISION*. https://www
.prnewswire.com/news-releases/oreo-is-the-1-brand-among-kids-6-12-300163953
.html.

Profitworks (n.d.). How Nike became successful and the leader in the sports product market. https://profitworks.ca/blog/marketing-strategy/545-nike-strategy-how-nike -became-successful-and-the-leader-in-the-sports-product-market.html.

River Island (n.d.). Anti-bullying week: troll talks. https://www.riverisland.com/ inspiration/blog/anti-bullying-week-troll-talks.

River Island (n.d.). Official website. https://www.riverisland.com/ss-campaign #firstPage.

Rizwan, A., Brohi, H., Bhutto, A., Prithiani, J., Khubchandani, R., Kumar, S., & Abbas, Z. (2016). Strategic marketing plan of Nike. doi:10.13140/RG.2.1.1558.3122.

Safdar, K. (2016). Target goes after millennials with small, focused stores; retailer opens shops in cities and college towns as sales slow at big-box suburban outlets. *Wall Street Journal* (Online). https://search-proquest-com.ezproxy.aub.edu .lb/docview/1825599680?accountid=8555.

Safdar, K. (2019). Nike's strategy to get a lot more personal with its customers. *Dow Jones Institutional News* [also found in *The Wall Street Journal*, May 13, 2019].

Saini, S. (2018). Tim Hortons vs. Starbucks: The power of brand. https://medium.com/ @sssaini/tim-hortons-vs-starbucks-the-power-of-brand-4cd4daff144f.

Salesforce (2016). Dunkin' Donuts strengthens customer loyalty using Salesforce. https://www.prnewswire.com/news-releases/dunkin-donuts-strengthens-customer -loyalty-using-salesforce-300339585.html.

Sandler, E. (2020). How e.l.f. Cosmetics is using personalization to drive e-commerce sales. https://www.glossy.co/beauty/how-e-l-f-cosmetics-is-using-personalization -to-drive-e-commerce-sales/.

Sedacca, M. (2017). The business strategy behind Oreo's constant, weird new flavors. *GQ Culture*. https://www.gq.com/story/the-business-strategy-behind-oreos-constant -weird-new-flavors.

Sharma, K. (2019). How Spotify used its '3 Billion Playlists' to stand out in the clutter: Case study. *Business Insider*. https://www.businessinsider.in/advertising/ ad-tech/article/how-spotify-used-its-3-billion-playlists-to-stand-out-in-the-clutter/ articleshow/71940944.cms.

Shaw, M. (2014). Doritos: Testing customer loyalty with 'mystery' flavors. https:// www.customerinsightgroup.com/loyaltyblog/doritos-testing-customer-loyalty-with -mystery-flavors/.

Smart Insights (2018). Campaign of the week: How Spotify showed the power of data analytics in their marketing campaign. https://www.smartinsights.com/traffic -building-strategy/campaign-of-the-week-how-spotify-showed-the-power-of-data -analytics-in-their-marketing-campaign/.

SomeSpotify (2018). Spotify target audience: Millenials. *Wordpress*. https:// somespotify.wordpress.com/2018/03/08/spotify-target-audience-millenials/.

Spotify (2019). What is Spotify? *Spotify Home*. https://support.spotify.com/us/using _spotify/getting_started/what-is-spotify/.

Starbucks Secret Menu (n.d.). Official website. https://starbuckssecretmenu.net/.

Sweeney, E. (2018). Capri Sun unveils 'The Together Table' to drive awareness of bullying. https://www.marketingdive.com/news/capri-sun-unveils-the-together-table-to -drive-awareness-of-bullying/539856/.

Team Gary Vee (2020). Instagram Reels vs. Tiktok: 13 things you need to know. https://www.garyvaynerchuk.com/instagram-reels-vs-tiktok/.

Tirico, K. (2016). Target revamps stores to attract millennial shoppers. *Retail Touch Points*. https://retailtouchpoints.com/features/trend-watch/target-s-store-revamp -aims-to-attract-millennials.

Trefis Team (2016). Starbucks' challenges and how it can overcome them. https://
    www.forbes.com/sites/greatspeculations/2016/12/05/starbucks-challenges-and-how
    -it-can-overcome-them/?sh=240ba2b74be9.
Unilever (n.d.). Building body confidence & self-esteem. https://www.unilever.com/
    sustainable-living/improving-health-and-well-being/health-and-hygiene/building
    -body-confidence-and-self-esteem/.
Vilá, O.R., & Bharadwaj, S. (2017). Competing on social purpose. *Harvard Business
    Review.*
Wasserman, T. (2013). Starbucks 'Tweet-a-Coffee' campaign prompted $180,000
    in purchases. https://mashable.com/2013/12/05/starbuckss-tweet-a-coffee-180000/
    ?europe=true.
Weiner, J. (2014). The problem with the new cookie dough Oreos: The critics of the
    new cookie dough Oreos. *Vanity Fair.* https://www.vanityfair.com/style/2014/
    01/the-problem-with-the-new-cookie-dough-oreos-is-the-critics-of-the-new-cookie
    -dough-oreos.
Wertz, J. (2019). Personalization is boosting retail sales: Here are 3 ways to do it
    right. *Forbes.* https://www.forbes.com/sites/jiawertz/2019/03/23/personalization-is
    -boosting-retail-sales-here-are-3-ways-to-do-it-right/#1adcdb4e69ca.
Wharton University of Pennsylvania (2016). How Target and Amazon are changing
    the rules of retailing. https://knowledge.wharton.upenn.edu/article/how-target-and
    -amazon-are-changing-the-rules-of-retail/.
Willigan, G.E. (1992). High-performance marketing: An interview with Nike's Phil
    Knight. *Harvard Business Review.*

Index

Printed and bound by CPI Group (UK) Ltd, Croydon, CR0 4YY

16/04/2025

14658491-0004